CLASSICAL MONOLOGUES

FROM
AESCHYLUS
TO
BERNARD SHAW

CLASSICAL MONOLOGUES

FROM
AESCHYLUS
TO
BERNARD SHAW

Volume One: **Young Men's Roles**

edited with introductions by **Leon Katz**
with the assistance of **Georgi Iliev**

APPLAUSE
THEATRE & CINEMA BOOKS

Classical Monologues
From Aeschylus to Bernard Shaw
Edited with Introductions by Leon Katz

Copyright © 2002 by Leon Katz
All rights reserved.

ISBN: 1-55783-575-6

Library of Congress Cataloging in Publication Data
Classical monologues from Aeschylus to Bernard Shaw / edited with
introductions by Leon Katz with the assistance of Georgi Iliev.
  p. cm.
  ISBN 1-55783-575-6
1. Monologues.
2. Drama—Collections.
3. Young men—Drama.
I. Katz, Leon, 1919-
  PN2080 .C58 2002
  808.82′45—dc21
  2002004863

British Library Cataloging in Publication Data
A catalogue record for this book is available from the British Library.

Applause Theatre & Cinema
151 West 46th Street
New York, NY 10036
Phone: 212-575-9265
Fax: 646-562-5852
Email: info@applausepub.com

Sales and Distribution

in North America:
HAL LEONARD CORP.
7777 West Bluemound Road
P.O. Box 13819
Milwaukee, WI 53213
Phone: 1-414-774-3630
Fax: 1-414-774-3259
Email: halinfo@halleonard.com
Internet: www.halleonard.com

in the United Kingdom:
COMBINED BOOK SERVICES LTD.
Units I/K, Paddock Wood Distribution Centre
Paddock Wood, Tonbridge, Kent TN12 6UU
Phone: (44) 01892 837171
Fax: (44) 01892 837272
United Kingdom

CONTENTS

TRAGEDY/DRAMA

ELIZABETHAN/JACOBEAN

XVII CENTURY FRENCH/SPANISH

RESTORATION

XVIII CENTURY ENGLISH/GERMAN

XIX CENTURY ENGLISH/FRENCH

COMEDY

GREEK

ITALIAN RENAISSANCE

XVII CENTURY FRENCH

XVIII CENTURY ENGLISH

XIX/XX CENTURY GERMAN/SCANDINAVIAN/ENGLISH

This anthology consists of more than five hundred entries in four volumes, the first two of men's monologues (v.I, for younger, v.II, for older men's roles), the other two for women (v.III for younger, v.IV for older women's roles)[1].

The initial question is of course: what is "classic" and what is "classical"? "Classic" is more easily defined: every movie more than a year old. "Classical" as it pertains to plays is necessarily more difficult to pin down. For practical purposes, it involves some sort of separation from "modern," and the guidelines for that separation might be these: 1) texts that are "classical" are restricted by date to those that are roughly a century away (with a few exceptions which conscience did not permit to be excluded), and 2) texts that are recognizably at a distance from contemporary speech, and that demand a reasonable, sometimes considerable, stretch from an actor's normal rhetorical habits. Under these guidelines, it seems reasonable to include, for example, some 19th century texts from farce and melodrama that have currently unfamiliar dialectal twists (see, for example, Sailor William in *Black-Ey'd Susan*, I, #70)[2], as well as translations that though friendly to contemporary ears are still sufficiently distant from current speech to qualify. These demarcations, like the Mexican border, may be a bit porous, but for practical purposes of audition and workshop, they should hold.

Similarly, the division between "younger" and "older" is also porous. What's young? Before our own age of lengthening longevity, it was more or less the rule, right through the 19th century, that "young" hardly extended beyond the twenties — men possibly to very early thirties, women at the very best to early twenties. But not to be too harsh or doctrinaire, there is added here another, more malleable criterion: the weight of authority, the weight of experience, the dignity of title. Between the two the decision regarding the age of characters remains of course subjective, but the harm to characters' standing or reputation, in whatever category or anthology volume they find themselves, is at most slight.

* * *

Emotion is the beginning, the wellspring, from which we naively suppose actors channel and shape their performances and bring them to life. Well, in a way, yes. But consider: a sequence of thoughts can, conceivably, be expressed with no particular emotion, be understood and accepted as rational communication. Try it the other way around — expressing emotion

---

1 Volumes III and IV to be published in the Fall of 2003

2 Cross-references are cited by Volume and Monologue Number, e.g., "(See II,#45)."

with no particular thought — and you'd be certifiable. Emotion is the ephemera of thought. And the actor's performance begins inside the line of logical connections — not emotional connections — of a text's moment to moment.

This anthology is devoted to the proposition that the intelligence of textual analysis is the first, the primary instrument of performance, and it gives the occasion, in a large number of its instances, for the actor to draw significantly on intellectual acuity preceding any emotional urges. To put it another way, a speech's emotional progression is its logical progression at a second remove. And the particularity and finesse of emotional performance corresponds precisely to the particularity and finesse of its intellectual perception.

With that proposition in mind, the headnotes preceding each of the monologues are of three kinds — sometimes featured singly, sometimes all in one: a description of the speech's strategy; a breakdown of its logical progression; a description of its context. Let's go over them one at a time:

Strategy: (1) The speaker's strategy (his/her intention.) Sometimes it's uniform throughout the speech, and in the labor of defining it, I've seen many, many actors stuck trying to articulate what that uniform intention might be. ("I want love" — no, says the mentor, that's not specific. Alright, "I want to get her into bed" — no, says the mentor, that's not the motive behind the motive. OK, "I want to dominate" — Well, let's talk further about this.) But articulated precisely or not, as likely as not that initial intent may not stay fixed throughout the speech. When it doesn't, the vagaries of the character's mind may dance through a jungle of intents (have a look at Lorenzaccio's remarkable speech when he's getting ready to murder de Medici (see I, #76)) or the speaker taking cues from his listener's silent or spoken reaction, or his own, may alter its direction, or qualify it, or change it altogether. The tendency in classically structured soliloquy is of course to stay doggedly on track, since the soliloquy's private conference with the self is usually working toward the resolution of a dilemma, or working through the likely obstacles to a plan of action, or — and these are the most interesting ones — are governed by battles of conscience whose fixed ideals and unspoken beliefs overwhelm practical intent. Whatever the case may be, the tracking of the "intent's" progress is one task assumed in these headnotes.

(2) The playwright's strategies: They're not formulas but habits. Major speeches tend to fall into distinguishable kinds, and tend to be shaped, by both habit and tradition, into certain formal patterns that remain fairly

fixed throughout the course of Western drama. Some of the most powerful speeches — in, for example, Euripides, Seneca, Schiller, Buchner, and Shaw — are almost identical in their rhetorical structure. Some examples of the most usual ones (it might be helpful if we give them names): the Speech of Justification (among the greatest, the Emperor Augustus in Corneille's *Cinna*); the Speech of Persuasion (among the most moving, Jocasta in Seneca's *Phoenician Women*); the Speech of Denunciation (in which the decibels run from wrath — Theseus in Euripides' *Hippolytus* — to barely audible contempt — Mr. O'Connell's great speech in Granville-Barker's *Waste*); the Formal Narrative Speech (Messengers' recitations of off-stage catastrophes in Greek tragedy, or Rodrigue's recounting of his battlefield triumph in *Le Cid*). All of these formally shaped addresses in which, over and above their dramatic function and emotional investment (which is sometimes enormous and sometimes nil), the actor has also to catch the sheer display involved in the music and the epic scaling of their rhetoric. The playwright's strategy in these passages usually comes as close to aria as it does to flat speech, and not to honor that dimension is like muttering under your breath instead of singing the lyrics of a song.

Logical (sometimes alogical) Progression: Whether rational or deranged, the mind is moving from one notion to the next in a chain of changing assertions that link. Figuring out the exact continuity of those links can be easy — in narratives or in expositions which merely detail a sequence of ordered events. But when the connections are either muffled or random, the work of the actor begins. The headnotes try particularly hard to be helpful in this respect: at the risk of being accused of childishness, they sometimes enumerate unashamedly and naively the steps of these progressions; sometimes — can you believe it? by the numbers. Why such silliness? Because it is precisely these progressions of linked-but-difficult-to-grasp sense that provide the basis for the emotional progressions which become, only then, the sustaining life of soliloquies.

Context: Obviously, there's the plot, the character, the situation just before, and the surrounding situation that provide the immediate context for individual monologues. The headnotes of course provide necessary information concerning these facts. But there's the larger, enormously significant perspective — the mindset, the contexts of beliefs and assumptions which the plays and their texts inevitably reflect — that the headnotes dwell on too. It's within these structures of belief that plays and speeches harbor their ultimate meanings, and their exploration, certainly in the greatest performances I've been privileged to see, give the ultimate richness of meaning and effect to actors' interpretations.

* * *

On the question of translation, Voltaire still, I think, has the last word. It's discouraging. How close can translation get — to meaning, to tone, to deftness of statement — in translatorese? Voltaire in the 18th century had this to say, and nobody has yet spoken the bad news better:

> It is impossible to convey through any modern language, all the power of Greek expressions; they describe, with one stroke, what costs us a whole sentence…That language had not only the advantage of filling the imagination with a word, but every word, we know, had its peculiar melody, which charmed the ear while it displayed the finest pictures to the mind; and for this reason all our translations from the Greek poets are weak, dry, and poor; it is imitating palaces of porphyry with bricks and pebbles.

What's true for Greek remains as true for modern language translation as well: no language can give up its peculiar music/sense to equivalents in another language. What Molière, for example, suffers in transit from French to English is possibly an exceptionally grim instance of bricks and pebbles making believe they're porphyry. His clarity, his ease, his perfect accommodation of plain sense to the straitjacket of hexameter couplets, when imitated precisely in English, converts into deadly banality, insufferable in expression and plainly laughable in sense. (Goethe, another victim, this editor felt it best to sidestep altogether. Faust in English sometimes marches to the tune and sense of Jack and Jill.)

What to do? Without hoping for true equivalence, for the purposes of actors speaking texts intended to stand in for some of the greatest dramatic passages in other languages, the uneasy solution is simply to avoid the unspeakable, in both senses. No rigid policy was followed: for example, of using only up-to-date, "relevant" (and sometimes hopelessly removed from the original) translations on the one hand, or scrupulously "faithful" (and sometimes hopelessly unspeakable) versions on the other. Compromises, of course, abound — some for reasons of availability, others in the interest of sampling different tacks to a single author's texts when multiple selections from the same author are included. The criterion was, roughly, this: how comfortably can the text sit on the actor's tongue, and how far can it reach toward the overall effect, admittedly very approximate, of the original? And admittedly, you can't win.

1

ORESTES IS JUBILANT, THEN UNCERTAIN, OVER HIS REVENGE

(458 BC) AESCHYLUS, Libation Bearers, *tr. R. Lattimore*

The doors of the palace are thrown open and Orestes stands over the bodies of the dead Clytemnestra and Aegisthus. This recalls with bitter irony the final scene of the previous play of the Oresteia trilogy, *Agamemnon,* in which Clytemnestra stood in the same posture over the slain bodies of her husband Agamemnon and his slave-paramour Cassandra, with the "net," that is, the blood-stained robe of Agamemnon, covering their bodies. It recalls the "net" in which all the actors in the trilogy are caught, the "net" of inevitability that is made up of both human passions and divine injunctions.

Orestes was captured in the "net" when he returned from exile under the prompting of the God Apollo to avenge the murder of his father Agamemnon, and plotted successfully with his sister Electra and his companion Pylades to murder his mother Clytemnestra and her lover and co-ruler, Aegisthus. Before the double murder, Orestes, in a long and powerfully lyrical scene, had undergone a ritual of dedication to his task at the tomb of Agamemnon. Steeled to his purpose, he first murdered Aegisthus, and then after a violent encounter with his mother in which her begging for mercy brought only his pitiless response, he slew her.

It's Orestes' intention at this moment, as it had been Clytemnestra's, to persuade the citizens (the chorus) of his triumphant certainty and his well-earned glory in the Apollo-sanctioned necessity of his bloody act. But as with Clytemnestra, in the very throes of jubilation, a doubt creeps in: "my victory is soiled." The doubt will lead quickly to the unhinging of his mind, and the terrifying sight of the Furies—avengers of victimized women—approaching.

ORESTES

Behold the twin tyrannies of our land, these two
who killed my father and sacked my house. For a time
they sat upon their thrones and kept their pride of state,
and they are lovers still. So may you judge by what
befell them, for as they were pledged their oath abides.
They swore together death for my unhappy sire
and swore to die together. Now they keep their oath.

Behold again, o audience of these evil things,
the engine against my wretched father they devised,
the hands' entanglement, the hobbles for his feet.
Spread it out. Stand around me in a cricle and
display this net that caught a man. So shall, not my
father, but that great father who sees all, the Sun,
look on my mother's sacrilegious handiwork
and be a witness for me in my day of trial
how it was in all right that I achieved this death,
my mother's: for of Aegisthus' death I take no count:
he has his seducer's punishment, no more than law.

But she, who plotted this foul death against the man
by whom she carried the weight of children underneath
her zone, burden once loved, shown hard and hateful now,
what does she seem to be? Some water snake, some viper
whose touch is rot even to him who felt no fang
strike, by that brutal and wrong daring in her heart.
And this thing: what shall I call it and be right, in all
eloquence? Trap for an animal or winding sheet
for dead man? Or bath curtain? Since it is a net,
robe you could call it, to entangle a man's feet.
Some highwayman might own a thing like this, to catch
the wayfarer and rob him of his money and
so make a living. With a treacherous thing like this
he could take many victims and go warm within.
May no such wife as she was come to live with me.
Sooner, let God destroy me, with no children born.

Did she do it or did she not? My witness is
this great robe. It was thus she stained Aegisthus' sword.
Dip it and dip it again, the smear of blood conspires
with time to spoil the beauty of this precious thing.
Now I can praise him, now I can stand by to mourn
and speak before this web that killed my father; yet
I grieve for the thing done, the death, and all our race.
I have won; but my victory is soiled, and has no pride.
I would have you know, I see not how this thing will end.
I am a charioteer whose course is wrenched outside
the track, for I am beaten, my rebellious senses
boilt with me headlong and the fear against my heart
is ready for the singing and dane of wrath. But while
I hold some grip still on my wits, I say publicly
to my friends: I killed my mother not without some right.
My father's murder stained her, and the gods' disgust.

As for the spells that charmed me to such daring, I
give you in chief the seer of Pytho, Loxias. He
declared I could do this and not be charged with wrong.
Of my evasion's punishment I will not speak:
no archery could hit such height of agony.
And look upon me now, how I go armored in
leafed branch and garland on my way to the centrestone
and sanctuary, and Apollo's level place,
the shining of the fabulous fire that never dies,
to escape this blood that is my own. Loxias ordained
that I should turn me to no other shrine than this.
To all men of Argos in time to come I say
thay shall be witness, how these evil things were done.
I go, an outcast wanderer from this land, and leave
behind, in life, in death, the name of what I did.

No!
Women who serve this house, they come like gorgons, they
wear robes of black, and they are wreathed in a tangle

of snakes. I can no longer stay.
These are no fancies of affliction. They are clear,
and real, and here; the bloodhounds of my mother's hate.
Ah, Lord Apollo, how they grow and multiply,
repulsive for the blood drops of their dripping eyes.
You can not see them, but I see them. I amn driven
from this place. I can stay here no longer.
                    (He rushes out)

the Sun: the god Apollo **water snake…fang strike**: some sea snakes' skins are
more venomous than any ground snake's fangs **the seer of Pytho, Loxias**: the
god Apollo **the bloodhounds of my mother's hate**: the Furies who will pursue
Orestes for vengeance

2

JASON DEFENDS HIS
ABANDONMENT OF MEDEA

(431 BC) EURIPIDES, Medea, *tr. F. Prokosch*

Nietzsche said of Euripides that he reduced the Sophoclean "Apollonian" mythic-poetic man to the level of the "theoretical" man; that is, the man who argues like a cunning intellectual in the marketplace. It was a cruel judgment, but not altogether unwarranted. Euripides' characters do tend to argue their "case" like lawyers in a courtroom or like logicians in a debating society. His characteristic speeches of self-justification—like the one below—are rationally structured and logically argued: firstly, secondly, thirdly, etc. And frequently his actors address and clarify for their auditors the shape of the argument they are about to offer: I will begin with this thesis, go on to examples, and conclude with my summary point. But what he apparently lost in mythic scope he reconstituted in all-too-recognizable human passion and studies of subtly human self-delusion. In the very act of justifying themselves with careful argument, the characters—like Jason here—are unaware that they are condemning themselves by the spuriousness or irrelevance of those very arguments.

In this scene, Jason gets the chance to respond to Medea's vituperation, and—in characteristic Euripidean vein—takes up her points one by one, like a lawyer responding to his opposite number in court. The situation he is addressing—made fairly clear in the speech itself—is this: Medea, when Jason came to Colchis in quest of the golden fleece, fell in love with him, aided him, fled with him, and for him slew her own brother and later Jason's treacherous uncle. After ten hospitable years of their exile in Corinth, and the birth of their two sons, King Creon offers Jason his daughter in marriage and succession to his throne. Because of Medea's violent reaction to the marriage and her threats of vengeance, Creon orders her banishment, fearing also her reputation for sorcery. She has a day's grace. Jason in this scene meets her, assures her that she brought her banishment on herself, and offers her money for her journey. It is Medea's passionate, bitter reply to this offer that provokes Jason's point-by-point response.

It is a response of easily-worn self-justification, the intention of which is—because of his undervaluing of Medea's intensity of grief over her betrayal— to force her to recognize, as he argues, the womanly illogic of her position, her overlooking the possibility of accommodating to her new situation because she supposes everything to be judgeable by the female measure of "love."

For the actor, Jason's monologue is a study in the *intensity of meaning* in a speech intended to convince, and yet in incredible, enormous contrast to the intensity of Medea's meanings. He is in no way consciously trifling with argument, is in no way dismissive of his argument or its occasion. But it is the completely inaccurate measure he takes of Medea's *intensity of moral revulsion* that reveals—*unknown to him*—the mereness of his own.

> JASON
> The time has come, it seems, when I must speak, and speak well, and like a good helmsman reef up my sail and weather the tempest of your tongue…And since you dwell so heavily on all the favors you did me, Medea, I am certain that I owe the safety of my voyage to Aphrodite alone among gods and men. Not that I doubt your skill; but all the same, I prefer not to dwell on this notion that love, with all its irresistible power, compelled you to save my life. I don't think we need go into details. I admit that you meant well, and did your best. But when it comes to this matter of my safety, let me point out that you got rather more than you gave. First of all, instead of living in a barbaric land, you've come to Greece and enjoyed contact with a country where justice and law prevail, and not brute force; and what is more,

the Greeks thought rather highly of you. You even acquired a certain
fame here. Whereas, if you had stayed on in that outer fringe of the
world, your name would now be quite unknown. Frankly, I'd rather
have real fame and distinction than mighty stores of gold in my halls
or the talent to sing more sweetly than Orpheus. That is my answer to
your version of all my labors; remember, it was you who brought up
this matter.

As for your bitter attack on my marriage with the princess, I think
I can prove first of all that it was a shrewd move; secondly, a thoroughly sober one; and finally, that I did it in your interest and that of your
children…Wait! Please remain calm…Since I had come from Iolcos
involved in every kind of trouble, and an exile, what could be luckier
for me than marriage with the King's own daughter? It was not—since
it is this that seems to rankle in you—it was not that I grew weary of
going to bed with you, and began to look around for a new wife. Nor
was it that I was anxious to have more children. The two we have are
quite enough; I don't complain. No, it was this, first of all: that we
might live in comfort, and not in poverty. Believe me, I have learned
how a man's friends desert him the moment he is penniless…And
then I wanted to bring up my sons in a manner worthy of my position; I even hoped that by having more sons, who would live as
brothers to yours, we might draw the entire family into harmony, and
all be happy. You yourself need no more children; but I would do well
to help the sons I have through the sons I hope to have. Do you dis-
agree with all this? You would agree if it weren't for this matter of love
which rankles in you. But you women have developed such curious
notions: you think that all is well as long as your life at night runs
smoothly. But if something happens which upsets your way of love,
then all that you once found lovely and desirable you now find hateful. Believe me, it would have been better far if men could have
thought up some other way of producing children, and done away
with women; then no evil would ever have come to men.

reef: to shorten sail by tying in one or more reefs **Iolcos**: a port in Thessaly, ruled
by Pelias, Jason's uncle who had usurped the throne from Jason's father, and later
sent Jason and the Argonauts to bring back the Golden Fleece

3

THE MESSENGER REPORTS JOCASTA'S SUICIDE AND OEDIPUS' SELF-BLINDING

(430-25 BC) SOPHOCLES, Oedipus the King, *tr. W. B. Yeats*

Messengers' speeches in classical drama—whether in Greek or Roman or French neo-classical—were understood to be anything but neutral reports of an event. They were its present-tense realization in words, just as a film sequence of a battle or murder or suicide is their present-tense realization in image; both are expected to have the same evocative power, with the difference that the Messenger on stage is humanly invested in the event's recapitulation. Some of the greatest actor's moments in Greek drama are in these speeches, one of which is this Messenger's report of the suicide of Jocasta and the self-blinding of Oedipus. "So far as words can serve, you shall see it," he promises, and makes good his promise.

The speech is constructed as preamble, then body of report, then peroration. There are two distinct phases to his delivery: 1) his orienting his listeners to what is coming, and at the end to what has been spoken, and 2) his immersion in the event itself during his evocation of it. From the first word, the Messenger establishes his *personal* relation to the House and to the horrific event, and—most important—immediately invites his listeners to share entirely, to enter entirely into, that same relation, from which vantage they will see what he still sees and feel what he feels. The *seeing* of the event currently is the occasion for the Messenger's immersion into its progress—as though it is currently happening and currently being felt exactly as at first.

The events preceding the Messenger's speech are almost too well known to need repeating. Briefly, Oedipus and Jocasta discover that he was, in ignorance, the murderer of his father Laius and the subsequent husband of his mother Jocasta, with whom he sired four children. The violation of the double taboo of parricide and incest, discovered in a single moment to the horror of both Oedipus and Jocasta, leads to the terrible consequences that the Messenger "reports," that is to say, once again lives through.

MESSENGER
Friends and kinsmen of this house! What deeds must you look upon, what burden of sorrow bear, if true to race you still love the House of Labdacus. For not Ister nor Phasis could wash this house clean, so many misfortunes have been brought upon it, so many has it brought upon itself, and those misfortunes are always the worst that a man brings upon himself.

A short tale in the telling: Jocasta, our Queen, is dead. By her own hand. It cannot be as terrible to you as to one who saw it with his eyes, yet so far as words can serve, you shall see it. When she had come into the vestibule, she ran half-crazed towards her marriage-bed, clutching at her hair with the fingers of both hands, and once within the chamber dashed the doors together behind her. Then called upon the name of Laius, long since dead, remembering that son who killed his father and upon the mother begot an accursed race. And wailed because of that marriage wherein she had borne a twofold race—husband by husband, children by her child. Then Oedipus with a shriek burst in and running here and there asked for a sword, asked where he could find the wife that was no wife but mother who had borne his children and himself. Nobody answered him, we all stood dumb; but supernatural power helped him, for, with a dreadful shriek, as though beckoned, he sprang at the double doors, drove them in, burst the bolts out of their sockets, and ran into the room. There we saw the woman hanging in a swinging halter, and with a terrible cry he loosened the halter from her neck. When that unhappiest woman lay stretched upon the ground, we saw another dreadful sight. He dragged the golden brooches from her dress and lifting them struck them upon his eyeballs, crying out, 'You have looked enough upon those you ought never to have looked upon, failed long enough to know those you should have known; henceforth you shall be dark.' He struck his eyes, not once, but many times, lifting his hands and speaking such or like words. The blood poured down and not with a few slow drops, but all at once over his beard in a dark shower as it were hail.

He cries for some one to unbar the gates and to show to all the men of Thebes his father's murderes, his mother's—the unholy word must not be spoken. It is his purpose to cast himself out of the land that he may not bring all this house under his curse. But he has not the strength to do it. He must be supported and led away. The curtain is parting; you are going to look upon a sight which even those who shudder must pity.

Labdacus: father of Laius, who was father of Oedipus **Ister, Phasis**: two rivers; Ister is the lower Danube river, Phasis is a river in Colchis

4

HIPPOLYTUS CURSES WOMEN AND ADULTERY AFTER LEARNING OF PHAEDRA'S PASSION FOR HIM
(428 BC) EURIPIDES, Hippolytus, *tr. M. Hadas and J. H. McClean*

On the face of it, the action of the tragedy of *Hippolytus* is foreordained: in the play's prologue, the Goddess of Love Aphrodite determines that Hippolytus, ignoring her worship and devoting his allegiance instead to Artemis, the Goddess of the hunt and of chastity, will be punished by death. She will arrange that his father Theseus will discover his wife Phaedra's secret passion for Hippolytus, and so lead to Phaedra's suicide and Hippolytus' violent demise.

But there is sometimes an odd disconnect between Euripides' schematic functions of the Gods and the human urgencies that follow out their dictates, in the sense that the human urgencies alone need no more than themselves to accomplish the same ends. The absolutes of those godly injunctions are dramatically displaced by the absolute power of the humans' emotional obsessions, and need no other causative propulsion than themselves.

That's the key to the overwhelming force of the motives operating in this tragedy: they are absolute, unqualified. Hippolytus' absolute devotion to his chastity is accompanied by his equally absolute detestation of women. And Phaedra's incestuous love for him—she is, after all, his step-mother—is an uncontrollable desire so enormous that she imagines death as its only possible constraint. It is the Nurse, Phaedra's confidante, who, being helpful as she supposes to her mistress, informs Hippolytus of Phaedra's passion. And it is the news that a woman, his detestation, and most particularly his father's wife, offers her love that sends Hippolytus into a frenzy of disgust and vituperation. Note that when in the course of this speech he confronts Phaedra directly, openly, there is not even a minimal vestige of human regard for her person or position—she is nothing to him but the hated fact of woman's existence. He is, in this speech, clearing his body and mind of a revulsion; he is using word and argument as a weapon, an axe, an instrument of murder flung in the face of the hated woman Phaedra and her revolting love.

HIPPOLYTUS

Zeus! Why did you let women settle in this world of light, a curse and a snare to men? If you wished to propagate the human race you should have arranged it without women. Men might have deposited in your temples gold or iron or a weight of copper to purchase offspring, each to the value of the price he paid, and so lived in free houses, relieved of womankind.

Here is a proof that woman is a great nuisance. The father who begot her and brought her up pays a great dowry to get her out of his house and be rid of the plague. The man who receives the poisonous weed into his home rejoices and adds beautiful decorations to the useless ornament and tricks her out in gowns—poor fool, frittering away the family property. Happiest is he who has a cipher for a wife, a useless simpleton to sit at home. A clever woman I hate; may there never be in my house a woman more intellectual than a woman ought to be. Mischief is hatched by Cypris in clever women; the helpless kind is kept from misconduct by the shortness of her wit. No maids should be allowed near a wife; beasts that can bite but cannot talk should be her only company in the house, so that they could neither address anyone or receive speech in return. As it is, the vile women weave their vile schemes within, and the maids carry word outdoors.

So you, sorry wretch, come to me to procure incest in my father's bed. But I will scour it away, sluicing fresh running water in my ears. How could I be base, who feel polluted by the mere hearing? Know well, woman, it's only my piety that saves you. If I had not been unaware by sacred oaths I should never have kept from telling my father this. Now I will stay away from the house as long as Theseus is out of the country, and I shall keep my mouth shut. But I shall watch, when I come back with my father, how you will look at him, you and that mistress of yours. Then I shall know fully the brazenness of which I have had the taste.

Curse you! *Let* people say I am always harping on the same theme. Still I shall never tire of hating women. For that matter, *they* never tire of wickedness. Either teach them to be chaste or leave me to assail them always.

5

HIPPOLYTUS DEFENDS HIS INNOCENCE
BEFORE HIS FATHER
(428 BC) EURIPIDES, Hippolytus, *tr. D. Grene*

Rejected violently and ignominiously by Hippolytus [see I, #4], Phaedra, her great love turned to as great a hate, determines to destroy herself and Hippolytus in one action: she hangs herself, but ties a note to her wrist accusing Hippolytus of violating her. Theseus, assuming the truth of the note, at once prays to Poseidon to kill his son in retribution. When his son approaches, he greets him at first in silence, then in absolute rage.

Note the temper and style of Hippolytus' self-defense against this fatherly rage. As with the confrontation of Jason and Medea [see I, #2], there is an enormous gap between the emotional level of Theseus' rage and the level of Hippolytus' rather careful, measured, lawyerlike response. For all his swearing by "earth and sea" to his innocence, he structures his defense with an astonishing coolness, the consequence of his certainty of his own innocence, to be sure, but fatal in tone to the perception by his father of his revolting and criminal guilt. His arguments do not answer to that perception, and in tone condemn him even more. Note too how Euripides, with a sly subtlety rarely matched, characterizes Hippolytus' cool assurance—based on his confidence in its absolute truth—as the assurance of a somewhat doltish young man, asserting proudly the propriety of his spending all his time training at the gymnasium, and so has never had time or inclination for a thought about sex at all.

It is the intention of Hippolytus in this speech to neutralize his father's accusations entirely by the elaborate and relatively calm assurance with which it is offered. Cruelly, every word, every point made, more and more accomplishes the opposite.

HIPPOLYTUS
Your mind and intellect are subtle, father:
here you have a subject dressed in eloquent words;
but if you lay the matter bare of words
the matter is not eloquent. I am
no man to speak with vapid, precious skill
before a mob, although among my equals
and in a narrow circle I am held
not unaccomplished in the eloquent art.
That is as it should be. The demagogue
who charms a crowd is scorned by cultured experts.
But here in this necessity I must speak.
First I shall take the argument you first
urged as so refutable and deadly.
You see the earth and air about you, father?

In all of that there lives no man more chaste
than I, though you deny it.
There is one thing that I have never done, the thing
of which you think that you convict me, father.
I am a virgin to this very day.
Save what I have heard or I have seen in pictures
I'm ignorant of the deed. Nor do I wish
to see such things, for I've a maiden soul.
But say you disbelieve my chastity.
Then tell me how it was your wife seduced me:
was it because she was more beautiful
than all the other women in the world?
Or did I think, when I had taken her,
to win your place and kingdom for a dowry
and live in your own house? I would have been
a fool, a senseless fool, if I had dreamed it.
Was rule so sweet? Never, I tell you, Theseus,
for the wise. A man whom power has so enchanted
must be demented. I would wish to be
first in the contests of the Hellenic Games
but in the city I'd take second place
and an enduring happy life among
the best society who are my friends.

I swear to you by Zeus, the God of Oaths,
by this deep rooted fundament of earth,
I never sinned against you with your wife
nor would have wished or thought of it.
If I have been a villain may I die
unfamed, unknown, a homeless, stateless beggar,
an exile! May the earth and sea refuse
to give my body shelter when I am dead!
Whether your wife took her own life because
She was afraid, I do not know. I may not speak
further than this.
Virtuous she was in deed although not virtuous:
I that have virtue used it to my ruin.

Hellenic Games: the origin of the Olympic Games

6

THE MESSENGER REPORTS THE GRUESOME DEATH OF HIPPOLYTUS

(428 BC) EURIPIDES, Hippolytus, *tr. D. Grene*

As with the Messenger's speech in *Oedipus the King* [see I, #3], the personal investment of the Messenger in this account must be as powerful as the narrative in his report. It is not only his love and respect for the dying Hippolytus that moves him, but the injustice of Theseus' condemnation. But since, as he professes, he is "only a slave in [Theseus'] household," his accusation against Theseus' blindness to his own son's inherent innocence, though stated and even underscored, is nevertheless muted. It is a delicate balance—between the judgment he yearns to express strongly against Theseus, and the limit to which he can do so. Two intentions, warring against one another, is the drama of the speech, over and above the revulsion the Messenger feels toward the event itself that he is reporting.

MESSENGER
King Theseus,
I bring you news worthy of much thought
for you and all the citizens who live
in Athens' walls.
Hippolytus is dead: I may almost say dead:
he sees the light of day still, though the balance
that holds him in this world is slight indeed.
It was the horses of his car that killed him,
they, and the curses of your lips,
the curses you invoked against your son,
and prayed to the Lord of Ocean to fulfil them.

We were combing our horses' coats beside the sea
where the waves came crashing to the shore. And we were crying
for one had come and told us that our master,

Hippolytus, should walk this land no more,
since you had laid hard banishment upon him.
Then he came himself down to the shore to us,
with the same refrain of tears.
But at last he gave over crying and said:
"Why do I rave like this? It is my father
who has commanded and I must obey him.
Prepare my horses, men, and harness them.
This is no longer a city of mine."
Then every man made haste. Before you could say the words,
there was the chariot ready before our master.
He put his feet into the driver's rings,
and took the reins from the rail into his hands.
But first he folded his hands like this and prayed:
"Zeus, let me die now, if I have been guilty!
Let my father know that he has done me wrong,
whether I live to see the day or not."
With that he took the goad and touched the horses.
And we the servants followed our master's car.

When we were entering the lonely country
the other side of the border, a rumbling
deep in the earth, terrible to hear,
growled like the thunder of Father Zeus.
The horses raised their heads, pricked up their ears,
and gusty fear was on us all to know,
whence came the sound. As we looked towards the shore,
where the waves were beating, we saw a wave appear,
a miracle wave, lifting its crest to the sky.
To the shore it came,
swelling, boiling, crashing, casting its surf around,
to where the chariot stood.
But at the very moment when it broke,
the wave threw up a monstrous savage bull.
Its bellowing filled the land, and the land echoed it,
with shuddering emphasis. And sudden panic
fell on the horses in the car. But the master,—
he was used to horses' ways,—all his life long

he had been with horses—took a firm grip of the reins
and lashed the ends behind his back and pulled
like a sailor at the oar. The horses bolted:
their teeth were clenched upon the fire-forged bit.
They heeded neither the driver's hand nor harness
nor the jointed car. As often as he would turn them
with guiding hand to the soft sand of the shore,
the bull appeared in front to head them off,
maddening the team with terror.
But when in frenzy they charged towards the cliffs,
the bull came galloping beside the rail,
silently following until he brought disaster,
capsizing the car, striking the wheel on a rock.
Then all was in confusion. Axles of wheels
and lynch-pins flew up into the air,
and the unlucky driver, tangled in the reins,
was dragged along in an inextricable
knot and his dear head pounded on the rocks,
his body bruised. He cried aloud and terrible
his voice rang in our ears: "Stand, horses, stand!
You were fed in my stables. Do not kill me!
My father's curse! His curse! Will none of you
save me? I am innocent. Save me!"
Many of us had will enough, but all
were left behind in the race. Getting free of the reins
somehow he fell. There was still life in him.
But the horses vanished and that ill-omened monster
somewhere, I know not where, in the rough cliffs.

I am only a slave in your household, King Theseus,
but I shall never be able to believe
that your son was guilty, not though the tribe of women
were hanged for it, not though the weight of tables
of a high pine of Ida, filled with writing,
accused him,—for I know that he was good.

the Lord of Ocean: Poseidon **Argos**: ancient Greek kingdom, the capital was
Thebes **Ida**: a mountain near Troy

7

TALTHYBIUS RECOUNTS TO HECUBA
THE SLAYING OF HER DAUGHTER

(417-415 BC?) EURIPIDES, Hecuba, *tr. J. Lembke and K. J. Reckford*

The Trojan War has ended. Hecuba, Queen of the Trojans and now a captive of the Greeks, has only the consolation that two of her children, Polyxena and Polydorus, are still alive and are still with her. But at the play's beginning, the Greeks have decided to put Polyxena to death; a sacrifice, as Odysseus explains, demanded by the ghost of the dead hero, Achilles. Hecuba's laments and entreaties count for nothing, and Polyxena, with dignity and courage, leaves to face her doom.

A Greek soldier, Talthybius, comes to recount for Hecuba the event of her daughter's sacrifice. It is the Greek soldier's compassion for Hecuba's suffering, and his awe at the rare nobility and courage of Polyxena during the ceremony of her murder, that makes this "Messenger's" speech one of the most moving and most admired in Greek tragedy. Talthybius enters in tears. The intent of his speech is to be at one with Hecuba's grief, and to show her how the Greek soldiers themselves were stricken with both grief and admiration for the conduct of her daughter during her sacrifice.

> **TALTHYBIUS**
> My lady, you ask me to reap my tears twice.
> My eyes filled when I watched your child die.
> Now memory must see her die again.
>
> They were all there—the Greek army in full strength,
> there by the tomb for your girl's sacrifice.
> And Achilles' son took Polyxena's hand
> and placed her on top of the grave-mound. I stood nearby.

And young soldiers, specially chosen, followed,
hands ready to keep your calf from bolting.
And the son of Achilles takes in his two hands
a brimming goblet, pure gold, and raises
libations to his dead father. And he signals me
to call the whole army to silence.

I took my station and called out the order:
"Silence, Greeks. All keep silence.
Keep still. Silence." And not a ripple swept the crowd.
And he spoke: "O son of Peleus, my father,
receive this wine that summons up and calms
the dead. And come, taste a darker drink,
a girl's unwatered blood, the army's gift and mine.
And turn your dead eyes peacefully on us at last
and let the hulls go, let the hawsers loose,
and let the ships sail from Troy in peace,
grant us all a safe return home."

So he spoke, and the whole army echoed, "Safe return home."
Then, taking his sword by the gold-covered hilt,
he unsheathed it and gave a quick nod
to the chosen young men: Take the virgin.
But she saw him and gave her own clear orders:
"Listen, Greeks who laid my city waste,
I volunteer my death. Let no hand touch me,
for I am glad to offer you my throat.
Set me free so, by the gods, I die free
when you do your killing. Born a queen, I
would feel shame to be called slave among the dead."

A wave of approval broke, and Lord Agamemnon
told the young guards to let go of the virgin.
And they, the instant they heard that order
come from the chief in command, let her go.
And when she heard authority's words,

she grasped her robe and tore it wide open
from shoulder straight down to her navel
and showed breasts that gleamed like a statue's
carved to honor the gods, and she knelt on one knee
to say the most courageous last words:
"Look, young soldier. If you would strike
my breast, strike here. But if my throat
is what you want, my neck is bared—here."

And he, unwilling yet willing in his pity,
cuts her windpipe with the iron sword.
Springs gushed forth. But she even in her dying
took great care to fall modestly, hiding
all that should be hidden from men's eyes.

Then, when sacrifice had stopped her breath,
none of the Greeks performed the same labor,
but some strewed green leaves over her body,
while some brought pine logs to build her
a pyre.

Hecuba, your child
is dead. Of all the world's women, I see you
as luckiest in your child and most ill-used by Chance.

Achilles' son: Neoptolemus **son of Peleus, my father**: Achilles **turn your eyes...home**: the dying Achilles had begged that Polyxena be sacrificed on his tomb, and threatened to keep the fleet windbound in Troy until the Greeks fulfilled his demand **hulls**: n, ships **hawsers**: n, ropes

8

PHILOCTETES REVILES THE GREEKS
WHO ABANDONED HIM

(409 BC) SOPHOCLES, Philoctetes, *tr. D. Grene*

The war in Troy is at stalemate. The two great warrior heroes, Achilles and Ajax, are dead, and the Greeks have little prospect of moving their campaign forward. Two possibilities: if the son of Achilles, Neoptolemus, joined their force with his father's weapons; and—a more remote possibility—if the possessor of the magic bow of Heracles, Philoctetes, could be persuaded to join the army with his magic weapon, the Greeks would, according to oracular foretelling, win.

The problem lies in persuading Philoctetes. Years before, on the way to Troy, when the expedition stopped at a small island, one of their number, Philoctetes, was bitten in the foot by a serpent, and the wound, never healing, produced a stench so intolerable that he was put ashore on the uninhabited island of Lemnos. There he has lived alone for nine years with the unrelenting pain of his wound and his unrelenting hatred for the Greek commanders and Odysseus, who abandoned him; but he is still in possession of Heracles' magic bow.

Odysseus with Neoptolemus comes to the island, Odysseus having worked up a cunning scheme for winning the magic bow from Philoctetes. It begins with Neoptolemus meeting the abandoned warrior alone, professing who he is, but pretending to know nothing of the fate of the still-tortured man. Philoctetes, overjoyed to meet a Greek compatriot, pours out to him the story of his abandonment, his painful, solitary life, his continuing hatred of Odysseus and the Greek Generals.

Several motives creep into his bitter confessional. Sophocles is praised for the complexity with which he dramatized Philoctetes' character, and the complexity of motives is evident in this, his very first full articulation of his inner self—not merely his external history and condition. Note: first, his visiting on Neoptolemus the pride he takes in his endurance, in his Robinson Crusoe ingenuity in staying alive, fed and sheltered, and most particularly his pride, oddly enough, in his almost superhuman ability to endure unrelenting pain and unrelenting handicap. Note, as distinct from this, the opposite motive: his appeal for pity, and the accompanying appeal to be rescued (the pitiable example he gives of those who found him previously and left without him, once again as always, abandoned.) And overwhelming all other motives, the pent-up longing for the vengeance of a soul wracked with hatred of his long-ago betrayers. Behind his biographical narrative, multiple, contradictory intentions in its telling.

PHILOCTETES

Surely I must be vile! God must have hated me
that never a word of me, of how I live here,
should have come home through all the land of Greece.
Yet they that outraged God casting me away
can hold their tongues and laugh! While my disease
always increases and grows worse. My boy,
you are Achilles' son. I that stand here
am one you may have heard of, as the master
of Heracles' arms. I am Philoctetes
the son of Poias. Those two generals
and Prince Odysseus of the Cephallenians
cast me ashore here to their shame, as lonely
as you can see me now, wasting with my sickness
as cruel as it is, caused by the murderous bite
of a viper mortally dangerous.

I was already bitten when we put in here
on my way from sea-encircled Chryse.
I tell you, boy, those men cast me away here
and ran and left me helpless. They were happy

when they saw that I had fallen asleep on the shore
in a rocky cave, after a rough passage.
They went away and left me with such rags—
and few enough of them—as one might give
an unfortunate beggar and a handful of food.
May God give them the like!
Think, boy, of that awakening when I awoke
and found them gone; think of the useless tears
and curses on myself when I saw the ships—
my ships, which I had once commanded—gone,
all gone, and not a man left on the island,
not one to help me or to lend a hand
when I was seized with my sickness, not a man!
In all I saw before me nothing but pain;
but of that a great abundance, boy.

Time came and went for me. In my tiny shelter
I must alone do everything for myself.
This bow of mine I used to shoot the birds
that filled my belly. I must drag my foot,
my cursed foot, to where the bolt
sped by the bow's thong had struck down a bird.
If I must drink, and it was winter time—
the water was frozen—I must break up firewood.
Again I crawled and miserably contrived
to do the work. Whenever I had no fire,
rubbing stone on stone I would at last produce
the spark that kept me still in life.
A roof for shelter, if only I have fire,
gives me everything but release from pain.

Boy, let me tell you of this island.
No sailor by his choice comes near it.
There is no anchorage, nor anywhere
that one can land, sell goods, be entertained.
Sensible men make no voyages here.
Yet now and then someone puts in. A stretch

of time as long as this allows much to happen.
When they have come here, boy, they pity me—
at least they say they do—and in their pity
they have given me scraps of food and cast-off clothes;
that other thing, when I dare mention it,
none of them will—bringing me home again.

It is nine years now that I have spent dying,
with hunger and pain feeding my insatiable
disease. That, boy, is what they have done to me,
the two Atridae, and that mighty Prince
Odysseus. May the Gods that live in heaven
grant that they pay, agony for my agony.

Cephallenians: inhabitants of the island of Cephallenia, named after the mythical hero Cephalus **Chryse** (also Krisa): a town in Phocis on the gulf of Corinth **Atridae**: Agamemnon and Menelaos, members of the house of Atreus

9

PHILOCTETES CURSES NEOPTOLEMUS FOR HIS THEFT OF THE MAGIC BOW

(409 BC) SOPHOCLES, Philoctetes, *tr. D. Grene*

Inherently innocent and honorable, Neoptolemus has been persuaded by Odysseus to share in the betrayal of Philoctetes for the sake of Greek victory in Troy [see I, #8]. Acting as agent for Odysseus (who remains carefully concealed), he wins Philoctetes' complete trust, and pretends to be taking him back to his beloved father and homeland. At the last moment, the ruse about to be put into effect, Neoptolemus suffers a revulsion from the lie, and confesses to the real plan: the magic bow now in his own hands, Philoctetes is to be taken aboard ship and brought, captive, to Troy for the sake of the Greek army's then-foreordained victory.

The betrayal is doubly outrageous to Philoctetes—to his fully developed trust in Neoptolemus, and to his loss of possession of the bow, on which his life's sustenance on this island depends. His response is double too: from the height of his rage, he cries anathema on this vile betrayer; on his knees, he fawns, begs, appeals to the hopefully still innocent, the hopefully still "true self" of "son" Neoptolemus. He is alternately the powerful one and the helpless one; the proud, the cringing. And another opposition: on the one hand hoarsely whispering his appeals to the silent Neoptolemus, on the other crying aloud, at the top of his voice, to the caverns and crags and headlands of his landscape, the familiar great auditors of his griefs, who are also silent.

> **PHILOCTETES**
> You fire, you every horror, most hateful engine
> of ruthless mischief, what have you done to me,
> what treachery! Have you no shame to see me
> that kneeled to you, entreated you, hard of heart?
>
> You robbed me of my livelihood, taking my bow.
> Give it back, I beg you, give it back, I pray, my boy!
> By your father's Gods, do not take my livelihood.
> He does not say a word,
> but turns away his eyes. He will not give it up.
> Caverns and headlands, dens of wild creatures,
> you jutting broken crags, to you I raise my cry—
> there is no one else that I can speak to—
> and you have always been there, have always heard me.
> Let me tell you what he has done to me, this boy,
> Achilles' son. He swore to bring me home;
> he brings me to Troy. He gave me his right hand,
> then took and keeps my sacred bow,

the bow of Heracles, the son of Zeus,
and means to show it to the Argives,
as though in me he had conquered a strong man,
as though he led me captive to his power.
He does not know he is killing one that is dead,
a kind of vaporous shadow, a mere wraith.
Had I had my strength, he had not conquered me,
for, even as I am, it was craft that did it.
I have been deceived and am lost.
What can I do?

Give it back. Be your true self again. Will you not?
No word. Then I am nothing.

Two doors cut in the rock, to you again,
again I come, enter again, unarmed,
no means to feed myself! Here in this passage
I shall shrivel to death alone. I shall kill no more,
neither winged bird nor wild thing of the hills
with this my bow. I shall myself in death
be a feast for those that fed me. Those that I hunted
shall be my hunters now.
Life for the life I took, I shall repay
at the hands of this man that seemed to know no harm.

My curse upon your life!—but not yet still
until I know if you will change again;
if you will not, may an evil death be yours!

10

THE MESSENGER REPORTS THE CYNICALLY CONDUCTED TRIAL THAT CONDEMNED ORESTES TO DEATH

(408 BC) EURIPIDES, Orestes, *tr. J. Peck and F. Nisetich*

Again, the compassionate Messenger takes center stage [see I, #3, 6, and 7]. This time it is to report to Electra the proceedings of her trial (she, a woman, not in attendance) for the murder of her mother, Clytemnestra. He is compassionate as a former servant of their father Agamemnon who was murdered by Clytemnestra and her lover Aegisthus, and remains "loyal in the service of friends."

But the tone of his compassion is hardly tearful; it is shruggingly cynical. And his cynicism underlies his account of what he regards, throughout his report, as the casual corruption of justice. And that cynicism is thoroughly shared by Euripides.

It is not a week since Clytemnestra's murder. It was accomplished by Orestes by command of the god Apollo, who, unreliable god that he is, encouraged him with words but no real subsequent help. After the deed, Orestes, nursed by Electra, is suffering periodic lapses into madness, fits of seeing avenging Furies, and on each recovery recognizes with shame his own physical and mental disintegration. So does the family that's gathered—the respectable (one might say upper middle class) relatives of Clytemnestra: her father Tyndareus, her sister Helen and her husband Menelaus and their daughter Hermione. Tyndareus at once instigates the citizens of Argos to put Orestes and Electra on trial and condemn both to death by stoning. Menelaus carefully backs away from aiding Orestes in the face of civic opposition ("the usual policy," Orestes comments to his companion Pylades, "of faithless friends"), and the citizens at the trial—some for personal advantage, some out of conviction—discount Orestes' defense and that of one courageous citizen, and brother and sister are, as the Messenger reports, condemned.

Note the characterization not only of the arguments but of the personalities offering those arguments at the trial as the Messenger recapitulates them; their moral distinctions, as he summarizes them, carry not only his implied judgments of those principles but just as much his judgment of the perpetrators of those principles. The equation between the two clearly undercuts, for Euripides as for the Messenger, the pretensions of public discourse to being principled discourse. It is only one of the touches the play registers concerning human moral sham. So much and no more is the comfort the truly compassionate Messenger can offer Electra: only the bald truth.

> *(A MESSENGER, formerly a servant of Agamemnon, enters.)*

MESSENGER

Noble Electra! Daughter of Agamemnon,
hear what I have to say, unlucky though it is.
The Pelasgians have decreed that your brother,
and you with him, poor woman, must die today.
I happened to be coming through the gates from the fields,
wanting to see how things stood with you and Orestes.
For I always loved your father, and your house always supported me.
Peasant though I am I treat my friends nobly.
There was a crowd, then, going up the hill and filling the seats
where they say Danaos called the very first assembly,
when Aigyptos pressed his claims there. Seeing
all the citizens gathering, I asked one of them,
"What's happening in Argos? Has some threat of war
come from our enemies? Why all this disturbance?"
And he said, pointing: "Don't you see Orestes there,
coming this way, to run his deadly race?"
And then I saw a sight I didn't expect and wish
I'd never seen: Pylades and your brother on their way,
one limp and dejected, the other suffering with him

like a brother, helping and watching over him.
When there was a full crowd, a herald stood up and asked:
"Who wants to speak to the issue, whether or not
Orestes must be put to death
for killing his mother?" And thereupon
Talthybios rose, your father's henchman at Troy.
Always one to kowtow, he spoke both ways at once,
extolling your father but disparaging Orestes,
interweaving noble sentiments with vulgar ones,
to the effect that customs established by Orestes
would not bode well for parents. And he kept on
glancing and smiling at Aigisthos' men.
That's his type: heralds always go for the main chance.
Him too, sidling up to those in power.
After that Lord Diomedes addressed them.
He advised the city not to execute you and your brother,
but to do what religion demands, that is to banish you.
Shouts of approval greeted this, but others dissented.
And after that there rose the kind of man
who will say anything at all to get his way,
patriotic when it suits him, a hireling,
ready to stir up a row with his loose talk,
sure to entangle his audience in some crime.
He exhorted them to kill you and Orestes
by stoning; and it was Tyndareos
who coached your executioner.
Then another—not much to look at
but every inch a man—stood up and spoke against him.
Seldom seen in town or marketplace, he works the land
for himself, the kind of man our country relies on,
shrewd, though, and willing to press his points home.
Corruption couldn't touch him, not the way he's lived.
He said that Orestes, son of Agamemnon, ought
to be decorated for having dared to avenge
his father, to kill a whore and godless woman
who would have kept us from arming ourselves and going
off to war, afraid the stay-at-homes
would debauch the women while the men were gone.

He seemed to carry his point, too, at least
with respectable people.
And then
not a soul spoke up in support.
Your brother came forward
and said, "Citizens of Argos,
holders and protectors of the land
given to our fathers by Inachos,
in *your* defense, no less than my own father's,
I slew my mother. For if women get away
with killing men, if they are condoned, you are all
as good as dead, or you must become
slaves, women's slaves. You will be doing
the opposite of what you should do.
As of now, the woman who betrayed my father's bed
has died. But if you are bent on killing me,
the law becomes a mockery, and any man
is as good as dead. Mark my words:
they won't hold back from it."
But he didn't sway the crowd, for all his eloquence.
That scoundrel won—he carried the majority,
exhorting them to put your brother and you to death.
All that poor Orestes could do, to persuade them
to mitigate the sentence of public stoning, was to promise
that today both of you would take your own lives.
Pylades helped him to leave, weeping as he did so,
and other friends have joined them, commiserating, crying,
all on their way here now, a bitter spectacle.
So now you must prepare. Get a sword or a rope,
to make your way from the light. Noble birth has not saved you,
not even Pythian Apollo throned upon his tripod
has been your savior, but rather your destroyer.

Pelasgians: name of the primitive inhabitants of Greece **Danaos**: king of Argos, of Egyptian origin, ran away from a plot by his brother **Aigyptos** to kill him **Talthybius**: the herald of Agamemnon (see I, #7) **Diomedes**: king of the Bistones in Thrace, took part in the siege of Troy **Tyndareos**: king of Lacedemonia, father of Helen and Clytemnestra **Inachos**: founder of Argos, son of Oceanos and father of Io

11

POLYNEICES BEGS OEDIPUS' BLESSING BEFORE HIS BATTLE AGAINST HIS BROTHER

(406 BC) SOPHOCLES, Oedipus at Colonus, *tr. R. Fitzgerald*

Polyneices comes to blind and beggared Oedipus in Colonus for a fatherly blessing on his coming battle to win back the kingship of Thebes. He has a tough job. It was he and his brother Eteocles, and Creon, who 20 years before concurred in exiling Oedipus, and during the year when Polyneices was sole possessor of the throne, he failed to rescue or recall his wandering, suffering father. Since then, his younger brother Eteocles has taken over the kingship, and the banished Polyneices has now gathered an army to win it back. To win Oedipus' blessing for victory, he promises, if he defeats Eteocles, to return Oedipus to Thebes.

But Oedipus has already learned that an oracle has urged his being brought back to Thebes for final burial if the city is to prosper. Polyneices' motive for restoring him to Thebes, Oedipus understands, is as selfish as his motive had been for banishing him. Had it not been for King Theseus, whose hospitality has given Oedipus safe harbor in Colonus, and who supported Polyneices' attempt to approach his father, Oedipus would not have countenanced his son's presence at all. And had it not been for Antigone's encouraging Polyneices to continue his appeal in the face of Oedipus' refusal to answer, he would have given up. He makes this second attempt.

His argument: our plight is the same, both banished, both beggared, both wronged. With the army I've collected, and your now-magic blessing, I'll win; without your alliance against your other, your evil son, I'm doomed. It is characteristic of Greek tragedy's speeches of persuasion—both Euripides' and Sophocles'—that it is not the argument itself but the context in which the argument is uttered, that, if anything, undermines it [see I, #2]. Polyneices is aware of the potentially explosive wrath that could emanate from Oedipus in reply to his petition. But he is not conscious of the shameful inadequacy in Oedipus' mind of the arguments he poses to counter it. He speaks urgently—matter of life and death—with gathering assurance, and ends climactically posing the extreme alternatives of his victory or his doom. His tone is assured; his certainty is not.

> POLYNCEICES
> I will speak out then; your advice is fair.
> First, however, I must claim the help
> Of that same god of ocean from whose altars
> The governor of his land has lifted me
> And sent me here, giving me leave to speak
> And to await response, and a safe passage.
> These are the favors I desire from you,
> Strangers, and from my sisters and my father.
>
> And now, father, I will tell you why I came.
> I am a fugitive, driven from my country,
> Because I though fit, as the eldest born,
> To take my seat upon your sovereign throne.
> For that, Eteocles, the younger of us,
> Banished me—but not by a decision
> In argument or ability or arms;
> Merely because he won the city over.
> Of this I believe the Furies that pursue you
> Were indeed the cause: and so I hear
> From clairvoyants whom I afterwards consulted...
>
> Then, when I went into the Dorian land,
> I took Adrastus as my father-in-law,
> And bound to me in oath whatever men
> Were known as leaders or as fighters there;
> My purpose being to form an expedition
> Of seven troops of spearmen against Thebes—
> With which enlistment may I die for justice

Or else expel the men who exiled me!
So it is. Then why should I come here now?
Father, my prayers must be made to you!
Mine and those of all who fight with me!
Their seven columns under seven captains
Even now complete the encirclement of Thebes:
And it is I, your son—or if I am not
Truly your son, since evil fathered me,
At least I am called your son—it is I who lead
The fearless troops of Argos against Thebes.

Now in the name of these two children, father,
And for your own soul's sake, we all implore
And beg you to give up your heavy wrath
Against me! I go forth to punish him,
The brother who robbed me of my fatherland!
If we can put any trust in oracles,
They say that those you bless shall come to power.
Now by the gods and fountains of our people,
I pray you, listen and comply! Are we not beggars,
Both of us, and exiles, you and I?
We live by paying court to other men;
The same fate follows us.
But as for him—how insupportable!—
He lords it in our house, luxuriates there,
Laughs at us both!

If you will stand by me in my resolve,
I'll waste no time or trouble whipping him;
And then I'll re-establish you at home,
And settle there myself, and throw him out.
If your will is the same as mine, it's possible
To promise this. If not, I can't be saved.

god of ocean: Poseidon **Dorian**: Doris was an ancient country of Greece; home of the powerful Hellenic tribe **Adrastus**: a king of Argos, leader of the expedition of the Seven against Thebes who laid seige on the city on Polyneices' behalf **these two children**: Oedipus' daughters and Polyneices' sisters Antigone and Ismene

12

THE MESSENGER RECOUNTS THE
TRANSFIGURATION AND DEATH OF OEDIPUS

(406 BC) SOPHOCLES, Oedipus at Colonus, *tr. R. Fitzgerald*

A Messenger who tells of a miracle: the mysterious, sanctified death of Oedipus. His speech completes the story of Oedipus' transformation from the ostracized, beggared and polluted king who left his native Thebes cast out by his people and his own sons, to the long enduring journeyer who won sanctuary in Colonus, to the figure of overwhelming moral force who condemns the crimes against human propriety of Creon his erstwhile lieutenant and of his embattled sons, to the sanctified man who is beckoned by the gods themselves to join them in a way and in a place it is not feasible for any man—but Oedipus' savior, Theseus—to know. As the Messenger reports, what happened at the last "was no simple thing:" the transfiguration of a man into almost a god.

The Messenger is conscious of reciting wonders. He begins with the evidence his auditors saw with their own eyes—blind Oedipus without aid guiding a retinue—and continues with the facts as he observed them, each step of the way becoming more awesome, and finally transgressing human understanding. As with all Messenger speeches in Greek tragedy [see I, #3, 6, 10, 21], his intention is primarily evocative, his at-oneness with the experience he underwent as witness carrying the conviction of its truth, its reality. But unlike other Messenger speeches, this one is not intent on his auditors sharing the Messenger's emotion—his compassion or his anger or his cynicism toward what he is reporting. In this case, his own awe at the mystery of what he's witnessed is enough for him: if you think I'm exaggerating, he concludes, who cares? The man is a convert; he has no argument; he's seen the glory.

MESSENGER

Citizens, the briefest way to tell you
Would be to say that Oedipus is no more;
But what has happened cannot be told so simply—
It was no simple thing.

You know, for you were witnesses, how he
Left this place with no friend leading him,
Acting, himself, as guide for all of us.
Well, when he came to the steep place in the road,
The embankment there, secured with steps of brass,
He stopped in one of the many branching paths.
This was not far from the stone bowl that marks
Theseus' and Pirithous' covenant.

Half-way between that place of stone
With its hollow pear tree, and the marble tomb,
He sat down and undid his filthy garments;
Then he called his daughters and commanded
That they should bring him water from a fountain
For bathing and libation to the dead.
From there they could see the hill of Demeter,
Freshener of all things: so they ascended it
And soon came back with water for their father;
Then helped him properly to bathe and dress.

When everything was finished to his pleasure,
And no command of his remained undone,
Then the earth groaned with thunder from the god below;
And as they heard the sound, the girls shuddered,
And dropped to their father's knees, and began wailing,
Beating their breasts and weeping as if heartbroken.
And hearing them cry so bitterly,
He put his arms around them, and said to them:

"Children, this day your father is gone from you.
All that was mine is gone. You shall no longer

Bear the burden of taking care of me—
I know it was hard, my children.—And yet one word
Makes all those difficulties disappear:
The word is love. You never shall have more
From any man than you have had from me.
And now you must spend the rest of life without me."

That was the way of it. They clung together
And wept, all three. But when they finally stopped,
And no more sobs were heard, then there was
Silence, and in the silence suddenly
A voice cried out to him—of such a kind
It made our hair stand up in panic fear:
Again and again the call came from the god:
"Oedipus! Oedipus! Why are we waiting?
You delay too long; you delay too long to go!"

Then, knowing himself summoned by the spirit,
He asked that the lord Theseus come to him;
And when he had come, said: "O beloved one,
Give your right hand now as a binding pledge
To my two daughters; children, give him your hands.
Promise that you will never willingly
Betray them, but will carry out in kindness
Whatever is best for them in the days to come."

And Theseus swore to do it for his friend,
With such restraint as fits a noble king.
And when he had done so, Oedipus at once
Laid his blind hands upon his daughters, saying:
"Children, you must show your nobility,
and have the courage now to leave this spot.
You must not wish to see what is forbidden,
Or hear what you may not afterward be told.
But go   go quickly. Only the lord Theseus
May stay to see the thing that now begins."

This much every one of us heard him say,
And then we came away with the sobbing girls.
But after a little while as we withdrew
We turned around—and nowhere saw that man,
But only the king, his hands before his face,
Shading his eyes as if from something awful,
Fearful and unendurable to see.
Then very quickly we saw him do reverence
To Earth and to the powers of the air,
With one address to both.

But in what manner
Oedipus perished, no one of mortal men
Could tell but Theseus. It was not lightning,
Bearing its fire from God, that took him off,
No hurricane was blowing.
But some attendant from the train of heaven
Came for him; or else the underworld
Opened in love the unlit door of earth.
For he was taken without lamentation,
Illness or suffering; indeed his end
Was wonderful if mortal's ever was.

Should someone think I speak intemperately,
I make no apology to him who thinks so.

Pirithous: Theseus' friend and follower; after a contest, Theseus and Pirithous
filled with admiration for each other swore brotherhood; later Pirithous helped
Theseus carry off Persephone from Hades, from which adventure they were rescued by Heracles

Tragedy/Drama

ELIZABETHAN/JACOBEAN

13

TAMBURLAINE PERSUADES AN ENEMY CAPTAIN TO JOIN HIM
(1587-88) CHRISTOPHER MARLOWE, Tamburlaine the Great, *Act 1, Sc. 2*

It was the Elizabethan actor Edward Alleyn who was reputed to make bombast real, and who first roared with conviction the role of Marlowe's *Tamburlaine,* and made welcome to Elizabethan audiences the remarkable fanfare of Marlowe's lines. Hopeless to treat Tamburlaine as the intimate of his own inner self, addressing his thoughts inward to his own percipient bosom. Not until the last act of the double-length play does he speak with any measure of intro-spection or with, so to speak, self-address. Not until he is on the verge of dying. Until then, just as he cuts a wide swath through the known world, so he cuts a very wide swath through his throat's vocables.

But this is *not*, and has little relation to, what we think of as 'char-acterization.' Here is a different relation between the actor and the words coming out of his mouth, a relation that is never wholly lost in classical tradition, one that was revived by Brecht: the actor is not *being* the character subjectively, but *reports on* the character objective-ly, by so to speak "quoting" his words. As between consciousness of the character's rhetoric, and identity with the character's emotional inwardness, he is far closer to the first. Just as the Messenger's speech in Greek tragedy evokes completely *in words* the reality of the scene described but *is not in* the scene described, so the actor evokes the con-dition, the nature, the emotion, the intentions, of the character *in words,* but is not *being* the character. The contemporary equivalent of this is the great singer-actors of opera, who no matter how close they may feel they are getting to the subjectivity of the role they are singing, uppermost in their focus and in the spectator's focus is the *musical description* of those emotions, not the actualized replication of them. And rhetoric, like music, has formalities, limitations and strategies of its own that can be violated just so much in the service of behavioral literalism before the art of rhetoric and the art of duplicating real behavior collapse together into foolishness.

Tamburlaine is one of the Renaissance's early instances of the conqueror living by cruelty only to be kind. He does not, as did his later counterparts, bring guns and bibles to the benighted and the weak, but the example of himself as the new and strenuous instance of Man. His greatness is in his boundlessness and shamelessness, in the limitless thrust of his ambition, and in his limitless violation of the humane. The shock, for us but not perhaps for the Elizabethans, is the proximity within the compass of his ideals of what might still be thought of as noble striving and bottomless savagery. Marlowe generally tests and defines the limits of human possibility.

The Persian Captain Theridamas has been sent by his Emperor with 1,000 horses to get rid of what he thinks of as an upstart annoyance, the shepherd Tamburlaine who has come to invade Persepolis with 500 men. So raw, so outnumbered, Tamburlaine turns to persuasion rather than force. And in this first display for us of his prowess, we discover along with Theridamas that it is bravely, rashly, hugely, and largely verbal. But it is as overwhelmingly successful as though it had been martial. Through this speech alone, the Persian Captain, taking the measure of his man, is overwhelmed, totally conquered, and joins him.

> TAMBURLAINE
> In thee, thou valiant man of Persia,
> I see the folly of thy emperor.
> Art thou but captain of a thousand horse,
> That by characters graven in thy brows,
> And by thy martial face and stout aspect,

Deserv'st to have the leading of an host!
Forsake thy king, and do but join with me,
And we will triumph over all the world.
I hold the Fates bound fast in iron chains,
And with my hand turn Fortune's wheel about:
And sooner shall the sun fall from his sphere
Than Tamburlaine be slain or overcome.
Draw forth thy sword, thou mighty man-at-arms,
Intending but to raze my charmed skin,
And Jove himself will stretch his hand from Heaven
To ward the blow and shield me safe from harm.
See how he rains down heaps of gold in showers,
As if he meant to give my soldiers pay!
And as a sure and grounded argument,
That I shall be the monarch of the East,
He sends his Soldan's daughter, rich and brave,
To be my Queen and portly Empress.
If thou wilt stay with me, renowned man,
And lead thy thousand horse with my conduct,
Besides thy share of this Egyptian prize
Those thousand horse shall sweat with martial spoil
Of conquer'd kingdoms and of cities sack'd.
Both we will walk upon the lofty clifts,
And Christian merchants that with Russian stems
Plough up huge furrows in the Caspian sea,
Shall vail to us, as lords of all the lake.
Both we will reign as consuls of the earth,
And mighty kings shall be our senators.
Jove sometime masked in a shepherd's weed,
And by those steps that he hath scal'd the Heavens
May we become immortal like the gods.
Join with me now in this my mean estate,
(I call it mean because, being yet obscure,
The nations far remov'd admire me not,)
And when my name and honour shall be spread
As far as Boreas claps his brazen wings,

Or fair Bootes sends his cheerful light,
Then shalt thou be competitor with me,
And sit with Tamburlaine in all his majesty.

Fates bound fast: Tamburlaine's claim is that he himself has stopped the
progress of the Fates in governing the length of life **Soldan**: the Sultan of Egypt,
Zenocrate's father **portly**: of noble bearing **conduct**: direction **clifts**: cliffs **stems**:
ships **vail**: i.e. shall lower their flags in salute **as far as Boreas**: to the farthest
North **Bootes**: a northern constellation containing Arcturus

14

TAMBURLAINE CELEBRATES HIS LOVE FOR ZENOCRATE AND FOR HIMSELF
(1587-88) CHRISTOPHER MARLOWE, Tamburlaine the Great, *Act 5, Sc. 2*

This is the fullest expression of Tamburlaine's two primary devotions described in the previous note [see I, #13]. The occasion is
the demise of Egypt, Zenocrate's home, on the verge of being conquered by Tamburlaine, portending the possible destruction of its
ruler, her father. Zenocrate, at the previous night's banquet, has pleaded gently for a measure of mercy from Tamburlaine in the coming
battle, and he's reassured her. But now, in apparent contradiction of
his characteristic ruthlessness, his lack of compassion for any, he is
deeply moved by Zenocrate's plea of the night before. But his praise
for the beauty of her compassion is inevitably tied, in his conclusion,
to praise for himself as well.

TAMBURLAINE
Ah, fair Zenocrate! divine Zenocrate!
Fair is too foul an epithet for thee,
That in thy passion for thy country's love,
And fear to see thy kingly father's harm,

With hair dishevell'd wip'st thy watery cheeks;
And, like to Flora in her morning's pride
Shaking her silver tresses in the air,
Rain'st on the earth resolved pearl in showers,
And sprinklest sapphires on thy shining face,
Where Beauty, Mother of the Muses, sits
And comments volumes with her ivory pen,
Taking instructions from thy flowing eyes;
Eyes when that Ebena steps to Heaven,
In silence of thy solemn evening's walk,
Making the mantle of the richest night,
The moon, the planets, and the meteors, light.
There angels in their crystal armours fight
A doubtful battle with my tempted thoughts
For Egypt's freedom, and the Soldan's life;
His life that so consumes Zenocrate,
Whose sorrows lay more siege unto my soul,
Than all my army to Damascus' walls:
And neither Persia's sovereign, nor the Turk
Troubled my senses with conceit of foil
So much by much as doth Zenocrate.
What is beauty, saith my sufferings, then?
If all the pens that ever poets held
Had fed the feeling of their master's thoughts,
And every sweetness that inspir'd their hearts,
Their minds, and muses on admired themes;
If all the heavenly quintessence they still
From their immortal flowers of poesy,
Wherein, as in a mirror, we perceive
The highest reaches of a human wit:
If these had made one poem's period,
And all combin'd in beauty's worthiness,
Yet should there hover in their restless heads
One thought, one grace, one wonder, at the least,
Which into words no virtue can digest.
But how unseemly is it for my sex,
My discipline of arms and chivalry,

My nature, and the terror of my name,
To harbour thoughts effeminate and faint!
Save only that in beauty's just applause,
With whose instinct the soul of man is touch'd;—
And every warrior that is rapt with love
Of fame, of valor, and of victory,
Must needs beauty beat on his conceits:
I thus conceiving and subduing both
That which hath stoop'd the tempest of the gods,
Even from the fiery-spangled veil of Heaven,
To feel the lovely warmth of shepherds' flames
And mask in cottages of strowed weeds,
Shall give the world to note, for all my birth,
That virtue solely is the sum of glory,
And fashions man with true nobility.

passion: sorrow **Flora**: goddess of vegetation **resolved pearl**: tears **Ebena**: called "a drowsy deity", and so, worshipped by sleepers, who are said to "sacrifice to the God of Ebena" **the Turk**: the sultan of the Ottoman Empire, the most powerful Mohammedan kingdom at the time when *Tamburlaine* was written **conceit of foil**: thought of being defeated, overthrown **still**: distill **virtue**, mental energy, effort **strowed**: spread around **virtue…the sum of glory**: the "genius" of the exceptional person in valor rather than intellect

15
TAMBURLAINE SHOWS HIMSELF
MAGNANIMOUS IN VICTORY
(1587-88) CHRISTOPHER MARLOWE, Tamburlaine the Great, *Act 5, Sc. 2*

Tamburlaine, having conquered the Turks, the Egyptians, the Persians, the known Eastern world with unparalleled efficiency and cruelty, is ready, at the end of Part One, to lay down arms and "put on scarlet robes," rewarding his followers in arms with sundry kingdoms and principalities. Dead and defeated emperors and kings are lying at his feet in heaps, among them the Emperor and Empress of Turkey—having just dashed out their brains—and the King of Arabia—having just expired of wounds received in the previous moment's battle. But one among the defeated potentates who is to share in Tamburlaine's geographical spoils, is sacred to him—the father of his beloved, the "divine Zenocrate." It is she, his captive, who from the beginning of the play to this moment's end has shared his progress, she unwillingly, he enraptured, worshipful, sexually, piously abstaining from her, his vision of perfect beauty. His is equally a devotion to the absolute dominance of arms and to absolute self-abnegation at the feet of beauty.

To the end Tamburlaine continues to voice his loftiest, his most fulsome apostrophes to these two visions—himself as the conqueror of universes and as the Godhead of the gods, invincible over destiny, over what is, and Zenocrate, the ultimate of beauty. In this concluding moment of Part One of the play, he has reached what, in the play's context, is to be understood as the apogee of accomplishment, as well as the apogee of devotion. With the largesse of the all-powerful, he offers earthly kingdoms to his warriors, and holy marriage to his paragon.

TAMBURLAINE
'T was I, my lord, that gat the victory,
And therefore grieve not at your overthrow,
Since I shall render all into your hands,
And add more strength to your dominions
Than ever yet conform'd th' Egyptian crown.
The god of war resigns his room to me,
Meaning to make me general of the world.
Jove, viewing me in arms, looks pale and wan,
Fearing my power shall pull him from his throne.
Where-er I come the Fatal Sisters sweat,

And grisly Death, by running to and fro,
To do their ceaseless homage to my sword.
And here in Afric, where it seldom rains,
Since I arriv'd with my triumphant host,
Have swelling clouds, drawn from wide-gasping wounds,
Been oft resolv'd in bloody purple showers,
A meteor that might terrify the earth,
And make it quake at every drop it drinks.
Millions of souls sit on the banks of Styx,
Waiting the back return of Charon's boat;
Hell and Elysium swarms with ghosts of men
That I have sent from sundry foughten fields,
To spread my fame through hell and up to Heaven.
And see, my lord, a sight of strange import,
Emperors and kings lie breathless at my feet.
The Turk and his Great Empress, as it seems,
Left to themselves while we were at the fight,
Have desperately dispatch'd their slavish lives;
With them Arabia, too, has left his life:
All sights of power to grace my victory.
And such are objects fit for Tamburlaine;
Wherein, as in a mirror, may be seen
His honour that consists in shedding blood,
When men presume to manage arms with him.
Then sit thou down, divine Zenocrate;
And here we crown thee Queen of Persia,
And all the kingdoms and dominions
That late the power of Tamburlaine subdu'd.
Egyptians, Moors, and men of Asia,
From Barbary unto the Western Indie,
Shall pay a yearly tribute to thy sire;
And from the bounds of Afric to the banks
Of Ganges shall his mighty arm extend.
And now, my lords and loving followers,
Hang up your weapons on Alcides' post,
For Tamburlaine takes truce with all the world.
Thy first-bethroted love, Arabia,

Shall we with honour, as beseems, entomb,
With this great Turk and his fair Empress.
Then, after all these solemn exequies,
We will our rites of marriage solemnise.

gat: got **Fatal Sisters**: the Fates in Greek mythology, three sisters who measured the length of everyone's life on a thread of wool **the Turk**: the sultan of the Ottoman Empire, the most powerful Mohammedan kingdom at the time when *Tamburlaine* was written **Latona's daughter**: Artemis, the goddess of the hunt **Barbary**: from the west and central coast of northern Africa **Ganges**: the sacred river in India **Alcides' post**: door-post of the temple of Hercules **exequies**: funeral rites (mod., obsequies)

16

FAUSTUS REJECTS SCHOLASTIC LEARNING, YEARNS FOR NECROMANTIC KNOWLEDGE
(c1589) CHRISTOPHER MARLOWE, The Tragical History of Doctor Faustus, *Act 1, Sc. 1*

Faustus, having just been awarded his doctorate at the University of Wittenberg, reviews in turn the subjects he had most diligently studied—logic, medicine, law, theology—for their "end," that is, their ultimate value for the self. But as with Tamburlaine, the self has itself an ultimate value: omnipotence. The failure Faustus mourns in his studies is their failure to grant him that: "Yet art thou but Faustus and a man." Faustus sitting in his study with a heap of texts surrounding him, rejecting them one after the other until he comes to the text concealed at the bottom of the heap—the book of spells—is the image of the ultimate of human frustration and human yearning as it was reconstituted in the Renaissance, not as the imitation of Christ, but as the imitation of Godhead itself: omnipotence through omniscience. (At least, so reconstituted by Marlowe.) The chopped, descending, failing rhythms of the first part of the soliloquy are succeeded by the brilliant, sustained rhythmic arcs of the second part, as though with the opening of the volume of necromantics, the weight of Faustus's frustration is thrown off, and the random instances of omnipotence, both skittish and serious, which he calls up suddenly light the dark study in which he has been brooding, and out of that darkness emerges a triumphant intent: "Here tire my brains to gain a deity!"

FAUSTUS
Settle thy studies, Faustus, and begin
To sound the depth of that thou wilt profess;
Having commenced, be a divine in show,
Yet level at the end of every art,
And live and die in Aristotle's works.
Sweet Analytics, 'tis thou hast ravished me—
(Reads)
Bene disserere est finis logices.
Is to dispute well logic's chiefest end?
Affords this art no greater miracle?
Then read no more, thou hast attained the end;
A greater subject fitteth Faustus' wit:
Bid ὄν χαι μή ὄν farewell; Galen come,
Seeing *Ubi destinit philosophus, ibi incipit medicus*;
Be a physician, Faustus, heap up gold,
And be eternized for some wondrous cure.

(Reads)
Summum bonum medicinae sanitas,
The end of physic is our body's health.
Why, Faustus, hast thou not attained that end?
Is not thy common talk sound aphorisms?
Are not thy bills hung up as monuments,
Whereby whole cities have escaped the plague,
And thousand desperate maladies been eased?
Yet art thou still but Faustus and a man.
Wouldst thou make men to live eternally,
Or, being dead, raise them to life again,

Then this profession were to be esteemed.
Physic, farewell.—Where is Justinian?

(Reads)
Si una eademque res legatur duobus, alter rem, alter valorem rei, etc.
A pretty case of paltry legacies!

(Reads)
Exhaereditare filium non potest pater nisi, etc.
Such is the subject of the Institute
And universal body of the law.
His study fits a mercenary drudge,
Who aims at nothing but external trash;
Too servile and illiberal for me.
When all is done divinity is best;
Jerome's Bible, Faustus, view it well.

(Reads)
Stipendium peccati mors est. Ha! *Stipendium, etc.*
The reward of sin is death. That's hard.

(Reads)
Si peccasse negamus, fallimur, et nulla est in nobis veritas.
If we say that we have no sin we deceive ourselves, and there's no truth in us.
Why, then, belike we must sin, and so consequently die.
Ay, we must die an everlasting death.
What doctrine call you this, *Che sera sera,*
What will be, shall be? Divinity, adieu!

settle: to define **commenced...divine**: graduated (doctorate in theology) **level**: aim **Analytics**: Aristotle's logic, dominant in medieval curriculum, consisted of "prior" and "posterior" analytics **bene dissere est finis logices**, Lat: (translated in the next line) good dispute is logic's chiefest end ον χαι μη ον, Gr: the Aristotelian "being and not being," i.e. philosophy **Galen**: the standard classical work on medical science **Ubi desinit philosophus ibi incipit medicus**, Lat:"where the philosopher stops, the doctor begins" **summum bonum medidicae sanitas**, Lat: (translated in the next line), the highest good of medicine is health **sound aphorisms**: valid precepts (the medical precepts of Hippocrates, the father of medicine, were called Aphorisms) **bills hung up as monuments**: prescriptions used to be posted in public places as enduring examples of medical art The Byzantine Emperor **Justinian** I the Great (483-565): the Justinian Code is the textbook of Roman law *Si una eademque res legatur duobus, alter rem, alter valorem rei*, Lat: "if the same thing is bequeathed to two persons, let one have the thing, and the other its equivalent in other property," a quote from Justinian's Code *Exhaereditare filium non potest pater nisi*, Lat: "a father cannot disinherit his son unless…" **the Institute**: Justinian's *Institutes*, aka the Code **Jerome's Bible**: the Latin version of the Scriptures, accepted as the authorized version of the Roman Catholic Church, prepared by Jerome at the end of the 4th century *Stipendium peccati mors est*, Lat: the reward of sin is death *Si peccasse negamus, fallimur, et nulla est in nobis veritas*, Lat: (translated in the next line) *Che sera sera*, It: (translated in the next line)

17
FAUSTUS ENVISIONS THE BLESSINGS OF CONJURING
(c1589) CHRISTOPHER MARLOWE, The Tragical History of Doctor Faustus, *Act 1, Sc. 1*

[see I, #16]

FAUSTUS
These metaphysics of magicians
And necromantic books are heavenly;
Lines, circles, signs, letters, and characters:
Ay, these are those that Faustus most desires.
Oh, what a world of profit and delight,
Of power, of honor, of omnipotence
Is promised to the studious artisan!
All things that move between the quiet poles
Shall be at my command: emperors and kings
Are but obeyed in their several provinces,
Nor can they raise the wind or rend the clouds;
But his dominion that excels in this
Stretcheth as far as doth the mind of man:

A sound magician is a demi-god;
Here tire my braines to get a deity!

How am I glutted with conceit of this!
Shall I make spirits fetch me what I please,
Resolve me of all ambiguities,
Perform what desperate enterprise I will?
I'll have them fly to India for gold,
Ransack the ocean for orient pearl,
And search all corners of the new-found world
For pleasant fruits and princely delicates.
I'll have them read me strange philosophy
And tell the secrets of all foreign kings;
I'll have them wall all Germany with brass
And with swift Rhine circle fair Wittenberg;
I'll have them fill the public schools with silk
Wherewith the students shall be bravely clad.
I'll levy soldiers with the coin they bring
And chase the Prince of Parma from our land
And reign sole king in all our provinces;
Yea, stranger engines for the brunt of war
Than was the fiery keel at Antwerp's bridge
I'll make my servile spirits to invent.

Come German Valdes and Cornelius,
And make me blest with your sage conference.
Valdes, sweet Valdes, and Cornelius,
Know that your words have won me at the last
To practice magic and concealed arts;
Yet not your words only, but mine own fantasy,
That will receive no object, for my head
But ruminates on necromantic skill.
Philosophy is odious and obscure,
Both law and physic are for petty wits,
Divinity is basest of the three,
Unpleasant, harsh, contemptible, and vile;

'Tis magic, magic, that hath ravished me.
Then, gentle friends, aid me in this attempts,
And I, that have in concise syllogisms
Graveled the pastors of the German church,
And made the flowering pride of Wittenberg
Swarm to my problems as the infernal spirits
On sweet Musaeus when he came to hell,
Will be as cunning as Agrippa was,
Whose shadow made all Europe honor him.

Then come and dine with me, and after meat
We'll canvass every quiddity thereof,
For ere I sleep I'll try what I can do:
This night I'll conjure though I die therefor.

metaphysics…necromantic books: supernatural arts and books of black magic **artizan**: virtuoso **quiet poles**: the stationary north and south poles **wall all Germany with brass**: suggested by the legend of Friar Bacon, who meant to wall England with brass **Rhine circled fair Wittenberg**: to divert the course of the Rhine river to enclose the university town of Wittenberg, the city of Faustus **public schools**: university classrooms **the Prince of Parma**: later Duke, was Philip II's governor for the Spanish crown in the Netherlands **provinces**: of the Netherlands **fiery keel**: a fire-ship employed by the defenders of Antwerp in 1585 to blow up Parma's bridge **graveled**: confounded **problems**: demonstrations **Musaeus**: ancient Thracian poet, when he descended to the underworld the shadows of the dead swarmed around him to hear his music **Agrippa** von Nettesheim (1486-1535): a reputed magician who apparently created "**shadows**" who "in the moment they were seen were of any shape one would conceive" (Lyly's Campassepy Prologue) **quiddity**: essential element, a scholastic term

18

FAUSTUS PRAYS IN HIS LAST HOUR TO ESCAPE DAMNATION

(c1589) CHRISTOPHER MARLOWE, The Tragical History of Doctor Faustus, *Act 5, Sc. 2*

Faustus's pact with the devil is specific: in exchange for his immortal soul, he will win access to all knowledge. Knowledge is the key to his quest, since having all knowledge at his command, he'd be capable subsequently—and on his own—of grasping unlimited power. But to grasp, in turn, the densely packed ironies of this, Faustus's last soliloquy, one must be clear about what it is that Faustus has, through the course of the play, lost—for the play describes the step-by-step journey of Faustus toward an end of total loss. But loss of what? Not merely, as one might suppose from the medieval folk legend, his immortal soul, but the crippling loss of what it is that makes that loss inevitable: the loss of the ability to accumulate knowledge, the ability to know at all.

There's a theological substratum to the logic of Faustus's demise that would be inappropriate to detail here, but the fundamental notion is this: that knowing anything at all is dependent on a triad of commitments: knowledge-faith-love, none of which is attainable without the other. And all knowledge is dependent on the triad's commitment to the primacy of God, who is at the apex and is also the ultimate embrace of all power and all knowledge. If that is abrogated—as it is by Faustus's commitment to Lucifer—then the structure of all knowledge (dependent as it is on definable distinctions that hinge on and find meaning only through the recognition of the primacy of God) collapses into a mass of non-distinctions, and finally, even into the equivalencies of opposites.

Faustus, in his pursuit of power through knowledge, suffers the growing inconvenience of increasingly constraining limits on what he can know through his mentor, Mephistopheles. Each time Faustus reaches the very threshold of a final answer—in each instance, the answer is "God"—and so Mephistopheles must frustrate his inquiry. And each time Faustus reaches for one of the sacraments—marriage, for example—Mephistopheles can only offer him its gross equivalent—whoredom. Faustus's soul's damnation is preceded by his intellectual damnation. Note its consequence in his final soliloquy, in which the greatest and the least, the most sacred and the most damned, the most enduring and the most ephemeral, merge and become indistinguishable. It is presaged by his appeal to the earlier image of Helen: "Make me immortal with a kiss." And in the end, his increasing desperation leads to increasingly blind, increasingly unknowing equivalencies in his appeals for rescue: for time to stand still, for this hour to become a year, for his matter to become mist, for the limitless to have limit, for body to turn into air, or into water-drops—in a word, for his temporal presence to become eternal absence. But most tellingly, when Christ's blood is revealed to him— his assurance of redemption—he cries, almost in a breath, "Ah my Christ!…Spare me Lucifer!" As midnight approaches, and Faustus's terrified yearning for an alternative to damnation increases, his intellect, brilliantly inventive as ever, flailing about for avenues of escape, is nevertheless frustrated by its incapacity and imprisonment in an ultimate and unknowing darkness. His wan promise at the end to correct his life's error—"I'll burn my books!"—is the capping irony.

(The clock strikes eleven.)

FAUSTUS
Ah Faustus,
Now hast thou but one bare hour to live,
And then thou must be damned perpetually.
Stand still thou ever-moving spheres of heaven,

That time may cease and midnight never come;
Fair nature's eye, rise, rise again and make
Perpetual day; or let this hour but be
A year, a month, a week, a natural day,
That Faustus may repent and save his soul.
O lente lente currite noctis equi!
The stars move still, time runs, the clock will strike,
The devil will come, and Faustus must be damned.
Oh, I'll leap up to my God! Who pulls me down?
See see where Christ's blood streams in the firmament!
One drop would save my soul, half a drop. Ah my Christ!—
Rend not my heart for naming of my Christ;
Yet will I call on him: oh, spare me Lucifer!—
Where is it now? 'Tis gone: and see where God
Stretcheth out his arm and bends his ireful brows.
Mountains and hills, come, come and fall on me
And hide me from the heavy wrath of God!
No, no:
Then will I headlong run into the earth.
Earth gape! O no, it will not harbor me.
You stars that reigned at my nativity,
Whose influence hath allotted death and hell,
Now draw up Faustus like a foggy mist
Into the entrails of your laboring clouds,
That when they vomit forth into the air,
My limbs may issue from their smoky mouths,
So that my soul may but ascend to heaven.

(The watch strikes.)

Ah, half the hour is passed; 'twill all the passed anon.
O God,
If thou wilt not have mercy on my soul,
Yet for Christ's sake, whose blood hath ransomed me,
Impose some end to my incessant pain;
Let Faustus live in hell a thousand years,
A hundred thousand, and at last be saved!

Oh, no end is limited to damned souls.
Why wert thou not a creature wanting soul?
Or why is this immortal that thou hast?
Ah, Pythagoras' metempsychosis, were that true
This soul should fly from me and be changed
Unto some brutish beast: all beasts are happy,
For when they die
Their souls are soon dissolved in elements;
But mine must live still to be plagued in hell.
Cursed be the parents that engendered me!
No Faustus, curse thyself, curse Lucifer
That hath deprived thee of the joys of heaven.

(The clock striketh twelve.)
It strikes, it strikes! Now body, turn to air,
Or Lucifer will bear thee quick to hell!

(Thunder and lightning.)
O soul, be changed to little water-drops
And fall into the ocean, ne'er be found.

(Enter devils.)
My God, my God! Look not so fierce on me!
Adders and serpents, let me breathe awhile!
Ugly hell, gape not! Come not Lucifer;
I'll burn my books!—Ah, Mephistopheles!

(Exeunt with him.)

nature's eye: the sun ***O lente lente currite noctis equi!***, Lat: slightly altered from Ovid's *Amores*, "Run slowly, slowly, horses of the night" **limited**: measured out **Pythagoras' metempsychosis**: the doctrine of Pythagoras of Samos concerning the transmigration of souls appealed powerfully to the Elizabethan imagination **elements**: earth, air, fire, water **quick**: alive

19

GAVESTON, THE NEW KING'S FAVORITE, MAKES PLANS

(c1592) CHRISTOPHER MARLOWE, The Tragedy of Edward II, *Act 1, Sc. 1*

Gaveston had been banished from England by Edward's father, and now with the old king's death, he's welcomed back by the son, Edward II. We meet Edward II through Gaveston's enthusiastic description of the King's likely appetite for the entertainments of Gaveston's imagination. And we meet Gaveston, for the first time, in these words. Thrilled with the news of Edward's sudden ascension to the throne, learning that his exile in boring France is over, at once leaping in dream to his beloved Edward and dismissing from thought the extraneous appendages of the London scene when he gets there— the city itself, its multitudes, its noble peers—he calls up two visions: one, his lying enfolded in the king's bosom, a willing lover, and two, his manipulating the king at his pleasure.

And so Gaveston's intent is double: to be ruled by his love of the king, and to rule the king's love. The meshing of the two opposite motives in a euphoria of anticipation gives us a fixed definition of Gaveston, but only a preliminary, initial insight into Edward.

What will his stage-managed entertainment of Edward be? He sees it clearly, describes it in synopsis—a masque exalting nubile boys. But inadvertently, Gaveston previsions his Edward's, his "Actaeon's" fate: turned into a fugitive by an angry 'goddess' for "peeping" at such entertainment, Edward will be 'pulled down by yelping hounds' and die.

> *(Enter Gaveston, reading on a letter that was brought to*
> *him from the King)*

GAVESTON

"My father is deceas'd! Come, Gaveston,
And share the kingdom with thy dearest friend."
Ah! words that make me surfeit with delight!
What greater bliss can hap to Gaveston
Than live and be the favourite of a king!
Sweet prince, I come; these, these thy amorous lines
Might have enforc'd me to have surum from France,
And, like Leander, gasp'd upon the sand,
So thou would'st smile, and take me in thy arms.
The sight of London to my exil'd eyes
Is as Elysium to a new-come soul;
Not that I love the city, or the men,
But that it harbors him I hold so dear—
The king, upon whose bosom let me lie,
And with the world be still at enmity.

Farewell, base stooping to the lordly peers!
My knee shall bow to none but to the king.
As for the multitude, that are but sparks
Rak'd up in embers of their poverty,—
Tanti! I'll fawn first on the wind
That glanceth at my lips, and flyeth away.

These are not men for me:
I must have wanton poets, pleasant wits,
Musicians, that with touching of a string
May draw the pliant king which way I please.
Music and poetry is his delight;
Therefore I'll have Italian masks by night,
Sweet speeches, comedies, and pleasing shows;
And in the day, when he shall walk abroad,
Like sylvan nymphs my pages shall be clad;

My men, like satyrs grazing on the lawns,
Shall with their goat-feet dance an antic hay.
Sometime a lovely boy in Dian's shape,
With hair that gilds the water as it glides,
Crownets of pearl about his naked arms,
And in his sportful hands an olive tree,
To hide those parts which men delight to see,
Shall bathe him in a spring; and there hard by,
One like Actaeon peeping through the grove
Shall by the angry goddess be transform'd
And running in the likeness of an hart
By yelping hounds pull'd down, and seem to die;—
Such things as these best please his majesty.

Leander, in Greek mythology, swam across the Hellespont every night to visit his lover Hero **"what need the Arctic people…"**: allusion to arctic day/night which lasts several months *Tanti*, It: so much for them! **Italian masks**: i.e., the ones from the Festival in Venice in February were very much in vogue at the time **like silver nymphs…hay** (a lively rural dance): Gaveston is suggesting an imitation of the licentious Greek satiric festivals **Dian(a)**: the Roman goddess of hunting and the moon, when seen by Actaeon bathing, changed him into a stag

20

EDWARD DEFENDS HIS LOVE OF GAVESTON AGAINST HIS NOBLES
(c1592) CHRISTOPHER MARLOWE, The Tragedy of Edward II, *Act 2, Sc. 2*

Shocked by Edward's open display of affection for Gaveston, and furious at the thought of the king's mignon having court influence over themselves, the nobility confronts Edward and insists that he be rid of his favorite. Edward's response to their demand is a tribute to his steadfastness and loyalty, but also the sure sign of his political fatuity. Like Shakespeare's Richard II, he believes that ultimate power is guaranteed by the symbols alone of kingly office, but has no understanding at all of the realities that lie behind those symbols if they are to have any meaning. Richard claims the sufficiency of divine right— God, who makes kings, is obliged to protect them; Edward claims the sufficiency of his own absolute will. Both make elaborate display of their self-assurance, Richard almost unconsciously, as a matter of course, but Edward purposefully, aggressively, cheerfully flaunting kingly privilege as though it were power in itself.

It is this flaunting that is the essence of his intent in this scene. His will, he tells the barons, is immovable by appeal or threat. "I am that cedar, shake me not too much." And rising to the height of his assertion of ultimate privilege, with deliberate mockery of their authority and influence, he makes a show of fawning over Gaveston before them, and then—ultimate insult—requires them to pay homage to his lover, to welcome him as their equal, or more than equal.

When in disgust they turn their backs on him, he is caught in the vice of his kingly posture, fragile at best and now, with the barons' outraged defection, becoming unsupported and insupportable. This is the moment that determines Edward's doom: his posture is all that is left to him, but he pursues policy—war against these barons—now, almost literally tilting at windmills.

> EDWARD
>
> They love me not that hate my Gaveston.
> I am that cedar, shake me not too much;
> And you the eagles; soar ye ne'er so high,
> I have the jesses that will pull you down;
> And *Aeque tandem* shall that canker cry
> Unto the proudest peer of Britainy.
> Though thou compar'st him to a flying fish,
> And threatenest death whether he rise or fall,
> 'Tis not the hugest monster of the sea,

Nor foulest harpy that shall swallow him.
Look where his lordship comes.

(Enter Gaveston.)

My Gaveston!
Welcome to Tynemouth! welcome to thy friend!
Thy absence made me droop and pine away;
For, as the lovers of fair Danae,
When she was locked up in a brazen tower,
Desired her more, and waxed outgareous,
So did it fare with me: and now thy sight
Is sweeter far than was thy parting hence
Bitter and irksome to my sobbing heart.
Will none of you salute my Gaveston?
Still will these earls and barons use me thus.
Convey hence Gaveston; they'll murder him.
Dear shall you abide this riotous deed.
Out of my presence! come not near the court.
Nay, all of them conspire to cross me thus;
But if I live, I'll tread upon their heads
That think with high looks thus to tread me down.
Come, Edmund, let's away and levy men,
'Tis war that must abate these barons' pride.

jesses: the straps around a hawk's legs, to which the falconer's leash was fastened *Aeque tandem*, Lat: "equally in length" (the canker will be as high as the eagle) **canker**: canker worm **harpy**: Greek mythology, a monstrous bird with the head of a maid **Danae**, Greek mythology: a maiden imprisoned in a brazen tower by her father Acrisius, king of Argos, to keep her away from potential lovers; Zeus visited her in the form of golden rain, and she bore him the son Theseus

21

EDWARD SWEARS REVENGE
AFTER GAVESTON'S MURDER

(c1592) CHRISTOPHER MARLOWE, The Tragedy of Edward II, *Act 3, Sc. 2*

Behind Edward's rage after the murder of Gaveston, there remains less and less of substance to support his pretensions to kingly authority, but visible though the fact may be to his enemies, it is invisible to him. And so his wrath is unqualified and genuinely majestic, a cardboard presence with the voice, the bearing, the glare, of genuine majesty. As with Shakespeare's Richard II, the more the figure of the king shrinks to small dimensions within the habiliments of royalty, the greater is the sound, the look, the presence, the inward dignity, the grandeur of his self-portrayal. Edward, like Richard, enlarges in stature to tragic enormity as he diminishes to the littleness of practical incapacity. His first 'challenge' to his enemies is to declare his love for a substitute Gaveston, the young Spencer, whom he claps to his bosom as though in defiance of the murderous barons.

How the barons planned and successfully executed Gaveston's murder is this: Gaveston, captured by the nobles led by Mortimer, Lancaster and Warwick, were interrupted in their hurry to hang him by the arrival of an emissary from King Edward, who begged for Edward the favor of seeing Gaveston once more before his death. Lord Pembroke undertook his safe passage and return, but during the journey, Warwick, betraying the noble's avowed intention to protect Gaveston during his journey, murders him en route. With the capture of the barons on the battlefield, Edward, for the moment victorious, condemns them severally to prison and death.

EDWARD

(kneeling) By earth, the common mother of us all,
By Heaven, and all the moving orbs thereof,
By this right hand, and by my father's sword,
And all the honours 'longing to my crown,
I will have heads, and lives for him, as many
As I have manors, castles, towns, and towers!—
Treacherous Warwick! traitorous Mortimer! *(Rises.)*
If I be England's king, in lakes of gore
Your headless trunks, your bodies will I trail,
That you may drink your fill, and quaff in blood,
And stain my royal standard with the same,
That so my bloody colours may suggest
Remembrance of revenge immortally
On your accursèd traitorous progeny,
You villains, that have slain my Gaveston!
And in this place of honour and of trust,
Spencer, sweet Spencer, I adopt thee here:
And merely of our love we do create thee
Earl of Gloucester, and Lord Chamberlain,
Despite of times, despite of enemies.

Now, lusty lords, now, not by chance of war,
But justice of the quarrel and the cause,
Vailed is your pride; methinks you hang the heads,
But we'll advance them, traitors; now 'tis time
To be avenged on you for all your braves,
And for the murder of my dearest friend,
To whom right well you knew our soul was knit,
Good Pierce of Gaveston, my sweet favourite.
Ah, rebels! recreants! you made him away.
Accursèd wretches, was't in regard of us,
When we had sent our messenger to request
He might be spared to come to speak with us,
And Pembroke undertook for his return,
That thou, proud Warwick, watched the prisoner,
Poor Pierce, and headed him 'gainst law of arms?

For which thy head shall overlook the rest,
As much as thou in rage outwent'st the rest.

Away with them, my lord of Winchester!
These lusty leaders, Warwick and Lancaster,
I charge you roundly—off with both their heads!
Away! Go take that haughty Mortimer to the Tower,
There see him safe bestowed; and for the rest
Do speedy execution on them all.
Begone!

(The captive Barons are led off.)
Sound drums and trumpets! March with me, my friends,
Edward this day hath crowned him king anew.

vail: to lower, sink, descend **recreants**: cowards **'gainst law of arms**: i.e., beheaded him in spite of the laws of war (which state that prisoners of war are not to be executed) **the Tower** of London: where royal and noble prisoners were kept

22

EDWARD FORCED TO RENOUNCE HIS CROWN, RAGES, SORROWS, FINALLY SURRENDERS
(c1592) CHRISTOPHER MARLOWE, The Tragedy of Edward II, *Act 5, Sc. 1*

What are kings when regiment is gone, / But perfect shadows in a sunshine day?" Edward concludes, finally understanding the realities of power. Like Richard II, Edward, in this deposition scene (echoed in considerable detail by Shakespeare) tests the limits of emotional show, the extravagances in turn of his self-pity, his kingly wrath, his sorrowful resignation, his whipping himself again to kingly fury, his wrathful surrender of his crown once again, his longing for death, his gracious commendation of himself to wife and son, and finally, his welcoming death as "felicity."

Again, as with Richard, the power of the scene lies in the brilliance of this now-helpless king's persuasiveness in performing each of his successive emotional postures. He performs each of them so well that we believe in the instant that each is entirely sincere, that each in succession, he thoroughly believes. What is lacking in the scene, and in the character of Edward, is the conscious irony of Shakespeare's helpless king, playing the game of feeling and of policy at one and the same time. There's a self-knowing smile, a conscious wit, behind Richard's emotional extravaganza; there's none behind Edward's.

EDWARD

Leicester, if gentle words might comfort me,
Thy speeches long ago had eased my sorrows;
For kind and loving hast thou always been.
The griefs of private men are soon allayed,
But not of kings. The forest deer, being struck,
Runs to an herb that closeth up the wounds;
But, when the imperial lion's flesh is gored,
He rends and tears it with his wrathful paw,
And highly scorning that the lowly earth
Should drink his blood, mounts up to the air.
And so it fares with me, whose dauntless mind
The ambitious Mortimer would seek to curb,
And that unnatural queen, false Isabel,
That thus hath pent and mewed me in a prison;
For such outrageous passions cloy my soul,
As with the wings of rancour and disdain,
Full often am I soaring up to Heaven,
To plain me to the gods against them both.
But when I call to mind I am a king,
Methinks I should revenge me of my wrongs,
That Mortimer and Isabel have done.
But what are kings, when regiment is gone,
But perfect shadows in a sunshine day?

My nobles rule, I bear the name of king;
I wear the crown, but am controlled by them,
By Mortimer, and my unconstant queen,
Who spots my nuptial bed with infamy;
Whilst I am lodged within this cave of care,
Where sorrow at my elbow still attends,
To company my heart with sad laments,
That bleeds within me for this strange exchange.
But tell me, must I now resign my crown,
To make usurping Mortimer a king?

Tis for Mortimer, not Edward's head;
For he's a lamb, encompassèd by wolves,
Which in a moment will abridge his life.
But if proud Mortimer do wear this crown,
Heavens turn it to a blaze of quenchless fire
Or like the snaky wreath of Tisiphon,
Engirt the temples of his hateful head;
So shall not England's vine be perishèd,
But Edward's name survives, though Edward dies.

Ah, Leicester, weigh how hardly I can brook
To lose my crown and kingdom without cause;
To give ambitious Mortimer my right,
That like a mountain overwhelms my bliss,
In which extreme my mind here murdered is.
But what the heavens appoint, I must obey!
Here, take my crown; the life of Edward too;

(Taking off the crown.)
Two kings in England cannot reign at once.
But stay awhile, let me be king till night,
That I may gaze upon this glittering crown;
So shall my eyes receive their last content,
My head, the latest honour due to it,
And jointly both yield up their wishèd right.
Continue ever, thou celestial sun;

Let never silent night possess this clime:
Stand still, you watches of the element;
All times and seasons, rest you at a stay,
That Edward may be still fair England's king!
But day's bright beam doth vanish fast away,
And needs I must resign my wishèd crown.
Inhuman creatures! nursed with tiger's milk!
Why gape you for your sovereign's overthrow!
My diadem I mean, and guiltless life.
See, monsters, see, I'll wear my crown again.

(He puts on the crown.)
What, fear you not the fury of your king?
But, hapless Edward, thou art fondly led;
They pass not for thy frowns as late they did,
But seek to make a new-elected king;
Which fills my mind with strange despairing thoughts,
Which thoughts are martyrèd with endless torments,
And in this torment comfort find I none,
But that I feel the crown upon my head;
And therefore let me wear it yet awhile.

O would I might! but heavens and earth conspire
To make me miserable! Here receive my crown;
Receive it? no, these innocent hands of mine
Shall not be guilty of so foul a crime.
He of you all that most desires my blood,
And will be called the murderer of a king,
Take it. What, are you moved? pity you me?
Then send for unrelenting Mortimer,
And Isabel, whose eyes, being turned to steel,
Will sooner sparkle fire than shed a tear.
Yet stay, for rather than I'll look on them,
Here, here!

(Gives the crown.)
Now, sweet God of Heaven,
Make me despise this transitory pomp,
And sit for aye enthronizèd in Heaven!

Come, death, and with my fingers close my eyes,
Or if I live, let me forget myself.
Bear this to the queen,
Wet with my tears, and dried again with sighs;

(Gives a handkerchief.)
If with the sight thereof she be not moved,
Return it back and dip it in my blood.
Commend me to my son, and bid him rule
Better than I. Yet how have I transgressed,
Unless it be with too much clemency?
I know the next news that they bring
Will be my death; and welcome shall it be;
To wretched men, death is felicity.

allay: to appease, alleviate **mew**: to confine **plain**: to complain **regiment**: royal authority **Tisiphon**: one of the Furies (see Glossary) **Engirt**: may it surround **watches of the element**: stars in the sky **fondly**: foolishly **pass not**: don't care

23

EDWARD PLEADS WITH, BRAVES, SUCCUMBS TO HIS MURDERERS
(c1592) CHRISTOPHER MARLOWE, The Tragedy of Edward II, *Act 5, Sc. 5*

Edward, once deposed, is hounded to his death by Mortimer and his now adulterous Queen. Mortimer instructs two followers, Matrevis and Gurney, to pursue and add to Edward's torments and, when he is at last imprisoned in the bowels of Berkeley Castle and left standing for ten days in the castle's sewage, these two and a hired murderer accomplish his assassination.

Edward, at first alone with the hired assassin, urges his pity, but soon recognizes the man's indifference and determination, and falls to begging—at first, not for his life but for the privilege of seeing the fatal blow coming, so that "my mind may be more steadfast on my God." But cruelly, Marlowe gives Edward no heroic death. His plea descends from this first, relatively noble prayer to a shivering, quaking helplessness in which he begs not for time to dwell on his oneness with God, or for God to receive his soul, but, at the very last moment, to be despatched "in a trice," so that he will not be aware of the oncoming blow. The grossness of the murder—he is thrown under a table and stomped to death while he screams in fright—completes the course of Edward's reduction from the illusion of his impregnable authority to the nonentity of incapacitated helplessness.

EDWARD

Who's there? what light is that? wherefore com'st thou?
Small comfort finds poor Edward in thy looks.
Villain, I know thou com'st to murder me.
Weep'st thou already? list awhile to me.
And then thy heart, were it as Gurney's is,
Or as Matrevis', hewn from the Caucasus,
Yet will it melt, ere I have done my tale.
This dungeon where they keep me is the sink
Wherein the filth of all the castle falls.
And there in mire and puddle have I stood
This ten days' space; and, lest that I should sleep,
One plays continually upon a drum.
They give me bread and water, being a king;
So that, for want of sleep and sustenance,
My mind's distempered, and my body's numbed,
And whether I have limbs or no I know not.
O, would my blood dropped out from every vein,
As doth this water from my tattered robes.
Tell Isabel, the queen, I looked not thus,
When for her sake I ran at tilt in France,
And there unhorsed the Duke of Cleremont.

These looks of thine can harbour nought but death:
I see my tragedy written in thy brows.
Yet stay; awhile forbear thy bloody hand,
And let me see the stroke before it comes,
That even then when I shall lose my life,
My mind may be more steadfast on my God.
One jewel have I left; receive thou this. *(Giving jewel.)*
Still fear I, and I know not what's the cause,
But every joint shakes as I give it thee.
O, if thou harbourest murder in thy heart,
Let this gift change they mind, and save thy soul.
Know that I am a king: O, at that name
I feel a hell of grief! where is my crown?
Gone, gone! and do I still remain alive?

But that grief keeps me waking, I should sleep;
For not these ten days have these eye-lids closed.
Now as I speak they fall, and yet with fear
Open again. O wherefore sitt'st thou here?

                    (Sleeps. Then waking)
O let me not die yet! O stay a while!
Something still buzzeth in mine ears,
And tells me if I sleep I never wake;
This fear is that which makes me tremble thus.
And therefore tell me, wherefore art thou come?
To rid me of my life.
I am too weak and feeble to resist:—
Assist me, sweet God, and receive my soul!
O spare me, or despatch me in a trice.

24

MENDOZA, NEW COURT LACKEY, ENVISIONS HIS PLEASURES IN OFFICE

(c1603?) JOHN MARSTON, The Malcontent, *Act 1, Sc. 5*

The usurper Pietro has banished the rightful Duke Altofronto from his dukedom in Genoa. The new Duke's follower Mendoza plotted the marriage of Pietro and his Florentine Duchess, but Mendoza, the insatiable Machiavellian underling, has already made the Duchess his mistress.

Newly established at the Genoese court, trusted accomplice of the usurping Duke and lover of the Duchess, Mendoza is beside himself with the sheer glee of his new estate, and enumerates his anticipated joys: the courtiers who will stand gravely respectful in his presence, petitioners who will bow to the ground pleading their suit, the slippery "eels" at court who will look to him for every favor.

But his greatest joy of all is making a cuckold of his benefactor. Yet his rapture is not confined to his pleasure in the Duchess but in women *sui generis*, apostrophizing over their "pleasure[s] unutterable." And emulating one of the genteel hobbies of the proper courtier, the upstart Mendoza goes off to pen a sonnet to his mistress.

> **MENDOZA**
> Now, good Elysium! what a delicious heaven is it for a man to be in a prince's favour! O sweet God! O pleasure! O fortune! O all thou best of life! What should I think, what say, what do? To be a favourite, a minion! to have a general timorous respect observe a man, a stateful silence in his presence, solitariness in his absence, a confused hum and busy murmur of obsequious suitors training him; the cloth held up, and way proclaimed before him; petitionary vassals licking the pavement with their slavish knees, whilst some odd palace-lampreels that

engender with snakes, and are full of eyes on both sides, with a kind
of insinuated humbleness, fix all their delights upon his brow. O
blessed state! what a ravishing prospect doth the Olympus of favour
yield! Death, I cornute the duke! Sweet women! most sweet ladies!
nay, angels! by heaven, he is more accursed than a devil that hates you,
or is hated by you; and happier than a god that loves you, or is
beloved by you. You preservers of mankind, life-blood of society, who
would live, nay, who can live without you? O paradise! how majestical
is your austerer presence! how imperiously chaste is your more modest
face! but, O, how full of ravishing attraction is your pretty, petulant,
languishing, lasciviously-composed countenance! these amorous
smiles, these soul-warming sparkling glances, ardent as those flames
that sing'd the world by heedless Phaeton! in body how delicate, in
soul how witty, in discourse how pregnant, in life how wary, in favours
how judicious, in day how sociable, and in night how—O pleasure
unutterable! indeed, it is most certain, one man cannot deserve only to
enjoy a beauteous woman: but a duchess! In despite of Phoebus, I'll
write a sonnet instantly in praise of her. *(Exit.)*

timorous: fearful, timid **observe**: pay obsequious court to **training**: following
lampreels: lamprey eels **engender**: mate **cornute**: to make cuckold **Phaeton**:
son of Helios the Sun God, who heedlessly drove the chariot of the sun too close
to its heat and plunged to earth on fire

25

WENDOLL BATTLES WITH HIS CONSCIENCE
(1603) THOMAS HEYWOOD, A Woman Killed with Kindness, *Act 2, Sc. 3*

There is a very particular psychology underlying motive and act in
A Woman Killed with Kindness that supports the Puritan morality on which the one half of the play's plot is based: the story of the
seduction of Anne Frankfort, wife of the very worthy Christian gentleman John Frankfort, by his trusted guest and employee, Wendoll.

The lust that seizes Wendoll as he first observes Mistress Wendoll is to
his own mind a hideous sin he consciously detests. But though he
struggles mightily to overcome it, once having put himself in the way
of temptation, his struggle against it is futile. He is doomed—
damned, that is—from the start. His nature is foreordained, and his
struggle succumbs to its demands. His good will, his respect for this
household and for Mistress Frankfort, his love and gratitude and
devotion to his master, are no match in his struggle against the devil
in the flesh, that is, his inherently and from his beginning damned
nature that responds, finally, in the only way it can. Resignedly, bitterly, he concludes, "Be content…[v]illains, [even] when they would,
cannot repent."

(Enter WENDOLL, melancholy)

WENDOLL
I am a villain, if I apprehend
But such a thought! Then, to attempt the deed,
Slave, thou art damn'd without redemption.—
I'll drive away this passion with a song.
A song! Ha, ha! A song! As if, fond man
Thy eyes could swim in laughter, when they soul
Lies drench'd and drowned in red tears of blood!
I'll pray, and see if God within my heart
Plant better thoughts. Why, prayers are meditations,
And when I meditate (oh, God, forgive me!)
It is on her divine perfections.
I will forget her; I will arm myself
Not t'entertain a thought of love to her;
And, when I come by chance into her presence,
I'll hale these balls until my eye-strings crack,
From being pull'd and drawn to look that way.

O God, O God! With what a violence
I'm hurried to mine own destruction!
There goest thou, the most perfect'st man

That ever England bred a gentleman,
And shall I wrong his bed?—Thou God of thunder!
Stay, in Thy thoughts of vengeance and of wrath,
Thy great, almighty, and all-judging hand
From speedy execution on a villain,—
A villain and a traitor to his friend.
I never bound him to me by desert.
Of a mere stranger, a poor gentleman
A man by whom in no kind he could gain,
And he hath plac'd me in his highest thoughts,
Made me companion with the best and chiefest
In Yorkshire. He cannot eat without me,
Nor laugh without me; I am to his body
As necessary as his digestion,
And equally do make him whole or sick.
And shall I wrong this man? Base man! Ingrate!
Hast thou the power, straight with thy gory hands,
To rip thy image from his bleeding heart,
To scratch thy name from out the holy book
Of his remembrance, and to wound his name
That holds thy name so dear? Or rend his heart
To whom they heart was knit and join'd together?—
And yet I must. Then Wendoll, be content!
Thus villains, when they would, cannot repent.

apprehend: to conceive **fond**: foolish **hale these balls**: hold these eyeballs **kind**: way **whole**: well

26

FRANKFORT RECOILS AT REPORT OF HIS WIFE'S ADULTERY

(1603) THOMAS HEYWOOD, A Woman Killed with Kindness, *Act 3, Sc. 2*

Frankfort's most devoted servant Nicholas, having secretly observed Mistress Frankfort's surrender to Wendoll's plea, out of loyalty to his master and rage against the adulterers, reports the seduction and betrayal to his master. Frankfort's response—as is his later response when he himself observes and is confirmed in their iniquity—is deeply embedded in, and conforms perfectly to, his truly pious Christian nature: he cannot tolerate the possibility of either wife or friend being capable of such betrayal. At the same time, he struggles with the more conventional outrage of the cuckolded, dishonored husband. After hearing Nicholas's accusation, he struggles to reconcile this double response.

He rages at first at Nicholas for making such an accusation at all, and holds angrily to his disbelief, but then falls into agonized consideration of the sin's likelihood, and finally decides on circumspection: to determine without haste, to inquire further and so suspend for the present all judgment on his beloved wife and friend.

The soliloquy is preparation for his later discovery of the naked truth of Nicholas' accusation. For his final carefully balanced, carefully calculated decision, see I, #27.

> **FRANKFORT**
> Y'are a knave, and have much ado
> With wonted patience to contain my rage,
> And not to break thy pate. Th'art a knave.
> I'll turn you, with your base comparisons,
> Out of my doors.
> Thou hast kill'd me with a weapon, whose sharp point

Hath prick'd quite through and through my shiv'ring heart.
Drops of cold sweat sit dangling on my hairs,
Like morning's dew upon the golden flowers,
And I am plung'd into strange agonies.
What did'st thou say? If any word that touch'd
His credit, or her reputation,
It is as hard to enter my belief,
As Dives into heaven.

(Aside)

Though I durst pawn my life, and on their faith
Hazard the dear salvation of my soul,
Yet in my trust I may be too secure.
May this be true? Oh, may it? Can it be?
Is it in any wonder possible?
Man, woman, what thing mortal can we trust,
When friends and bosom wives prove so unjust?—
What instance hast thou of this strange report?
Thy eyes may be deceiv'd, I tell thee;
For should an angel from the heavens drop down,
And preach this to me that thyself hast told,
He should have much ado to win belief;
In both their loves I am so confident.

No more! To supper, and command your fellows
To attend us and the strangers! Not a word,
I charge thee, on thy life! Be secret then;
For I know nothing.

Away! Begone!—
She is well born, descended nobly;
Virtuous her education; her repute
Is in the general voice of all the country
Honest and fair, her carriage, her demeanour,
In all her actions that concern the love
To me her husband, modest, chaste, and godly.
Is all this seeming gold plain copper?
But he, that Judas that hath borne my purse,
Hath sold me for a sin. O God! O God!

Shall I put up these wrongs? No! Shall I trust
The bare report of this suspicious groom,
Before the double-gilt, the well-hatch'd ore
Of their two hearts? No, I will lose these thoughts;
Distraction I will banish from my brow,
And from my looks exile sad discontent.
Their wonted favours in my tongue shall flow;
Till I know all, I'll nothing seem to know.—
Lights and a table there! Wife, Master Wendoll,
And gentle Master Cranwell!

wonted: accustomed **pate**: head **Dives**: the rich man in the parable of Luke 6:19-31; any rich man **instance**: evidence **double-gilt**: pure gold **well-hatch'd**: richly inlaid

27

FRANKFORT PRONOUNCES HIS VERDICT OVER HIS WIFE'S ADULTERY
(1603) THOMAS HEYWOOD, A Woman Killed with Kindness, *Act 4, Sc. 5*

As between the obligation of the Christian soul to redeem the sinner, and the demand of the code of honor to exact bloody revenge, Frankfort determines on a course that will satisfy both. At his first moment of outraged discovery of his wife's and her lover's adultery, Frankfort raises a sword over the lover Wendoll's head ready to strike. But the intervention of a housemaid who "like a ministering angel" stays his hand, recalls Frankfort to his Christian self, and the doom he visits on Wendoll is simply to abandon him to the judgment of his own conscience. But for his wife, Frankfort undergoes lengthy debate—at one moment going off to pray for divine guidance—before coming to his decision.

As a betrayed, outraged husband, he separates himself at once from their conjugal connection: she is now, he tells her, an abandoned strumpet, and her infection cannot remain in his home or close to their children. But the Christian shepherd in him visits punishment on her that leaves the door open for her salvation. He offers her comfortable exile in his country house where—and this is the understood logic of his verdict—by voluntary surrender of the fruits of her sin, with penance and with prayer for forgiveness, she can (though it is a distant hope) yet save her soul.

Frankfort's speech arriving at this edict is hardly a coldly judgmental one. With his wife, he at first suffers their mutual shame. Then he questions her about his deficiency as husband or lover. And moving from painfully compassionate examination to obligatory moral contempt, he stops on the threshold of "martyring" her, substituting instead his verdict to "kill [her] even with kindness."

FRANKFORT

Spare thou thy tears, for I will weep for thee;
And keep thy count'nance, for I'll blush for thee.
Now, I protest, I think 't is I am tainted,
For I am most asham'd; and 't is more hard
For me to look upon thy guilty face
Than on the sun's clear brow.
My God, with patience arm me!—
Rise, nay, rise,
And I'll debate with thee. Was it for want
You play'dst the strumpet? Wast thou not suppli'd
With every pleasure, fashion, and new toy,—
Ay, even beyond my calling?
Was it, then, disability in me;
In thine eye seem's he a properer man?
Did I not lodge thee in my bosom?
Wear thee in my heart?
Witness my tears, I did—
Oh, Nan! Oh, Nan!

If neither fear or shame, regard of honour,
The blemish of my house, nor my dear love,
Could have withheld thee from so lewd a fact;
Yet for these infants, these young, harmless souls,
On whose white brows thy shame is character'd,
And grows in greatness as they wax in years,—
Look but on them, and melt away in tears!—
Stand up! Stand up! I will do nothing rashly.
With patience hear me! I'll not martyr thee,
Nor mark thee for a strumpet; but with usage
Of more humility torment thy soul,
And kill thee even with kindness.
Hear thy judgement!
Go make thee ready in thy best attire;
Take with thee all thy gowns, all thy apparel;
Leave nothing that did ever call thee mistress,
Or by whose sight, being left here in the house,
I may remember such a woman by.
Choose thee a bed and hangings for thy chamber;
Take with thee everything which hath thy mark,
And get thee to my manor seven mile off,
Where live;—'t is thine; I freely give it thee.
My tenants by shall furnish thee with wains
To carry all thy stuff within two hours;
No longer will I limit thee my sight.
Choose which of all my servants thou lik'st best,
And they are thine to attend thee.
But, as thou hop'st for Heaven, as thou believ'st
Thy name's recorded in the book of life,
I charge thee never after this sad day
To see me, or to meet me; or to send,
By word or writing, gift or otherwise,
To move me, by thyself, or by thy friends;
Nor challenge any part in my two children.
So farewell, Nan; for we will henceforth be
As we had never seen, ne'er more shall see.

fact: deed **wain**: a cart, wagon

28

BUSSY, YOUNG AND POOR, EQUATES POVERTY WITH VIRTUE

(c1604) GEORGE CHAPMAN, Bussy d'Ambois, *Act 1, Sc. 1*

The historical Bussy d'Ambois was, like the Bussy of the play, a ferocious dueler and an adulterous lover in the court of Henry III of France. He was murdered in 1579 by the husband of his mistress (the Duchess Tamyra in the play) in a plot joined by the Duke de Guise, his sworn enemy, and by the King himself. As in most Jacobean tragedies, the French or Italian court is the contemned repository of iniquity, but at the same time a garish intimation of the current English court.

Bussy is Marlowe's Tamburlaine in too small a world, one so reduced in scale that his grandiloquence becomes only bluster, and his attempted soaring to "greatness" a brutally truncated flight. Chapman's play reflects in fact the tragedy of Marlovian heroics becoming a mere anachronism in the world of the Jacobean Court, its superhuman ambitions caged and nullified in a milieu of malice, cunning and treachery.

Monsieur, the King's brother, recognizes in Bussy "a man of spirit beyond the reach of fear," and supposes that, being both poor and afire for advancement, is corruptible. He is, but on his own terms. The contempt Bussy voices for the Court politician's world in this speech measures the distance he thinks he will maintain from their delusions of greatness (his, he supposes, will be real) and from their corruptibility. Ironically, virtue, the "safe port" he supposes is his permanent home, is one he is destined to leave quickly under Monsieur's maneuvering, and with the train of powerful enemies he collects at each of his thrusts toward "greatness," his "soaring" becomes instead a steady progress toward his doom.

This speech, his first in the play, is his initial credo, bitterly, enviously uttered—and innocently. Almost from the moment it is uttered, his betrayal of it begins.

BUSSY
Fortune, not Reason, rules the state of things,
Reward goes backwards, Honour on his head;
Who is not poor, is monstrous; only need
Gives form and worth to every human seed.
As cedars beaten with continual storms,
So great men flourish; and do imitate
Unskillful statuaries, who suppose,
In forming a Colossus, if they make him
Straddle enough, strut, and look big, and gape,
Their work is goodly: so men merely great
In their affected gravity of voice,
Sourness of countenance, manners' cruelty,
Authority, wealth, and all the spawn of fortune,
Think they bear all the kingdom's worth before them;
Yet differ not from those colossic statues,
Which, with heroic forms without o'erspread,
Within are naught but mortar, flint, and lead.
Man is a torch borne in the wind, a dream
But of a shadow, summ'd with all his substance.
And as great seamen, using all their wealth
And skills in Neptune's deep invisible paths,
In tall ships richly built and ribb'd with brass,
To put a girdle round about the world,
When they have done it (coming near their haven)
Are fain to give a warning-piece, and call
A poor, staid fisherman, that never past
His country's sight, to waft and guide them in:
So when we wander furthest through the waves
Of glassy Glory, and the gulfs of State,

Topp'd with all titles, spreading all our reaches,
As if each private arm would sphere the earth,
We must to Virtue for her guide resort,
Or we shall shipwrack in our safest port.

Colossus: one of the seven wonders of the ancient world, a giant bronze statue in Rhodes dedicated to Helios **without**: externally **summ'd...substance**: when he and all he owns are estimated **warning-piece**: a signal-gun warning of arrival

29

MONSIEUR THE KING'S BROTHER MOCKS THE LADY'S ARGUMENT: "SIR, I HAVE A HUSBAND!"

(c1604) GEORGE CHAPMAN, Bussy d'Ambois, *Act 2, Sc. 2*

The practiced Machiavellian Monsieur, the King's brother, above the commonplaces of morality, faces facts. He woos the Duchess Tamyra, the wife of Montsurry, who, though she finds him detestable, puts him off with protestations of "my husband...my honor." Monsieur is repelled not by her refusal but by its triteness. Putting to one side the language of gallantry, he confronts her bluntly with four cogent arguments: 1) a married woman has already lost her maidenhead and can't lose it twice; 2) a sensible woman keeps both options open: a husband and a lover; 3) wives don't display themselves at court for their husbands—they can have them at home—but for our "common sports;" 4) on the other hand, telling me bluntly you dislike me is plain and also manageable, because it leaves open the ultimate argument: take me for a string of pearls, not for love but out of "wisdom." Intent on seduction without pretense, Monsieur takes for granted that the Duchess, as well as any other woman when reduced to honesty, bargains essentially in the commonest coin.

MONSIEUR

Honour, what's that? Your second maidenhead!
And what is that? A word. The word is gone,
The thing remains: the rose is pluck'd, the stalk
Abides; an easy loss where no lack's found.
Believe it, there's as small lack in the loss
As there is pain i' th' losing. Archers ever
Have two strings to a bow; and shall great Cupid
(Archer of archers both in men and women,)
Be worse provided that a common archer?
A husband and a friend all wise wives have.
Still you stand on your husband! so do all
The common sex of you, when y' are encounter'd
With one ye cannot fancy. All men know
You live in Court here by your own election,
Frequenting all our common sports and triumphs,
All the most youthful company of men:
And wherefore do you this? To please your husband?
'Tis gross and fulsome: if your husband's pleasure
Be all your object, and you aim at honour
In living close to him, get you from Court;
You may have him at home. These common put-offs
For common women serve: "My honour! Husband!"
Dames maritorious ne'er were meritorious.
Speak plain, and say, "I do not like you, sir,
Y' are an ill-favour'd fellow in my eye;"
And I am answer'd.
Then have at you, here!
Take (with a politic hand) this rope of pearl,
And though you be not amorous, yet be wise:
Take me for wisdom; he that you can love
Is ne'er the further from you.
Could I but please your eye,
You would give me the like, ere you would lose me.
"Honour and husband!"

30

MONSIEUR IS INVITED TO DRAW FOR BUSSY HIS "CHARACTER"

(c1604) GEORGE CHAPMAN, Bussy d'Ambois, *Act 3, Sc. 2*

Monsieur has sponsored Bussy for Court advancement with the understanding that he would reciprocate by assassinating the King and so helping Monsieur, the King's brother, to the throne. Bussy has indeed "advanced" at Court, killing several courtiers in a duel, making a mortal enemy of the powerful Duke de Guise, and earning the awakened suspicions of the King that his leniency toward Bussy—forgiving his murders and outrages—may have been misplaced. But for Monsieur, his protege has "advanced" so far as to become his nemesis, especially since he can no longer be cajoled into assassinating the King, and especially too since Bussy has fully succeeded—in making the Duchess Tamyra his mistress—where Monsieur has so ignominiously failed.

The two have gradually become enemies rather than collaborators. But the bravado of Bussy and the aplomb of Monsieur maintain between them the charade of unimpaired camaraderie, talking love, friendship and fidelity with elaborately unconcealed non-meaning. In this guise of measured joviality, they invite each other to tell, in the spirit of honest friendship, what they think "freely and heartily" of one another. Each obliges.

> MONSIEUR
> I think thee then a man
> That dares as much as a wild horse or tiger,
> As headstrong and as bloody; and to feed
> The ravenous wolf of thy most cannibal valour,

(Rather than not employ it) thou wouldst turn
Hackster to any whore, slave to a Jew
Or English usurer, to force possessions
(And cut men's throats) of mortgaged estates;
Or thou woudst 'tire thee like a tinker's strumpet,
And murther market-folks, quarrel with sheep,
And run as mad as Ajax; serve a butcher,
Do anything but killing of the King:
That in thy valour th' art like other naturals
That have strange gifts in nature, but no soul
Diffus'd quite through, to make them of a piece,
But stop at humours that are more absurd,
Childish and villainous than that hackster, whore,
Slave, cut-throat, tinker's bitch, compar'd before;
And in those humours wouldst envy, betray,
Slander, blaspheme, change each hour a religion;
Do anything but killing of the King:
That in thy valour (which is still the dung-hill,
To which hath reference all filth in thy house)
Th' art more ridiculous and vain-glorious
Than any mountebank, and impudent
Than any painted bawd; which, not to soothe
And glorify thee like a Jupiter Hammon,
Thou eat'st thy heart in vinegar; and thy gall
Turns all thy blood to poison, which is cause
Of that toad-pool that stands in thy complexion,
And makes thee (with a cold and earthy moisture,
Which is the dam of putrefaction,
As plague to thy damn'd pride) rot as thou liv'st:
To study calumnies and treacheries;
To thy friends' slaughters like a screech-owl sing,
And do all mischiefs, but to kill the King.

How think'st thou? Do I flatter?
Speak I not like a trusty friend to thee?

hackster: a bully, pimp **tinker**: an itinerant mender of tinwear, and commonly thought of as unskilled and clumsy **naturals**: idiots **soothe**: flatter **dam of putre-faction**: "mother," or cause of putrefaction

31

BUSSY IS INVITED TO DRAW FOR MONSIEUR HIS "CHARACTER"

(c1604) GEORGE CHAPMAN, Bussy d'Ambois, *Act 3, Sc. 2*

[see I, #30]

BUSSY

What, utter plainly what I think of you?
Why, this swims quite against the stream of greatness;
Great men would rather hear their flatteries,
And if they be not made fools, are not wise.
So here's for me. I think you are (at worst)
No devil, since y' are like to be no king;
Of which, with any friend of yours, I'll lay
This poor stillado here, 'gainst all the stars,
Ay, and 'gainst all your treacheries, which are more:
That you did never good, but to do ill;
But ill of all sorts, free and for itself:
That (like a murthering piece, making lanes in armies,
The first man of a rank, the whole rank falling)
If you have wrong'd one man, you are so far
From making him amends that all his race,
Friends, and associates, fall into your chase:
That y' are for perjuries the very prince
Of all intelligencers; and your voice
Is like an eastern wind, that where it flies
Knits nets of caterpillars, with which you catch
The prime of all the fruits the kingdom yields:
That your political head is the curst fount
Of all the violence, rapine, cruelty,

Tyranny, and atheism flowing through the realm:
That y'ave a tongue so scandalous, 't will cut
The purest crystal; and a breath that will
Kill to that wall a spider. You will jest
With God, and your soul to the devil tender
For lust; kiss horror, and with death engender.
That your foul body is a Lernean fen
Of all the maladies breeding in all men:
That you are utterly without a soul;
And, for your life, the thread of that was spun
When Clotho slept, and let her breathing rock
Fall in the dirt; and Lachesis still draws it,
Dipping her twisting fingers in a bowl
Defil'd, and crown'd with virtue's forced soul.
And lastly (which I must for gratitude
Ever remember) that of all my height
And dearest life, you are the only spring,
Only in royal hope to kill the King.

stillado: stilleto **like a murdering piece...the whole rank falling**: a weapon, such as a cannon, "making lanes in armies" by shooting at the first man in line and automatically causing "the whole rank" to fall **chase**: persecution **intelligencers**: informers, spies **curst**: cursed **rapine**: a plunder **engender**: to copulate **Lernean fen**: the swamp in which Hercules slaughtered Hydra, the multiheaded monster **Clotho**: the Goddess of Fate who, of the three sisters, spins the thread **breathing rock**: distaff on which the thread of life is spun **Lachesis**: the Goddess of Fate who determines the length of life (Atropos cuts it off)

32

FLAMINEO DAMNS HIS MOTHER FOR HAVING INFLICTED ON HIM A LIFE OF POVERTY

(1609-12) JOHN WEBSTER, The White Devil, *Act 1, Sc. 2*

The "tool villain" in Elizabethan and Jacobean tragedy is the underling who does the criminal work for the well-placed and the powerful, but rarely, in the outcome, is the debt for his services either acknowledged or paid, he accumulates culpability and little else. Knowing the likelihood of his ultimately winning little or no reward, and aware too that he has neither means nor station nor access to power other than by way of his "protector," with no other option but to starve, he grimly serves.

Flamineo is the tool villain for the Duke Brachiano. He is largely the main agent of the play's action, and also the play's cynical center, observing accurately and maneuvering skilfully through its world of wolves among wolves. He knows his function and it humiliates him, and he sneeringly revels in it.

At play's opening, he is serving as procurer for his Duke, whose desire is for Flamineo's own sister, Vittoria Corombona. Flamineo has obligingly brought her. Vittoria is more than willing, and the assignation is underway with Flamineo watching from a distance and enjoying the encounter. But an outraged Cornelia, the mother of Flamineo and Vittoria, bursts in, cries anathema on all of them, and leaves Brachiano and Vittoria with no option but to flee.

More outraged than his mother, Flamineo in this speech excoriates the old lady for demanding virtue from her son and daughter without having had the sagacity to provide them with the means to support it. He visits his own felt shame and the humiliation of his penury on his horrified mother, who has not had the sense, he accuses, of the more careful prostitutes, who provide their offspring with many fathers rather than only one unforthcoming one.

> FLAMINEO
> Now, you that stand so much upon your honour,
> Is this a fitting time o' night, think you,
> To send a duke home without e'er a man?
> I would feign know where lies the mass of wealth
> Which you have hoarded for my maintenance,
> That I may bear my beard out of the level
> Of my lord's stirrup.
> Pray what means have you
> To keep me from the galleys, or the gallows?
> My father proved himself a gentleman,
> Sold all's land, and like a fortunate fellow
> Died ere the money was spent. You brought me up,
> At Padua I confess, where I protest,
> For want of means (the university judge me)
> I have been fain to heel my tutor's stockings
> At least seven years. Conspiring with a beard
> Made me a graduate, then to this Duke's service;
> I visited the court, whence I returned—
> More courteous, more lecherous by far,
> But not a suit the richer—and shall I,
> Having a path so open and so free
> To my preferment, still retain your milk
> In my pale forehead? No, this face of mine
> I'll arm and fortify with lusty wine
> 'Gainst shame and blushing.
> I would the common'st courtezan in Rome
> Had been my mother rather than thyself.
> Nature is very pitiful to whores
> To give them but few children, yet those children
> Plurality of fathers; they are sure
> They shall not want. Go, go,
> Complain unto my great Lord Cardinal;

Yet may be he will justify the act.
Lycurgus wondered much, men would provide
Good stallions for their mares, and yet would suffer
Their fair wives to be barren.

fain: gladly **bear my beard...stirrup**: keep my chin above the level of my lord's foot **my father...sold all's land**: alluding sarcastically to the contemporary practice of aristocracy selling their land to the rising bourgeosie **conspiring with a beard...graduate**: Flamineo probably earned his degree by reaching physical, rather than intellectual, maturity **courteous**: courtly **Lycurgus...barren**: according to Plutarch, Lycurgus advocated that men share their wives with other "worthy" men, not to fulfill the needs of barren women, but to provide the state with citizens of the best possible sort

33

BRACHIANO GREETS HIS WIFE WITH SULLEN CONTEMPT
(1609-12) JOHN WEBSTER, The White Devil, *Act 2, Sc. 1*

Determined to tolerate no opposition to union with Vittoria, Duke Brachiano nevertheless must face inconvenient obstacles: both he and Vittoria are wed, and his wife Isabella is favored with the support of her brothers, the Duke Ferdinand and the Cardinal Monticelso, both powerful, both ruthless. Inopportunely, Isabella, Brachiano's irritatingly devoted wife, arrives, having been alerted to the imminent danger of losing her husband. The prevision of her inevitable onslaught of pleas and protestations disgusts Brachiano, and he greets her sullenly at first, but then with studied insult, and swiftly transforms his diatribe against her to a *fait accompli*: divorce. To discourage her further, and to bolster his own assurance, he directs his rage against her inevitable prop and his inevitable adversary, her brother Ferdinand, belittling what he knows to be his certain retaliation.

BRACHIANO
You are in health we see.
What amorous whirlwind hurried you to Rome?
Devotion?
Is your soul charged with any grievous sin?
Take your chamber!
I do not use to kiss.
If that will dispossess your jealousy,
I'll swear it to you.

                    (Isabella attempts to embrace him.)
(He, turning away) O your breath!
Out upon sweetmeats, and continued physic.
The plague is in them.
Must I be haunted out, or was't your trick
To meet some amorous gallant here in Rome
That must supply our discontinuance?
Because your brother is the corpulent Duke,
— That is the great Duke—'Sdeath I shall not shortly
Racket away five hundred crowns at tennis,
But it shall rest upon record: I scorn him
Like a shaved Polack: all his reverent wit
Lies in his wardrobe; he's a discreet fellow
When he is made up in his robes of state.
Your brother the great Duke, because h'as galleys,
And now and then ransacks a Turkish fly-boat,
(Now all the hellish Furies take his soul),
First made this match—accursed be the priest
That sang the wedding mass, and even my issue.

Your hand I'll kiss:
This is the latest ceremony of my love,
Henceforth I will never lie with thee, by this,
This wedding ring: I'll ne'er more lie with thee.
And this divorce shall be as truly kept
As if the judge had doomed it: fare you well,
Our sleeps are severed.
Let not thy love

Make thee an unbeliever. This my vow
Shall never on my soul be satisfied
With my repentance: let thy brother rage
Beyond a horrid tempest or sea-fight,
My vow is fixed.
No more; go, go, complain to the great Duke.

sweetmeats: candy, etc. **I scorn...shaved Polack**: as of no account; Poles were said to shave their heads **Turkish fly-boat**: a fast-sailing boat **doomed**: judged, sentenced

34

FRANCISCO FASHIONS HIS REVENGE FOR ISABELLA'S MURDER WITH HER GHOST
(1609-12) JOHN WEBSTER, The White Devil, *Act 4, Sc. 1*

To rid himself of his wife Isabella definitively, Brachiano had the lips on his portrait, which the devoted Isabella kissed every night on retiring, painted with poison, and so disposed of her. Her brother Francisco now plans his long-awaited, slowly-germinated revenge—one that would cap the ingenuity and efficiency of his sister's murder. He's already visited with his brother the Cardinal Monticelso who has shared with him a comprehensive list of the city of Rome's villains and cut-throats. From these, Ferdinand chooses Lodovico, a "decayed count" who seeks his own revenge for his earlier banishment from the city.

But before the murder of Brachiano, Francisco plans an amusing prologue: to have a letter delivered to Vittoria at the house of conver-tites to which the corrupt court of justice has condemned her, with a message of love from himself, the letter to be delivered in Brachiano's presence. The poisoning pang of jealousy is to precede the pain of Brachiano's death by poisoning.

Now Francisco, to gird himself "more seriously" for revenge, calls
up in his mind the image of his sister's ghost. But since he is a "melancholic," one of the "humors" types subject to self-induced
hallucinations that seem utterly real (as in the Closet Scene in
Hamlet) he begins to address his own fiction, and then, realizing his
absurdity, commands the image to leave him ("out of my brain with
it!"), and turning back to the pressing question of the revenge, decides
then to begin with a bit of "idle mirth"—and so initiates the game of
making Brachiano suffer jealousy of himself (to make matters as insufferable as possible for Brachiano). Revenge by physical means alone is,
says Francisco, fitting only for the ingenuous whose "wit is shallow."

> FRANCISCO
> To fashion my revenge more seriously,
> Let me remember my dead sister's face:
> Call for her picture: no; I'll close mine eyes,
> And in a melancholic thought I'll frame
>
> *(Enter ISABEL[L]A's Ghost)*
> Her figure 'fore me. Now I ha't—d'foot! How strong
> Imagination works! How she can frame
> Things which are not! Methinks she stands afore me;
> And by the quick idea of my mind,
> Were my skill pregnant, I could draw her picture.
> Thought, as a subtle juggler, makes us deem
> Things supernatural which have cause
> Common as sickness. 'Tis my melancholy;
> How cam'st thou by thy death? How idle am I
> To question my own idleness? Did ever
> Man dream awake till now? Remove this object,
> Out of my brain with't: what have I to do
> With tombs, or death-beds, funerals, or tears,
> That have to meditate upon revenge?

(Exit Ghost)

So now 'tis ended, like an old wives' story.
Statesmen think often they see stranger sights
Than madmen. Come, to this weighty business.
My tragedy must have some idle mirth in't,
Else it will never pass. I am in love,
In love with Corombona, and my suit
Thus halts to her in verse.—*(Writes)*
I have done it rarely: O the fate of princes!
I am so used to frequent flattery,
That being alone I now flatter myself;
But it will serve; 'tis sealed.

(Enter Servant)

Bear this
To th'house of convertites; and watch your leisure
To give it to the hands of Corombona,
Or to the matron, when some followers
Of Brachiano may be by. Away.

(Exit Servant)

He that deals all by strength, his wit is shallow:
When a man's head goes through, each limb will follow.
The engine for my business, bold Count Lodowick;
'Tis gold must such an instrument procure,
With empty fist no man doth falcons lure.
Brachiano, I am now fit for thy encounter.
Like the wild Irish I'll ne'er think thee dead
Till I can play at football with thy head.

melancholy: of the four temperaments, melancholy caused by an excess of black bile, was thought to produce hallucinations **Now I ha't—d'foot!**: Now I've it, by God's foot!, a curse **pregnant**: fertile, imaginative **juggler**: a magician, conjuror **idleness**: delirium, folly **house of convertites**: Vittoria is imprisoned in a monastery for the conversion of women libertines **when a man's...follow**. proverbial, for a fox or snake; here applied to a man **wild Irish**: thought notoriously cruel

35

FLAMINEO USES PARABLE TO REMIND THE DUKE OF HIS INGRATITUDE FOR SERVICES

(1609-12) JOHN WEBSTER, The White Devil, *Act 4, Sc. 2*

By indirection, Flamineo reminds Brachiano that payment for his services has so far not been forthcoming. The indirection is whimsically roundabout. This is its path:

As the Duke Francisco intended [see I, #34], his letter to Vittoria inflamed Brachiano's jealousy and caused a raging quarrel between the lovers. It's calmed only, and finally, by Flamineo who urges them to kiss and make up, and for the Duke to recognize, and forgive, that it's those little "chimneys" like Vittoria that "do ever cast most smoke." Flamineo urges them in the same breath to take advantage of the confusion in the city to rescue Vittoria from the house of convertites and together escape from Rome. The confusion? The news of the Pope's sudden death and a new election (which will have grave consequences for these three, since it's one of Brachiano's murdered wife's vengeful brothers, Cardinal Monticelso, who is to be elected).

The lovers have agreed to his plan, and are ready to run, Flamineo seizes the moment—stopping their headlong action—for his elaborate lesson by example. Ostensibly he is chastising the ungrateful "crocodile" Vittoria for her ingratitude toward "the bird with the prick in the head" to whom she owes her life. The "crocodile" Flamineo is really addressing, Brachiano, understands the lesson well. But then Flamineo, with the *spirituelle* fantasy and intellectual resilience of Lear's Fool, suddenly turns to us and divulges his real, his bottommost strategy: "varying [his] shapes," playing games with multiple roles, his private, most genuine, and most mordant pleasure.

> **FLAMINEO**
> O, sir, your little chimneys
> Do ever cast most smoke. I sweat for you.

Couple together with as deep a silence
As did the Grecians in their wooden horse.

My lord, supply your promises with deeds.
'You know that painted meat no longer feeds.'
And no time fitter than this night, my lord;
The Pope being dead; and all the cardinals entered
The conclave for th'electing a new Pope;
The city in a great confusion;
We may attire her in a page's suit,
Lay her post-horse, take shipping, and amain
For Padua.

Stay, my lord, I'll tell you a tale. The crocodile, which lives in the river
Nilus, hath a worm breeds i'th'teeth of't, which puts it to extreme
anguish: a little bird, no bigger than a wren, is barber-surgeon to this
crocodile; flies into the jaws of't; picks out the worm; and brings present remedy. The fish, glad of ease but ingrateful to her that did it,
that the bird may not talk largely of her abroad for non-payment, closeth her chaps intending to swallow her and so put her to perpetual
silence. But nature loathing such ingratitude, hath armed this bird
with a quill or prick on the head, top o'th'which wounds the crocodile
i'th'mouth, forceth her open her bloody prison, and away flies the
pretty tooth-picker from her cruel patient.

You sister are the crocodile: you are blemished in your fame, my lord
cures it. And though the comparison hold not in every particle; yet
observe, remember, what good the bird with the prick i'th'head hath
done you; and scorn ingratitude.

(Aside) It may appear to some ridiculous
Thus to talk knave and madman; and sometimes
Come in with a dried sentence, stuffed with sage.
But this allows my varying of shapes,
'Knaves do grow great by being great men's apes'.

Lay her post-horse…Padua: provide her with relays of post-horses, embark and
sail with all speed to Padua **Nilus**: Nile **barber-surgeon**: barbers were also den-
tists **sentence**: aphorism, maxim **sage**: a pun on herb/wisdom

36

BRACHIANO, POISONED, SUFFERS AN EXCRUCIATING DEATH
(1609-12) JOHN WEBSTER, The White Devil, *Act 5, Sc. 3*

There are two kinds of madness in 17th century drama: Italian and English. Italian madness: the mind unhinged, its store of words having lost their moorings in sense, floating freely and rapidly, a verbal potpourri with only minimal vestiges of sequential meaning. The English: the mind distracted, leaping from one scene and one role to another, each scene a *non sequitur* from the one preceding, but each successively evoking the mind's total immersion in its reality. Ophelia's madness, for example, speeds her successively through different roles in different times and places (flower girl, grand lady, street singer of bawdy songs, etc); Lear in his hovel sheltered from the storm is more fixed in location (a court of law) and in role (a judge, an observer of court proceedings). But Brachiano in his madness is not so fortunate: suffering the agony of his poisoning, he gradually slips into "English" madness, but in the end is out again, and so loses entirely the madman's comparative comfort of being "elsewhere."

It was at his wedding with Vittoria that a disguised Duke Francisco succeeded in getting himself and his surrogate murderers, Gasparo and Lodovico, into the festivities. They in turn succeeded in poisoning Brachiano's metal helmet—an ironic reversion to his own scheme in murdering his wife by poisoning her most trusted object (her nightly kiss on the lips of his portrait). In his first agony as the poison begins to work through his brain and heart, Brachiano cries out for help to get his helmet off, then for Vittoria, then for physicians (the "screech-owls" whom, unable to give him no comfort, he faults for their failed "art to save") and then, with increasing rage and foreboding, against his death by violence, and then against death itself. But all this is with awareness, sanity. The poison settling, he moves into madness. First, he's an abused prince dismissing his steward when he learns of his corruption; then he's at table with his mortal enemy, now cohort, the Duke Francisco as he orders dishes (with double meanings): quail, then dog-fish, and sees approaching his banquet table the devil in quaintly old fashioned fancy dress; finally, a vision of Flamineo balanced on a tightrope with a moneybag in each hand "to keep him even," and a salivating lawyer waiting below for the money to fall.

Reverting to reason for a moment, he mocks Vittoria's bridal getup; then, succumbing again, sees rats on his pillow. At last, and for the last time, he comes out of his madness and is terrified at the sight of his murderers in monks' disguise over him, cries out for Vittoria, and suffers, knowingly, his strangulation.

> BRACHIANO
> An armourer! Ud's death, an armourer!
> Tear off my beaver.
> O my brain's on fire,
> The helmet is poisoned.
> There are some great ones that have a hand in this,
> And near about me.
> O I am gone already: the infection
> Flies to the brain and heart. O thou strong heart!
> There's such a covenant 'tween the world and it,
> They're loth to break.
> Where's this good woman? Had I infinite worlds
> They were too little for thee. Must I leave thee?
> What say yon screech-owls, is the venom mortal?
>
> Most corrupted politic hangman!
> You kill without book; but your art to save

Fails you as oft as great men's needy friends.
I that have given life to offending slaves
And wretched murderers, have I not power
To lengthen mine own a twelvemonth?
(To VITTORIA) Do not kiss me, for I shall poison thee.

This unction is sent from the great Duke of Florence.
O thou soft natural death, that art joint-twin
To sweetest slumber: no rough-bearded comet
Stares on thy mild departure: the dull owl
Beats not against thy casement: the hoarse wolf
Scents not thy carrion. Pity winds thy corse,
Whilst horror waits on princes.
How miserable a thing it is to die,
'Mongst women howling!

On pain of death, let no man name death to me,
It is a word infinitely terrible.

> *(These speeches are several kinds of distractions and in*
> *the action should appear so.)*

Away, you have abused me.
You have conveyed coin forth our territories,
Bought and sold offices, oppressed the poor,
And I ne'er dreamt on't. Make up your accounts;
I'll now be mine own steward.
Indeed I am to blame.
For did you ever hear the dusky raven
Chide blackness? Or was't ever known the devil
Railed against cloven creatures?

Let me have some quails to supper.
No: some fried dog-fish. Your quails feed on poison—
That old dog-fox, that politician Florence—
I'll forswear hunting and turn dog-killer.
Rare! I'll be friends with him: for mark you sir, one dog
Still sets another a-barking: peace, peace,
Yonder's a fine slave come in now.

Why, there.
In a blue bonnet, and a pair of breeches
With a great codpiece. Ha, ha, ha,
Look you his codpiece is stuck full of pins
With pearls o'th'head of them. Do not you know him?
Why 'tis the devil.
I know him by a great rose he wears on's shoe
To hide his cloven foot. I'll dispute with him.
He's a rare linguist.

See, see, Flamineo that killed his brother
Is dancing on the ropes there: and he carries
A money-bag in each hand, to keep him even,
For fear of breaking's neck. And there's a lawyer
In a gown whipt with velvet, stares and gapes
When the money will fall. How the rogue cuts capers!
It should have been in a halter.
'Tis there; what's she?

(Points to VITTORIA)

Vittoria!
Ha, ha, ha. Her hair is sprinkled with arras powder, that makes her
look as if she had sinned in the pastry. What's he?

(Points at GASPARO or LODOVICO)

He will be drunk: avoid him: th'argument is fearful when churchmen
stagger in't. Look you; six gray rats that have lost their tails crawl up
the pillow; send for a rat-catcher.
I'll do a miracle: I'll free the court
From all foul vermin.
Vi Horia! Vi Horia!

(He is strangled.)

the **beaver** attaches the helmet to the lower part of the face, torn off it frees the
poisoned helmet to be dislodged **loth**: loath, reluctant **screech-owls**: the physicians who can foretell but not prevent death **Most corrupted politic hangman**:

i.e., Death **unction**: medicinal oil; here, ironically, poison **no rough-bearded comet**: a tailed comet **dull owl...horse wolf**: prodigies associated with the fall of kings **carrion**: dead and putrefying flesh **corse**: corpse **have conveyed...territories**: the export of money was a serious offense **raven chide blackness**: equivalent to the pot calling the kettle black **quails**: birds supposed to feed on venomous seeds, and considered a culinary delicacy; satirically, courtesans **dogfish**: a small shark; satirically, a person **dog-fox**: symbol of cunning **codpiece...them**: prominent and lengthy decorated codpieces were out of fashion since Henry VIII's time **rose...foot**: large silk rosettes on shoes became fashionable ten years earlier **whipt**: trimmed **arras**: orris (iris root), used for whitening and perfuming hair **six gray rats...pillow**: probably a reference to witches, like the one in *Macbeth* who says, "Like a rat without a tail/I'll do, I'll do, and I'll do" ***Vi Horia!***: an attempt to cry "Vittoria!," or a misprint in text

37
FLAMINEO, VISITED BY BRACHIANO'S GHOST, SURMISES HIS FATE
(1609-12) JOHN WEBSTER, The White Devil, *Act 5, Sc. 4*

After a bitter quarrel between brothers, Marcello sends his sword to Flamineo, signifying a challenge to a duel. Flamineo returns it—not for a duel, but smoothly depositing it into his brother's bowels, instantly killing him. ("I have brought your weapon back.") Their mother Cornelia, observing this casually lethal gesture, goes mad.

Flamineo later stumbles on his mother winding Marcello's corpse for burial and singing "distractedly," that is, madly. For a moment— only a moment—Flamineo feels "a strange thing...compassion," but turns his attention at once to a more pressing need: to meet his sister Vittoria to discover what of Brachiano's wealth she's to bestow on him for past service. His mission is forestalled by the arrival of the murdered Brachiano's ghost. Like Molière's Don Juan meeting with his Stone Guest, Flamineo is equal in courage, or bravado, to the shock and terror of a beckoning ghost. And, *de rigeur* in Webster's tragedies, his worldly, curious, and inquiring villains take the occasion, on meeting ghosts already passed-over or the dying on the very edge of passing over, of cross-examining them on what they know, or at least what is already—but just—dimly visible to them, of the other side.

But when the Ghost vanishes, with the same bravado with which he greeted it, though he surmises the meaning of its portents—earth and skull—he brushes them aside and is back to business: the persuasive case he'll make to Vittoria to move her generosity—or if not, he'll "drown this weapon in her blood."

> FLAMINEO
> I have a strange thing in me, to th'which
> I cannot give a name, without it be
> Compassion.
> This night I'll know the utmost of my fate:
> I'll be resolved what my rich sister means
> T'assign me for my service. I have lived
> Riotously ill, like some that live in court;
> And sometimes, when my face was full of smiles
> Have felt the maze of conscience in my breast.
> Oft gay and honoured robes those tortures try:
> 'We think caged birds sing, when indeed they cry'.
>
> > *(Enter [BRACHIANO'S] Ghost. In his leather cassock
> > and breeches, boots, a cowl [and in his hand] a pot of
> > lily-flowers with a skull in't)*
>
> Ha! I can stand thee.
>
> > *(The Ghost approaches)*
>
> Nearer, nearer yet.
> What a mockery hath death made of thee? Thou look'st sad.
> In what place art thou? In yon starry gallery
> Or in the cursed dungeon? No? Not speak?

Pray, sir, resolve me, what religion's best
For a man to die in? Or is it in your knowledge
To answer me how long I have to live?
That's the most necessary question.
Not answer? Are you still like some great men
That only walk like shadows up and down
And to no purpose? Say—

>*(The Ghost throws earth upon him and shows him the
>skull.)*

What's that? O fatal! he throws earth upon me.
A dead man's skull beneath the roots of flowers.
I pray speak, sir. Our Italian churchmen
Make us believe dead men hold conference
With their familiars, and many times
Will come to bed to them and eat with them.

>*(Exit Ghost)*

He's gone; and see, the skull and earth are vanished.
This is beyond melancholy. I do dare my fate
To do its worst. Now to my sister's lodging
And sum up all these horrors: the disgrace
The Prince threw on me; next the piteous sight
Of my dead brother; and my mother's dotage;
And last this terrible vision. All these
Shall with Vittoria's bounty turn to good,
Or I will drown this weapon in her blood.

[s.d.] leather cassock: conventionally worn by ghosts in tragedies; **cowl,** monastic hood associated with Franciscan monks; the **lily:** foul in odor sits above the **skull:** the symbol of death **mockery**: counterfeit, shadow **starry gallery…dungeon**: in the theatre "the gallery" walk above and below stage "the dungeon" from which would appear devils and ghosts; ironically, heaven and hell **This is beyond melancholy**: i.e., this ghost is not a figment of the imagination; according to contemporary theories, beyond melancholy lay spiritual despair

38

FLAMINEO OUTFOXES HIS SISTER VITTORIA'S VILLAINY IN THEIR GAME OF PISTOLS

(1609-12) JOHN WEBSTER, The White Devil, *Act 5, Sc. 6*

Predictably, Flamineo's appeal to his sister Vittoria [see I, #37] to share between them the bounty of the dead Brachiano yields no fruit, and so he exits to return with other bounty left him by Brachiano   pistols, with which he prepares to play a grim game with his sister and her attendant, Zanche. They will all three die together, he suggests, and then suffers them to persuade him to die first, with their promise to follow. He prepares his way, wonders at the outcome of his final journey, gives them the pistols. They shoot, trample him with no intention of following, but so bring his game to its foregone conclusion: after mimicking descent through fire to the bottomless pit, he rises, confesses his deceit of no bullets in the pistols, and seizes the occasion to sermonize scaldingly on the cunning of women. But his pleasure in his trick and his sermon is short-lived. Francisco's henchmen, Lodovico and Gasparo, are outside the door, waiting to despatch all three.

> FLAMINEO
> Leave your prating,
> For these are but grammatical laments,
> Feminine arguments, and they move me
> As some in pulpits move their auditory
> More with their exclamation than sense
> Of reason or sound doctrine.
> Take these pistols,
> Because my hand is stained with blood already;
> Two of these you shall level at my breast,

Th'other 'gainst your own, and so we'll die,
Most equally contented. But first swear
Not to outlive me.

Then here's an end of me. Farewell daylight
And O contemptible physic! That dost take
So long a study only to preserve
So short a life, I take my leave of thee.
There are two cupping-glasses that shall draw
All my infected blood out—
Are you ready?

(Showing the pistols)

Whither shall I go now? O Lucian thy ridiculous purgatory! To find
Alexander the Great cobbling shoes, Pompey tagging points, and
Julius Caesar making hair buttons, Hannibal selling blacking, and
Augustus crying garlic, Charlemagne selling lists by the dozen, and
King Pippin crying apples in a cart drawn with one horse.

Whether I resolve to fire, earth, water, air,
Or all the elements by scruples, I know not
Nor greatly care—Shoot, shoot,
Of all deaths the violent death is best,
For from ourselves it steals ourselves so fast
The pain once apprehended is quite past.

(They shoot and run to him and tread upon him)

I am mixed with earth already: as you are noble
Perform your vows and bravely follow me.
Will you be perjured? What a religious oath was Styx that the gods
never durst swear by and violate? O that we had such an oath to minister, and to be so well kept in our courts of justice.

O I am caught with a springe!
Killed with a couple of braches.
O, the way's dark and horrid! I cannot see—

Shall I have no company?
O I smell soot,
Most stinking soot, the chimney is a-fire—
My liver's parboiled like Scotch holy-bread;
There's a plumber laying pipes in my guts, it scalds;
Wilt thou outlive me?
O cunning devils! Now I have tried your love
And doubled all your reaches.

(Riseth)

I am not wounded:
The pistols held no bullets; 'twas a plot
To prove your kindness to me and I live
To punish your ingratitude. I knew
One time or other you would find a way
To give me a strong potion. O men
That lie upon your death-beds and are haunted
With howling wives, ne'er trust them—they'll remarry
Ere the worm pierce your winding sheet, ere the spider
Make a thin curtain for your epitaphs.
How cunning you were to discharge! Do you practise at the Artillery
Yard? Trust a woman? Never, never. Brachiano be my precedent: we
lay our souls to pawn to the devil for a little pleasure and a woman
makes the bill of sale. That ever man should marry! For one
Hypermnestra that saved her lord and husband, forty-nine of her sis-
ters cut their husbands' throats all in one night. There was a shoal of
virtuous horse-leeches. Here are two other instruments.

(Enter Lodovico and Gasparo)

Lodovico and Gasparo.
You shall not take justice from forth my hands—
O let me kill her! I'll cut my safety
Through your coats of steel. Fate's a spaniel,
We cannot beat it from us.

grammatical...arguments: lamentations according to formal rules; weak arguments **take these pistols**: Flamineo offers Vittoria and her servant Zanche each

a pair of pistols; each of them points one at Flamineo, one at the other woman **physic**: medicine **cupping-glasses**: cup-shaped surgical vessels applied to the body, then heated to create a vacuum and thus draw off blood **Lucian...cobbling shoes**: from Lucian's *Menippos* Webster takes examples of great men reduced to ridiculous occupations **tagging points**: putting metal tags on the laces or points which held together Elizabethan clothing. The ironies, Caeser was bald, Hannibal of North Africa was black, **pippin** is a variety of apple **lists**: strips of cloth **by scruples**: by small degrees or portions **What a religious...violate?**: in Greek mythology the gods swore their oaths upon the Underground river Styx **springe**: a snare **brach**: a hound (here, a bitch, meaning Vittoria and Zanche) **parboiled**: partially boiled **Scotch holy-bread**: a sodden sheep's liver **doubled your reaches**: matched your plots **For one Hypemnestra...one night**: in Greek mythology, Danaus who was warned that he would be killed by one of his brother's sons, caused his 50 daughters to marry his brother's 50 sons. Hypermnestra alone disobeyed her father's command to cut her husband's throat. The myth is recounted in Aeschylus' *The Suppliants* **horse leeches**: blood suckers; double-tongued rhetoricians

39

FLAMINEO MORDANTLY BUT WITTILY OBSERVES THE PROCESS OF HIS OWN DYING
(1609-12) JOHN WEBSTER, The White Devil, *Act 5, Sc. 6*

Directly after Flamineo's pistol game with his sister and Zanche [see I, #38], Lodovico and three other murderers come in, throw off their disguises, and are ready to kill. They are met by the bravado of all three of their victims, Vittoria, Zanche and Flamineo, who, though frustrated that he cannot himself be his sister's executioner, nevertheless is struck with admiration by her courageous performance in outfacing her murderers.

But even Lodovico, in the midst of fulfilling his longed-for objective, so furiously bent on vengeance that he wishes he could kill Flamineo "forty times a day," suffers the Websterian longing to know: what, at his last moment before death, does Flamineo "think on?"

Flamineo, true to himself, maliciously disobliges his curiosity: "Of nothing," he reports. But once run through by Lodovico, he regards the fatal weapon stuck inside him, and as though manifesting in turn little more than curiosity, asks: "O, what blade is't? A Toledo or an English Fox?"

In keeping with his posture in life, Flamineo stares at advancing death with determined equanimity, upright and, at the last, defiantly enlarging the image of himself—a habit of Elizabethan and Jacobean villains and heroes at their last moment: rising to the height of their self-assertion, they spell out their own epitaphs, define their enormity in the face of this last moment when they're succumbing to extinction. Flamineo does it with the sneering aplomb and easy malice with which he performed his life. He gives short shrift to the physical pain he's enduring, belittles it, hides it beneath his study of his current state of still-being-alive, hides it beneath the wit that laughs at solemnity: "I have caught an everlasting cold." He enlarges his self-image to the point where it obliterates any other reality: "I do not look who went before, nor who shall follow me; No, at myself I will begin and end." And though pleased enough to leave the world of pain, he anticipates by some centuries Dylan Thomas's advice not to "go gently into that good night; rage," by demanding that the rage outlast him: "Strike thunder and strike loud at my farewell."

> **FLAMINEO**
> What do I think on?
> Nothing, of nothing: leave thy idle questions;
> I am i'th'way to study a long silence.
>
> *(They strike)*
> O what blade is't?
> A Toledo or an English fox?
> I ever thought a cutler should distinguish
> The cause of my death rather than a doctor.

Search my wound deeper: tent it with the steel
That made it.

Th'art a noble sister—
I love thee now. If woman do breed man
She ought to teach him manhood: fare thee well.
Know many glorious women that are famed
For masculine virtue have been vicious
Only a happier silence did betide them.
She hath no faults, who hath the art to hide them.
'Prosperity doth bewitch men seeming clear,
But seas do laugh, show white, when rocks are near.
We cease to grieve, cease to be Fortune's slaves,
Nay cease to die by dying.' Art thou gone?

(To VITTORIA)

False report
Which says that women vie with the nine Muses
For nine tough durable lives. I do not look
Who went before, nor who shall follow me;
No, at myself I will begin and end:
'While we look up to heaven we confound
Knowledge with knowledge'. O, I am in a mist.
I recover like a spent taper for a flash,
And instantly go out.
Let all that belong to great men remember th'old wives' tradition, to
be like the lions i'th'Tower on Candlemas day, to mourn if the sun
shine for fear of the pitiful remainder of winter to come.
'Tis well yet there's some goodness in my death,
My life was a black charnel. I have caught
An everlasting cold. I have lost my voice
Most irrecoverably. Farewell, glorious villains.
'This busy trade of life appears most vain,
Since rest breeds rest where all seek pain by pain.'
Let no harsh flattering bells resound my knell,
Strike thunder and strike loud to my farewell. *(Dies)*

cutler: a dealer in knives and cutting utensils **tent**: to scour the wound, explore it with the end of the steel **betide**: to happen, befall **Candlemas day...winter to come**: proverbially, if the sun shines on Candlemas day (February 2), winter will come back with a vengeance in February **lions i'th' Tower**: lions were kept in a small zoo in the Tower of London **charnel**: a repository where the dead are stored

40

BOSOLA IMPORTUNES THE CARDINAL FOR HIS REWARD

(1613-14) JOHN WEBSTER, The Duchess of Malfi, *Act 1, Sc. 1*

Bosola, as the tool-villain in *The Duchess of Malfi*, is under the same coercion as his counterpart Flamineo in *The White Devil* [see I, #34, 37]. But for two reasons, his condition is worse: first, his employers, the Cardinal and the Duke Francisco, are far more ominous—one a cynical hypocrite and the other mad—than Flamineo's. Second, unlike Flamineo, Bosola has—though it is thoroughly dormant at the first—a conscience. The pain of his resentment is unrelieved by Flamineo's armor of sick pleasure in his office.

Bosola, then, becomes the envenomed Malcontent, the bitterest, most caustic type in Elizabethan/Jacobean drama.

When the Cardinal leaves him, without reward for criminal services but with a bit of advice ("Would you could be honest!"), and Bosola is left with nothing but dismissive indifference for his pains, he turns to his companions in the scene, Antonio and Delio, and not only gives the "character" of the Cardinal and his brother the Duke Ferdinand, but also voices the bitter complaint of the subservient to the great, the ones who are forever waiting, like Tantalus, for the fruit to drop.

(Enter Cardinal and Bosola)

BOSOLA

I do haunt you still. I have done you better service than to be slighted
thus. Miserable age, where only the reward of doing well is the doing of it!

I fell into the galleys in your service; where, for two years together,
I wore two towels instead of a shirt, with a knot on the shoulder, after
the fashion of a Roman mantle. Slighted thus! I will thrive some way.
Blackbirds fatten best in hard weather; why not I in these dog-days?
Ah, you say, would I were honest? With all your divinity do but direct
me the way to it. I have known many travel far for it, and yet return
as arrant knaves as they went forth, because they carried themselves
always along with them.

(Exit Cardinal.)

Are you gone? Some fellows, they say, are possessed with the devil,
but this great fellow were able to possess the greatest devil, and make
him worse. His and his brother are like plum-trees that grow crooked
over standing-pools; they are rich and o'erladen with fruit, but none
but crows, pies, and caterpillars feed on them. Could I be one of their
flattering pandars, I would hang on their ears like a horseleech, till I
were full, and then drop off. (*To Delio*) I pray, leave me. Who would
rely upon these miserable dependances, in expectation to be advanc'd
tomorrow? What creature ever fed worse than hoping Tantalus? Nor
ever died any man more fearfully than he that hop'd for a pardon.
There are rewards for hawks and dogs when they have done us service;
but for a soldier that hazards his limbs in a battle, nothing but a kind
of geometry is his last supportation.

Ay, to hang in a fair pair of slings, take his latter swing in the
world upon an honourable pair of crutches, from hospital to hospital.
Fare ye well, sir: and yet do not you scorn us; for places in the court
are but like beds in the hospital, where this man's head lies at that
man's foot, and so lower and lower.

(Exit.)

galleys: servitude as a slave on galleys (ships) **standing-pools**: stagnant ponds
pies: magpies **pandar**: a go-between, pimp; here, lackey, flatterer **Tantalus**:
whose fate was in his hunger to reach for a fruit on a tree and forever to be out
of reach **a kind of geometry**: swinging on the two legs of compass (crutches)

41

BOSOLA RAILS AT COURTIER, WOMAN, AND "THE FORM OF MAN"

(1613-14) JOHN WEBSTER, The Duchess of Malfi, *Act 2, Sc. 1*

R ailing" is the sour entertainment of the tool-villain-malcontent
[see I, #40] at court, where he paints the iniquities of court custom in sickening but accurate detail, providing its indwellers with acid
images of themselves. His targets are hypocrisy, pretension, iniquity
and self-delusion, and he takes on himself the mission of excoriating
each malefactor to his face. But for the innocent, those still aspiring to
enter the magic circle of court preferment, he is mockingly helpful,
instructing the novice in how to become the ideal hypocrite, the con-
summate pretender, the perfect court parasite.

Bosola, in this set passage of raillery, takes on both of these types
in turn. First, the naively aspiring courtier Castruchio, an incipient
lawyer, born to the profession, Bosola tells him, with his native "night-
cap" (lawyer's) face and ears (large). He offers him four invariably
infallible lessons: the trick of twirling the strings dangling from his
robe; hemming and hawing at the ends of sentences; blowing his nose
awhile to cover his lapses of memory; and as presiding justice ("president") in a lawcourt, tantalizing with the opposite expression (smile or
frown) what his sentence is to be. The test of when he's made it: pretend to be dying, and know he's won if he's earned the people's curse.

When an old woman of the court joins them, Bosola aims his malice at her, cataloguing the ingredients of her "face-painting" as "a shop
of witchcraft" that makes the easy fortune of the cosmetic-physician.
He offers the two of them his "medication," which is his description
of the condition of "man," who hides from himself the reality of his
diseased, deformed and death-inherent self with a covering of fancy

clothes ("rich tissue"). And he dismisses the two with off-hand advice: to slip off, while the "lawyer's" wife is away in Rome, and "couple."

Unlike other Elizabethan/Jacobean malcontents, Bosola's railing is neither mockingly gleeful nor wrathfully venomous. It is merely sour, staring as he does always at the underbelly of reality, and affecting no surprise.

(Enter BOSOLA and CASTRUCHIO.)

BOSOLA
You say you would fain be taken for an eminent courtier?
Let me see: you have a reasonable good face for't already, and your night-cap expresses your ears sufficient largely. I would have you learn to twirl the strings of your band with a good grace, and in a set speech, at th'end of every sentence, to hum three or four times, or blow your nose till it smart again, to recover your memory. When you come to be a president in criminal causes, if you smile upon a prison, hang him; but if you frown upon him and threaten him, let him be sure to scape the gallows. Give out you lie a-dying, and if you hear the common people curse you, be sure you are taken for one of the prime night-caps.

(Enter an Old Lady.)

You come from painting now,…from your scurvy face-physic. To behold thee not painted inclines somewhat near a miracle. These in thy face here were deep ruts and foul sloughs the last progress. There was a lady in France that, having had the small-pox, flayed the skin off her face to make it more level; and whereas before she looked like a nutmeg grater, after she resembled an abortive hedge-hog . One would suspect your closet for a shop of witchcraft, to find in it the fat of serpents, spawn of snakes, Jews' spittle, and their young children's ordure: and all these for the face. I would sooner eat a dead pigeon taken from the soles of the feet of one sick of the plague, than kiss one of you fasting. Here are two of you, whose sin is the very patrimony of the physician; makes him renew his foot-cloth with the spring, and change his high-pric'd courtesan with the fall of the leaf. I do wonder you not loathe yourselves. Observe my medication now:

What thing is in this outward form of man
To be belov'd? We account it ominous,
If nature do produce a colt, or lamb,
A fawn, or goat, in any limb resembling
A man, and fly from 't as a prodigy.
Man stands amaz'd to see his deformity
In any other creature but himself.
But in our own flesh though we bear diseases
Which have their true names only ta'en from beasts,—
As the most ulcerous wolf and swinish measle,—
Though we are eaten up of lice and worms,
And though continually we bear about us
A rotten and dead body, we delight
To hide it in rich tissue: all our fear,
Nay, all our terror, is, lest our physician
Should put us in the ground to be made sweet.—
Your wife's gone to Rome: you two couple, and get you to the wells at
Lucca to recover your aches. I have other work on foot.

ordure: excrement **foot-cloth**: ornamental trappings for saddle-animals **ulcerus wolf**: a tubercular affection of the nose, known as *lupus* **swinish measle**: a disease of hogs

42

FERDINAND VILLIFIES THE DUCHESS AND HER UNSEEN "LOVER"

(1613-14) JOHN WEBSTER, The Duchess of Malfi, *Act 3, Sc. 2*

The brothers of the Duchess of Malfi, Duke Ferdinand and the Cardinal, have sworn her to absolute celibacy after her widowhood, and have hired Bosola—whom they've advanced to a post at her court—to spy on her lest any suitors come her way.

The Duchess does not wait for suitors; she chooses her own—
Antonio, her secretary. They marry secretly, live privately and secretly
for a few years; have children. But Bosola discovers their secret and
informs the Duke. The revelation sends the Duke into a frenzy; he
accosts the Duchess in her chamber, and certain that her "lover" is
concealed in the next room, directs his fury against both.

The politic, practical reasons for the brothers' keeping the Duchess
from marriage are casually specified (their desire to keep her from a
further marriage to the detriment of their inheritance), but
Ferdinand's private motives are not specified at all, although they drive
not only him but the action of the play. That he is mad is certain; his
wolfishness of soul eventually takes on the literal characteristics of a
wolf when at play's end he suffers a "wolfish" transformation. His
injunction had not been only against his sister's marriage but against
even the suggestion of sexual dalliance. And in his villification of her
and her concealed lover in the following tirade, it's obvious that more
than her loss of reputation is troubling him.

Ferdinand's monologue is a marvelous study in the deflection of
intent. His very rage against the Duchess's and her "lover's" imagined
promiscuity broadcasts his own jealousy and lust for her. His subsequent sadistic pursuit of vengeance against her through the rest of the
play ends in one of the most eloquent understatements of feeling in
Jacobean tragedy. Having accomplished her death, and now staring at
her inert body, he permits the fullness of his feeling only this: "Cover
her face; mine eyes dazzle; she died young."

But he is not at all understated when, at first discovery, he storms
the Duchess's chamber. And though he discovers too that the Duchess
is not the "strumpet" he rages at, but is married, the knowledge makes
no difference to his violent condemnation of her. What he appears to
be condemning issues, on the face of it, from the same sexual disgust
that Hamlet and similar Jacobean melancholics endure, but the suspi-

cion of tangled motives is aroused by the oddity of his determination not to discover the identity of the "hidden" husband. May he be hidden forever in the closest room, he instructs his sister, if the "vile woman" the Duchess wishes her "lecher to grow old in [her] embracements." Married or no, she is in his eyes a strumpet of lost reputation, whose "lechery," sanctioned by marriage or not, he reviles with a kind of mad disgust, but does not root out or end. It lingers in his imagination through the rest of the play while he inflicts on her instruments of torture, madness and finally death.

> FERDINAND
> Virtue, where art though hid? What hideous thing
> Is it that doth eclipse thee?
> Or is it true thou art but a bare name,
> And no essential thing?
> O most imperfect light of human reason,
> That mak'st us so unhappy to foresee
> What we can least prevent! Pursue thy wishes,
> And glory in them: there's in shame no comfort
> But to be past all bounds and sense of shame.
> Whate'er thou art that hast enjoy'd my sister,
> For I am sure thou hear'st me, for thine own sake
> Let me not know thee. I came hither prepar'd
> To work thy discovery; yet am now persuaded
> It would beget such violent effects
> As would damn us both. I would not for ten millions
> I had beheld thee: therefore use all means
> I never may have knowledge of thy name.
> Enjoy thy lust still, and a wretched life,
> On that condition.—And for thee, vile woman,
> If though do wish thy lecher may grow old
> In thy embracements, I would have thee build
> Such a room for him as our anchorites
> To holier use inhabit. Let not the sun
> Shine on him till he's dead; let dogs and monkeys

Only converse with him, and such dumb things
To whom nature denies use to sound his name;
Do not keep a paraquito, lest she learn it.
If thou do love him, cut out thine own tongue,
Lest it bewray him. Thou art undone;
And thou hast ta'en that massy sheet of lead
That hid they husband's bones, and folded it
About my heart.

Dost thou know what reputation is?
I'll tell thee,—to small purpose, since th'instruction
Comes now too late.
Upon a time Reputation, Love, and Death
Would travel o'er the world; and it was concluded
That they should part, and take three several ways.
Death told them, they should find him in great battles,
Or cities plagu'd with plagues; Love gives them counsel
To inquire for him 'mongst unambitious shepherds,
Where dowries were not talk'd of, and sometimes
'Mongst quiet kindred that had nothing left
By their dead parents. 'Stay,' quoth Reputation.
'Do not forsake me; for it is my nature,
If once I part from any man I meet,
I am never found again.' And so for you:
You have shook hands with Reputation,
And made him invisible. So, fare you well:
I will never see you more.

vild: vile **anchorites**: hermits **paraquito**: a parrot

43

FERDINAND, THE DUCHESS DEAD, CONDEMNS THE MURDERER HE ENJOINED

(1613-14) JOHN WEBSTER, The Duchess of Malfi, *Act 4, Sc. 2*

Ferdinand, staring at the dead body of his sister the Duchess, is moved to remember a different history from the one in which he brought about her murder [see I, #42]. They were twins, he remembers now, she an innocent, his dearest friend, and her marriage galled only because it deprived him of inheriting her wealth—in his memory now, there was no other cause. And in his memory now, it was in a moment of distraction that he bade the villain Bosola to murder her, which Bosola, villainous (according to Ferdinand) in his nature, did, rather than defend her from him and bear her off to safety.

Putting out of his mind his insanely sadistic pursuit of the Duchess through torture, madness and death, the slaughter of her children, and his rage against her sexuality—which he had condemned as bestial whether within marriage or not—he recognizes now only the villainy of the surrogate murderer Bosola, who had, he now accuses, no authority to murder. ("Was I her judge?…Did a complete jury deliver her conviction up?") And so, with the blame entirely Bosola's, the blameless Ferdinand condemns him: "thou shalt die for't."

Once again [as in I, #42] Ferdinand, deeply pained by the loss of the sister for whom he never admitted incestuous desire, deflects his real intent. He mourns her loss and punishes his own guilt by bitterly condemning his henchman-murderer.

> FERDINAND
> Cover her face; mine eyes dazzle: she died young.
> She and I were twins;
> And should I die this instant, I had liv'd
> Her time to a minute.

Let me see her face
Again. Why didst not thou pity her? What
An excellent honest man mightst thou have been,
If thou hadst borne her to some sanctuary!
Or, bold in a good cause, oppos'd thyself,
With thy advanced sword above thy head,
Between her innocent and my revenge!
I bade thee, when I was distracted of my wits,
To kill my dearest friend, and thou hast done 't.
For let me but examine well the cause:
What was the meanness of her match to me?
Only I must confess I had a home,
Had she continu'd widow, to have gain'd
An infinite mass of treasure by her death:
And that was the main cause,—her marriage,
That drew a stream of gall quite through my heart.
For thee (as we observe in tragedies
That a good actor many times is cur'd
For playing a villain's part) I hate thee for 't.
And, for my sake, say, thou hast done much ill well.
By what authority didst thou execute
This bloody sentence?
Was I her judge?
Did any ceremonial form of law
Doom her to not-being? Did a complete jury
Deliver her conviction up i' th' court?
Where shalt thou find this judgment register'd
Unless in hell? See, like a bloody fool,
Thou'st forfeited thy life, and thou shalt die for't.
The wolf shall find her grave and scrape it up,
Not to devour the corpse, but to discover
The horrid murther.
O horror,
That not the fear of him which binds the devils
Can prescribe man obedience!—
Never look upon me more.
Get thee into some unknown part o' th' world,
That I may never see thee.

44

BOSOLA REPENTS AFTER THE DUCHESS'S MURDER

(1613-14) JOHN WEBSTER, The Duchess of Malfi, *Act 4, Sc. 2*

B osola is no run-of-the-mill tool-villain; his uniqueness emerges fully in this speech. Through four acts, he has dutifully carried out the commands of his employer the Duke Ferdinand, scrupulously putting the Duchess through all the tortures demanded by him that brought her to the verge of madness, and at last, at the Duke's behest, murdered her and her children. For this gruesome employment, his reward [see I, #43] is the Duke's expressed loathing and condemnation, nothing more.

But Bosola, in startling contrast to the tool-villain's conventional role, is a man of conscience. His observation of the court's and the world's ways [see I, #41] fed not only his malcontent's contempt, but also his private moral revulsion. Steeped though he is, out of need, in the employ of a highly placed, powerful but mad criminal, following scrupulously his instructions for the Duchess's undoing, he nevertheless throughout that occupation gained more and more respect, admiration and a kind of love for the Duchess's inherent virtue.

Condemned and betrayed by the Duke, he's lost what reward he labored for, and so in a moment, throws aside "painted honor" (the coded loyalty he owed to his employer) and allows his dormant feelings to manifest themselves. He looks at once to the Duchess, attempting to revive her. He does for a moment, and in that instant, quickly tells her comforting lies. She dies, and he is left with the "manly sorrow… that we cannot be suffered to do good when we have a mind to it!" and he has little recourse but to let his tears, which were "frozen up," mark his penitence, and stare at his guilty conscience as though staring into hell.

One more gesture—disposing safely the body of the Duchess—and he's off to Milan, where he will plot to save the Duchess's husband Antonio, and execute vengeance against the Duchess's criminal brothers. In the end, he accomplishes his revenge, but true to the run of his fortune, he accomplishes also, inadvertently, both Antonio's and his own death.

BOSOLA
Let me know
Wherefore I should be thus neglected. Sir,
I serv'd your tyranny, and rather strove
To satisfy yourself than all the world:
And though I loath'd the evil, yet I lov'd
You that did counsel it; and rather sought
To appear a true servant than an honest man.

(Ferdinand exits.)
Off, my painted honour.
While with vain hopes our faculties we tire,
We seem to sweat in ice and freeze in fire.
What would I do, were this to do again?
I would not change my peace of conscience
For all the wealth of Europe.—She stirs; here's life:—
Return, fair soul, from darkness, and lead mine
Out of this sensible hell!—she's warm, she breathes:—
Upon thy pale lips I will melt my heart,
To store them with fresh colour.—Who's there?
Some cordial drink!—Alas, I dare not call:
So pity would destroy pity.—Her eye opes,
And heaven in it seems to ope, that late was shut,
To take me up to mercy.
Madam, Antonio is living;
The dead bodies you saw were but fegn'd statues.
He's reconcil'd to your brothers; the Pope hath wrought
The atonement.

O, she's gone again! there the cords of life broke.
O sacred innocence, that sweetly sleeps
On turtles' feathers, whilst a guilty conscience
Is a black register wherein is writ
All our good deeds and bad, a perspective
That shows us hell! That we cannot be suffer'd
To do good when we have a mind to it!
This is manly sorrow!
These tears, I am very certain, never grew
In my mother's milk. My estate is sunk
Below the degree of fear: where are
These penitent fountains while she was living?
O, they were frozen up! Here is a sight
As direful to my soul as is the sword
Unto a wretch hath slain his father.
Come, I'll bear thee hence,
And execute thy last will; that's deliver
Thy body to the reverend dispose
Of some good women: that the cruel tyrant
Shall not deny me. Then I'll post to Milan,
Where somewhat I will speedily enact
Worth my dejection.

(Exit with the body.)

turtles: turtle doves **dispose**: care **worth my dejection**: suitable to my distress

45

GIOVANNI, DISPUTING WITH THE FRIAR, ARGUES FOR THE PROPRIETY OF HIS INCESTUOUS LOVE

(1629-33) JOHN FORD, 'Tis Pity She's a Whore, *Act 1, Sc. 1*

Depending on one's religious or anti-religious perspective, Giovanni is either the villain or the hero of this tragedy. He is, in this his first speech, responding to Friar Bonaventura's arguments, which are not so much arguments as injunctions not to speak at all: "Dispute no more in this," cries the Friar at the opening, and concludes after speaking religious/moral orthodoxy, "No more! I may not hear it!"

Giovanni's response to this prohibition opens up for us one of the most subversive intellectual conflicts gathering force from the early days of the Renaissance: what was owing to the Christian God and what to the God of Chivalric Love. No mean contest, for the obligation to either was absolute, a vow; one dropped the knee before the Lady Love as vigorously and soulfully as before the more familiar God. That the two could be reconciled was more easily said than done, and Ford in this play puts the case of their irreconcilability as uncompromisingly as it can be put: the ultimate case—incest—in which true obeisance toward the one commits absolute sin toward the other.

To understand the tragic force of this dilemma one must understand too the powerful emotional rituals that attended the formal worship of Love: they are not simply "feelings," but codified rituals of feeling and belief that are so entirely equivalent in force to the rituals of feeling associated with conventional religion, that they can speak exactly the same words of justification and demand exactly the same intensity of devotion.

Note Giovanni's argument for the propriety of his love for his sister: "Are we not therefore each to other bound...by links...even of religion, to be ever one, / One soul, one flesh, one love, one heart, one all?" And so he is both votary as well as militant champion for the religion of Love, and exactly like the Renaissance champion of Christian faith, sworn in his soul to commit martyrdom or murder for its glorification. Eventually, he does both.

> GIOVANNI
> Gentle father,
> To you I have unclasped my burdened soul,
> Emptied the storehouse of my thoughts and heart,
> Made myself poor of secrets; have not left
> Another word untold, which hath not spoke
> All what I ever durst or think or know;
> And yet is here the comfort I shall have?
> Must I not do what all men else may,—love?
> Must I not praise
> That beauty which, if framed anew, the gods
> Would make a god of, if they had it there,
> And kneel to it, as I do kneel to them?
> Shall a peevish sound,
> A customary form, from man to man,
> Of brother and of sister, be a bar
> 'Twixt my perpetual happiness and me?
> Say that we had one father; say one womb—
> Curse to my joys!—gave both us life and birth;
> Are we not therefore each to other bound
> So much the more by nature? by the links
> Of blood, of reason? nay, if you will have't,
> Even of religion, to be ever one,
> One soul, one flesh, one love, one heart, one all?
> Shall, then, for that I am her brother born,
> My joys be ever banished from her bed?
> No, father; in your eyes I see the change

Of pity and compassion; from your age,
As from a sacred oracle, distils
The life of counsel: tell me, holy man,
What cure shall give me ease in these extremes?
It were more ease to stop the ocean
From floats and ebbs than to dissuade my vows.

peevish: trifling **distils**: extracts

46

GIOVANNI, TO PREVENT ANNABELLA'S MARRIAGE, MAKES A PACT WITH HER FOR HER MURDER
(1629-33) JOHN FORD, 'Tis Pity She's a Whore, *Act 5, Sc. 5*

Giovanni's sister Annabella, in the course of their secret assignations, is with child. But she is wooed by a nobleman, Soranzo, a
man of questionable morality (of either Giovanni's kind or the
Church's [see I, #45]), who abandons a mistress in his pursuit of
advantageous marriage with Annabella. She, feeling otherwise lost if
her child is born out of wedlock, does not protest vigorously enough
to stave off the marriage. It's accomplished, only for Soranzo to discover Annabella's adultery and pregnancy. On the verge of killing her
for her sin, he is prevented by his servant who has a better plan: speak
her gently, he advises, preserve her until she reveals the name of her
adulterer, and then take revenge on them both. The kind words suddenly coming from the mouth of Soranzo go to the heart of
Annabella, who is ready to repent, abandon her sin, and renounce her
love for her brother Giovanni.

Giovanni meanwhile makes his own plan: Annabella, in an as yet
unconsummated marriage, is in terms of his own code of Love, still

inviolate in her devotion to him and to their love, and so far "white in her soul." Although "the laws of conscience and of [conventional] civil use" would condemn them, her actual "innocence and sanctity" will nevertheless fill a throne in Heaven. And so true to his code,—which he assumes is still shared by Annabella—he will accomplish her death, and then his own.

The speech he utters during this, in effect, ritual murder is motivated by two intentions: one is to hold religiously to his gruesome purpose and at the same time justify that purpose to himself and to her; and the other is to bid her the tenderest of lover's farewells. And just as multitudes of husbands, brothers and lovers in Western drama have assassinated their daughters, sisters and beloveds to preserve the lady's chastity and their own honor, so Giovanni in his own terms declares, "Revenge [against the infidels who brought Annabella to wedlock] is mine; honor [by overcoming his tender feelings in order to live up to his code] doth love command."

A hero in his own terms, he goes forward with the rest of his plan—the most gruesome part of it yet ("Shrink not, courageous hand"), but the one that will accomplish his faith's ultimate glorification [see I, #47].

> GIOVANNI
> The schoolmen teach that all this globe of earth
> Shall be consumed to ashes in a minute.
> But 'twere somewhat strange
> To see the waters burn: could I believe
> This might be true, I could believe as well
> There might be hell or Heaven.
> A dream, a dream! else in this other world
> We should know one another.
> Have you heard? We shall?

But d'ye think
That I shall see you there?—You look on me.—
May we kiss one another, prate or laugh,
Or do as we do here?
Look up, look here; what see you in my face?
What see you in mine eyes?
These are the funeral tears
Shed on your grave; these furrowed-up my cheeks
When first I loved and knew not how to woo.
Fair Annabella, should I here repeat
The story of my life, we might lose time.
Be record all the spirts of the air,
And all things else that are, that day and night,
Early and late, the tribute which my heart
Hath paid to Annabella's sacred love
Hath been these tears, which are her mourners now!
Never till now did Nature do her best
To show a matchless beauty to the world,
Which in an instant, ere it scarce was seen,
The jealous Destinies required again.
Pray, Annabella, pray! Since we must part,
Go thou, white in thy soul, to fill a throne
Of innocence and sanctity in Heaven.
Pray, pray, my sister!
Kiss me. If ever after-times should hear
Of our fast-knit affections, though perhaps
The laws of conscience and of civil use
May justly blame us, yet when they but know
Our loves, that love will wipe away that rigour
Which would in other incests be abhorred.
Give me your hand: how sweetly life doth run
In these well-coloured veins! how constantly
These palms do promise health! but I could chide
With Nature for this cunning flattery.
Kiss me again:—forgive me.

Be dark, bright sun,
And make this mid-day night, that thy gilt rays
May not behold a deed will turn their splendour
More sooty than the poets feign their Styx!—
One other kiss, my sister.
To save thy fame, and kill thee in a kiss.

(Stabs her)

Thus die, and die by me, and by my hand!
Revenge is mine; honour doth love command.

When thou art dead
I'll give my reasons for't; for to dispute
With thy—even in thy death—most lovely beauty,
Would make me stagger to perform this act,
Which I most glory in.

She's dead, alas, good soul! The hapless fruit
That in her womb received its life from me
Hath had from me a cradle and a grave.
I must not dally. This sad marriage-bed,
In all her best, bore her alive and dead.
Soranzo, thou hast missed thy aim in this:
I have prevented now they reaching plots,
And killed a love, for whose each drop of blood
I would have pawned my heart.—Fair Annabella,
How over glorious art thou in thy wounds,
Triumphing over infamy and hate!—
Shrink not, courageous hand, stand up, my heart,
And boldly act my last and greater part!

be record: be witness **jealous Destinies**: the Fates in Greek mythology **feign**: to paint, represent **reaching**: overreaching

47

GIOVANNI BRINGS TO HIS SISTER'S WEDDING FEAST HER HEART ON HIS SWORD
(1629-33) JOHN FORD, 'Tis Pity She's a Whore, *Act 5, Sc. 6*

The most grisly half of Giovanni's promise at the end of the previous scene [see I, #46], to "boldly act my last and greatest part," is luckily fulfilled off-stage. It is to cut out the heart of the corpse of Annabella, and then to bring it to the guests, on the end of his sword, who have come to celebrate a feast hosted by her new-minted husband, Soranzo.

Like the Dostoyevski characters who live their lives intensely and wholly governed by an *idée fixe,* Giovanni to the last is governed entirely by the precepts of his faith, and bears out in his actions—literally even though grotesquely—his devotion to the temple of that faith: Annabella's heart. He brings it proudly to the feast, at the end of his sword, as the visible sign of the honor he's bestowed on his revenge against Soranzo, who by becoming Annabella's husband, despoiled and trampled on the sanctity of his and his sister's Love.

Pride and glee: these are the emotions of the triumphant Giovanni, throwing in the face of the assembled the purity, the perfection of both his love for Annabella and the revenge he's executed on its despoilers. Waving the heart of Annabella in the faces of the feast's guests, his claim is confirmed; his faith is proven.

An unbeliever has gone to check—has this lunatic really done this ghastly thing? He comes back shaken, and Giovanni, smiling, revels in its confirmation: "Is't true or no, sir?"

(Enter GIOVANNI with a heart upon his dagger)

GIOVANNI

Here, here, Soranzo! trimmed in reeking blood,
That triumphs over death, proud in the spoil
Of love and vengeance! Fate, or all the powers
That guide the motions of immortal souls,
Could not prevent me.
Be not amazed: if your misgiving hearts
Shrink at an idle sight, what bloodless fear
Of coward passion would have seized your senses,
Had you beheld the rape of life and beauty
Which I have acted!—My sister, O, my sister!
The glory of my deed
Darkened the mid-day sun, made noon as night.
You came to feast, my lords, with dainty fare:
I came to feast too; but I digged for food
In a much richer mine than gold or stone
Of any value balanced; 'tis a heart,
A heart, my lords, in which is mine entombed:
Look well upon't; d'ye know't?
'Tis Annabella's heart, 'tis:—why d'ye startle?—
I vow 'tis hers: this dagger's point ploughed up
Her fruitful womb, and left to me the fame
Of a most glorious executioner.
And, that times to come may know
How, as my fate, I honoured my revenge,
List, father, to your ears I will yield up
How much I have deserved to be your son.
Nine months have had their changes
Since I first throughly viewed and truly loved
Your daughter and my sister.
For nine months' space in secret I enjoyed
Sweet Annabella's sheets; nine months I lived
A happy monarch of her heart and her.—
Soranzo, thou know'st this: thy paler cheek
Bears the confounding print of thy disgrace;

For her too-fruitful womb too soon bewrayed
The happy passage of our stol'n delights,
And made her mother to a child unborn.
'Tis the oracle of truth;
I vow it is so.
Have you all no faith
To credit yet my triumphs? Here I swear
By all that you call sacred, by the love
I bore my Annabella whilst she lived,
These hands have from her bosom ripped this heart.
Is't true, or no, sir?

trimmed: dressed, arrayed **misgiving:** doubting, apprehensive **bewrayed:**
betrayed

XVII CENTURY FRENCH/SPANISH

48

RODRIGUE IMPORTUNES CHIMENE TO KILL HIM FOR HAVING TAKEN REVENGE AGAINST HER FATHER

(1638) PIERRE CORNEILLE, Le Cid, *tr. Paul Landis*, Act 3, Sc. 4

Don Diegue, Rodrigue's father, struck by Count Gomez during a quarrel, is too old and weak to avenge his honor by his own hand. Rodrigue, under obligation to redeem that honor, confronts an irresolvable dilemma: Count Gomez is the father of his pledged love, Chimene. To challenge or not to challenge, either way, he is doomed: his father's dishonor is his own as well: "Only in blood," his father exhorts him, "can such a stain be cleansed. Kill or be killed." But to kill the father of Chimene puts her in the same plight: to redeem her honor, she is under filial obligation to destroy her father's murderer.

The code is absolute and brooks no dispute, no questioning. The "Pundonor," the point of honor, governs life's every moment, since dishonor prolonged, however slight, literally signifies not merely disgrace among men, but one's absence from the benignity of God until honor is restored by the spilling of blood. In chivalric Spain (where the play, like its original, is set, and from where the code in its most rigid form was replicated by all of literary and court-centered Europe) it infused moral, legal and military law and custom; rigid public decorum became its symbolic representation. In *The Cid*, it is followed, at no matter what cost, with passion, its principal characters—Rodrigue, Chimene and the Infanta—its wholly submissive votaries.

The corresponding meaning and psychology of love corroborate the code. What alone is worthy of love is one's unblemished honor; and the condition of one's honor is one's whole self, one's being entirely so defined. "Your beauty," Rodrigue onfesses to Chimene, "might have turned the balance still, /But for the thought, stronger than all your charms, /That without honor, no man could deserve you."

So strenuous is the commitment to this belief that it becomes wholly internalized; no longer external constraint, but one's controlling internal dynamic. The fusion creates a paradox on which the entire action of the play hinges. For Rodrigue to refuse the burden of avenging his father would destroy his honor in the very eyes of Chimene; her incapacity to pursue vengeance against him would equally destroy hers, though its pursuit on the part of either nullifies their hope of reconciliation.

And yet the force of their love, reinforced by the nobility of person each sees in the other, produces a level of pain for which there is no absolution. The duel is fought by Rodrigue; the Count is killed; Chimene pleads with the King for vengeance against "this rash youth." And so Rodrigue, as compassionate toward "what honor bids" Chimene to do as toward what it commanded of him, seeks audience with her to urge her to avenge her honor against him with his own sword.

> RODRIGUE
> Permit me but a word.
> Then let me have your answer with this sword.
>
> Spare not my blood; without resistance taste
> The sweetness of my death and our revenge.
>
> I do your will, yet cherish still the wish
> Of ending at your hands my wretched life;
> Do not expect that love will stir in me
> A base repentance for a worthy deed.
> The fatal issue of too swift a wrath
> Disgraced my father and brought shame to me.
> You know how a man of courage takes a blow:

I shared the affront, and I sought out the author;
I found him, and upon his head avenged
My father and my honor; I should do it
All again, were all again to do.
And yet against my father and myself
My love for you long battled with my duty.
Judge of its power, when I could hesitate
To take revenge for such a bold affront.
Bound to bring you grief or suffer insult,
I thought perhaps my arm had been too swift,
Accused myself of too much violence;
Your beauty might have turned the balance still,
But for the thought, stronger than all your charms,
That without honor, no man could deserve you;
That spite of all the love you bear for me,
Who loves me noble, would despise me base;
And that to yield, to hear the voice of love,
Would render me unworthy of your choice.
Again I say, though not without a sigh,
And with my latest breath would I repeat:
I did you wrong, but had I not erased
This insult, I had proven unworthy of you;
Now, honor and my father satisfied,
I come to you to pay my final debt.
You see me here to offer you my life.
Half my duty done, I do the rest.
I know your father's death makes you my foe;
I have no wish to rob you of your victim.
Shrink not from offering up the blood of him
Who glories in the shedding of your father's.
Delay no longer what your honor bids you;
It asks my head, I offer it to you;
Make it a sacrifice to your revenge;
The sentence and the death-stroke will be sweet.
After my crime to wait upon slow justice
Removes the glory from my punishment.
I shall die happy, dying by your hand.

49

RODRIGUE BIDS FAREWELL TO CHIMENE BEFORE COMBAT

(1638) PIERRE CORNEILLE, *Le Cid, tr. Paul Landis, Act 5, Sc. 1*

Rodrigue's offer to die at Chimene's hands [see I, #48] is countered by her invoking a "point of honor" Rodrigue had apparently overlooked: "I have too much courage," she explains, "To let you share in what will be my glory. / My father and my honor would [i.e., must] owe nothing / Either to your love or to your wretchedness." Rodrigue's continued intent to die is diverted by the news that the Moors are on the verge of sacking the city, and he rushes to lead his forces in its defense. In the course of the afternoon (in the shortest engagement in military history), the Moors are defeated on land and sea, and Rodrigue returns, his honor capped by victory.

But neither Chimene nor Rodrigue deviate from their intent. Despite her anguish at the possible loss of Rodrigue's life, she appoints a champion to challenge Rodrigue, and he longs, in opposing a defender of Chimene's cause, to suffer defeat. "I cannot strike the arm that fights for you." In the encounter, he argues, "On my voluntary death will follow / Honor which only that [i.e., my death] could bring to you."

Both inconsolable, both flying in the face of their possible consolation, in the end, two factors mitigate their suffering. The King, whose prerogative allows him to qualify the demands of the code, and time itself, which may overcome the intensity of Chimene's intent. But before this outcome, amd before the fateful duel with Chimene's champion, Rodrigue, in what he sees as their final farewell, urges the propriety of his death at the hands of her champion, the only possible rescue for both their honors.

RODRIGUE

I go to die, madam, but ere I go
I come to offer you a last good-bye;
The changeless love which binds me to your will
Demands my homage even as I die.
Since you desire my death, my faithful heart
Knows no desire to preserve my life.
My heart is firm, but I can find no joy
In saving that which only brings you pain.
This night already had brought death to me
Had I been fighting for myself alone.
But for my king, his people, and my country,
I have been brave not to defend myself.
Life is not yet so hateful to my soul
That I would leave it stained with treachery:
Now it is only of myself I think,
You seek my death and I accept the sentence.
Your anger chose another hand to serve it.
I was not worthy to meet death at yours.
They shall not see me giving blow for blow.
I cannot strike the arm that fights for you.
I shall rejoice to think his blows are yours.
Since 'tis your honor that his arms maintain,
I'll bare my bosom gladly to his sword,
Worshiping as yours the hand that slays me.

The Count is dead. The Moors, defeated, fly.
Must I do more to prove my right to glory?
My fame demands not that I save myself.
I need no further proof that I am brave,
That I am powerful, that under heaven
Nothing is dearer to me than my honor.
No, in the coming combat, Roderick,
Whatever you may think, can meet his death
And never risk his honor; never fear
That anyone will dare impeach his courage,
Or say that he has met his conqueror.

Men will only say: "He adored Chimene,
He could not live the object of her hate.
He yielded willingly to that stern fate,
Which forced his mistress to pursue his death.
She sought his life; to his great soul it seemed
Refusal of her wish were criminal.
He lost his love to keep his honor bright
And to avenge his mistress gave his life;
Preferring still, whatever hope he cherished,
His honor to Chimene, Chimene to life.
And thus my death upon the field of honor
Far from destroying glory, will enhance it.
And on my voluntary death will follow
Honor which only that could bring to you.

50

NERO RECOUNTS HIS FALLING
IN LOVE WITH JUNIA

(1669) JEAN RACINE, Britannicus, *tr. Robert Henderson and Paul Landis, Act 2, Sc. 1*

Restive under his mother Agrippina's dominance, and knowing that Britannicus was favored in his love for Junia by the politically wily Agrippina, the young emperor Nero, hating his half-brother Britannicus, has Junia kidnapped this night and brought to the palace as his prisoner. Love of Junia, or hate of Britannicus—which feeling most impelled the act? The balance of opposite motives in Nero is sustained until the critical moment in the Fourth Act, when, in the context of his enmity for Britannicus and his desire for Junia, he makes the decision that seals the fate of Britannicus, of Nero and of Rome.

"The face of tyranny," warns Nero's mother Agrippina, "is always mild at first." *Brittanicus* is a study in the progress of the incipient tyrant Nero from mildness to savagery, mirroring within the compass of one incident the journey that marked his career as Caesar. The extraordinary subtlety of this, his first utterance in the play, lies in its previsioning that entire progress, encapsulating it from its first rapturous words: "Nero loves!...Junia is my idol!" to its grimly foreboding: "If Nero's jealous, he will have revenge."

The steps of his self-revelation: the attraction of Junia's "tear-stained face," which was accompanied by her "cries breaking the silence" after having been pulled out of bed by Nero's soldiers while sleeping, and surrounding her in her imprisonment with "turmoil...torch-lit darkness...the savage looks" of her captives, and Nero confessing to having been "bewitched by such a lovely sight," and loving "the very tears that I had caused to flow." Never having seen Junia before this night, it is these images of her, when she is terrified and in distress, which inflame his love.

Later, in solitude, he imagines his sighing like a penitent lover and begging her forgiveness, but imagining these scenes too as ending with his threats at her obduracy. "And thus I have been nursing this new passion." Then, his confession of "what piqued his love" even before he met her: her "wrath" against his possible murder of her brother, the grief and pride that kept her from the court and from his sight, her modesty and "scorn of the prize" of Nero that all other women at court so covet, her indifference to him altogether; irresistible attractions for Nero—her pride, scorn, indifference—in anticipating her subjection. Finally, an open threat against his rival Britannicus: if he possesses her love rather than her "anger," Nero's jealousy will destroy him.

The arc of the sequence: from the facade of an innocent and enraptured Nero to intimations of the impulses that lie within him, to the revelation of the Nero to come.

NERO

The die is cast, Narcissus. Nero loves!
Love? Said I love? Why, Junia is my idol!
I went tonight to see her when she came.
So sad! She raised her tear-stained eyes to Heaven.
They shone amid the flash of swords and spears—
A beauty unadorned, in simple dress,
As when they seized her, sleeping; and I know not
Whether that turmoil, and the torch-lit darkness,
The cries breaking the silence, and the faces,
The savage looks of those who took her captive,
Made sweeter still those sweet and timid eyes:
But quite bewitched by such a lovely sight,
I tried to speak, and found my tongue was tied.
I was amazed, I could not even move.
And so I let her go to her apartments.
I sought my chamber. There in solitude
I tried in vain to turn my thoughts from her,
But she was always present to my eyes.
And so it seemed I talked with her. I loved
The very tears that I had caused to flow.
And sometimes, yet too late, I asked forgiveness,
And often found my sighs would end in threats.
And thus I have been nursing this new passion.
I have not closed these eyes, watching for daylight.
Perhaps I conjure up too fair an image
Of her whom I first saw at such a time.

Who'd believe,
That she had lived so long unseen by me?
Moved by a wrath
That thought me guilty of her brother's death,
Or guarding still her pride with jealous care
That would not let me see her dawning charms,
True to her grief, and wanting dim seclusion,
She stole away. She shunned all admiration.

And it is this, a virtue new to the court,
That, persevering so, has piqued my love.
Is there another maiden here in Rome
Who would not grow more vain at such an honor
If I should love her? Is there one but tries
Her loving looks upon great Caesar's heart,
Soon as he knows their strength? But she alone,
The modest Junia, scorns the prize they covet.
It may be that she would not even deign
To try to learn if Caesar merits love,
Or if he knows its rapture.

Is young Brittanicus her lover? No.
He is too young.
He does not know himself, nor love's sweet poison.
Can this boy have won her heart and faith?
He is the more unhappy
He should wish her anger.
If Nero's jealous, he will have revenge.

51

HIPPOLYTUS CONFESSES HIS LONG-CONCEALED LOVE FOR ARICIA

(1677) JEAN RACINE, Phaedra, *tr. Robert Henderson, Act 2*

Theseus is reported dead. At once, a seismic shift in the political landscape of Athens, and of Troezen where the royal family resides, occurs. Theseus' son, Hippolytus, is immediately hailed as King. The life of Phaedra's own son, born to Theseus from their later marriage, is suddenly in jeopardy as a possible rival to Hippolytus for the throne. Aricia, who has been a closely held captive by Theseus during his reign for fear of her own claim (through the brothers who had been defeated and killed in battle by Theseus, but who still command loyalties in Athens), is herself once again a possible rival for the throne. But all this is written in sand, since by a later report, and one as sudden, Theseus is not dead, but on the verge of arriving home. And so the new agreements and alliances forged at the news of his death are irrelevant. Later, another turn—his sudden arrival—causes, again, a shift in the spectrum of political instabilities.

Behind the tragedy of Phaedra herself lies a sense of the mutable, the insubstantial, the almost immateriality of circumstance, but which nevertheless has tangible and terrible consequence no different from the consequences of the real.

At one of these turns, Hippolytus is moved to confess his love for Aricia; it is politically feasible for him to do so, given the death of his father, and Aricia's release from Theseus' suspicion and subjugation. Characteristic of Racine, the relation between them is complex. Like the Greek Hippolytus, Racine's famously holds himself aloof from women, but hardly out of indifference. During his father's life, he dares not show his feeling for Aricia. (She in turn is secretly smitten with him, but her reasons are as cruel as they are kind: she longs to win the victory of subjecting so difficult and proud a prize.) Now he approaches her cautiously, revealing his love hesitantly, gradually. First, he offers her her freedom—she is no longer, he tells her, captive. Then, politically, he grants her a victory: he will be satisfied to rule only Troezen; Phaedra's son, he determines, will be satisfied with his mother's home, Crete; and so Aricia, with his support in the popular vote, will win the throne of Athens. "Athens is yours, and I will do my best / To bring to you the votes which are divided between us two." She, having supposed that he had hated her, is stunned by his generosity. Hippolytus, horrified that she had so believed, in a burst of confidence, blurts out, "Could I resist this charm which caught my soul?"

Having so blurted, he allows his feelings to emerge in a rush. And those feelings fit handily into hers: confessing his former aloofness—not from Alicia but from the bondage of love itself—he confesses further the struggle he's undergone "carrying with me always that sharp arrow/ Which tears my heart," his secret love for her, which results now in his "humbleness," in his joining with all those "poor, shipwrecked mortals" who fall victim to passion.

One must be careful to distinguish between the happy lovers in other fictions, who though using much the same vocabulary of love's defeat, mean the opposite, and lovers in Racine, for whom as in most of classical tradition, love is an illness, a disease that once rooted causes not joy but terrible pain. By this persistent illness, he's been thrown off course ("I cannot find my old self again"), he's lost his taste for, or even memory of, his old hunter's ways, and he recognizes—in battlefield terms—that as a captive, he signifies his defeat by offering up not his sword but his heart.

> HIPPOLYTUS
> I have said too much
> Not to say no more. No prudence can resist
> The violence of passion. Now, at last,
> Silence is broken. I must tell you now
> The secret that my heart can hold no longer.
> You see before you an unhappy victim
> Of hasty pride — a prince who begs compassion.
> For I was long the enemy of love.
> I mocked his fetters, I despised his captives,
> And while I pities these poor, shipwrecked mortals,
> I watched the storms, and seemed quite safe on the land.
> And now I find that I have such a fate,
> And must be tossed upon a sea of troubles!
> My boldness is defeated in a moment,
> And all my boasted pride is humbleness.
> For nearly six months, ashamed, despairing,
> Carrying with me always that sharp arrow
> Which tears my heart, I struggle quite in vain
> To free me, both from you and myself.

I leave your presence; — leaving, I find you near,
And in the forest's darkness see your form.
Black night, no less than daylight brings the vision
Of charms that I avoid. All things conspire
To make Hippolytus your slave. The fruit
Of all my sighs is only that I cannot
Find my own self again. My bow, my spear,
Please me no longer. I have quite forgotten
My chariot, and the teaching of the Sea God.
The woods can only echo back my groans,
Instead of flinging back those joyous shouts
With which I urged my horses. Hearing this,
A tale of passion so uncouth, you blush
At your own handiwork. These are wild words
With which I offer you my heart, a captive
Held, strangely, by a silken jess. And yet
The off'ring should be dearer to your eyes,
Since such words come as strangers to my lips.
Nor do I scorn my vows, so poorly spoken
Since, but for you, they never had been formed.

coursers: horses

52

THERAMENES REPORTS THE GRUESOME DEATH OF HIPPOLYTUS

(1677) JEAN RACINE, Phaedra, *tr. Robert Henderson, Act 5*

To compare the account of Hippolytus' death in Euripides [see I, #6] with that in Racine [see I, #51] is to detect the difference between pragmatic Greek and French Baroque sensibility. Euripides sticks to the details; his narrator describes them with the accuracy and precision of a newspaper account. The emotion of the narrator lies over and above the text itself, which is bent most particularly on putting his listeners inside the scene, watching it through his words as precisely as he observed it in the event: "You are there." Racine, narrating the same event, is focused not so much on its photographic realism as on its emotional reverberation. The narrator, Theramenes, drenches the bare bones of his narrative in a universal, emotionally excited environment—Heaven itself "is struck with horror," earth was "in terror quakes," the very wave that threw up the monster bull out of the sea, when it finished its chore, "runs back in fear." For all the profound desperations that run through Racine's tragedy, the norms of that world—the court world of Louis XIV—are polite discourse and measured gesture. The shock of disorder, the eruption into the uncontrolled, evokes for its spectators what is in their experience and in their emotion uncontainable. And so the emotional afflatus surrounding Theramenes' account of Hippolytus' gruesome death is not a description of the event, but essentially a terrified response to the event. Its expression, both in the verse and in its delivery, does not particularize with studied emotional control as in Euripides, but swells its emotional clamor attempting to match the scope of unimaginable horror. The result is Baroque hyperbole, and the larger the shock of dismay Theramenes expresses, the more amplified the overcoloring of its presentation. Altogether, the effect is of chaos erupting through the norms of propriety.

> THERAMENES
> Your son is dead
> I have seen the very flower
> Of all mankind cut down; and I am bold
> To say that never man deserved it less.
> When we had scarcely passed the gates of Troezen —
> He, silent in his chariot, his guards
> Downcast and, silent, too, all ranged around him —

He tuned his steeds to the Mycenian road.
And, lost in thought, allowed the reins to lie
Loose on their backs, and hi high mettled chargers,
One time so eager to obey his voice,
Now seemed to know his sadness and to share it.
Then, coming from the sea, a frightful cry
Shatters the troubled air with sudden discord;
And groaning from the bosom of the earth
Answers the crying of that fearful voice.
It froze the blood within out very hearts!
Our horses hear, and stand with bristling manes.
Meanwhile there rises on the watery plain
A mountain wave, mighty, with foaming crest.
It rolls upon the shore, and as it breaks
It throws before our eyes a raging monster.
Its brow is armed with terrifying horns
And all its body clothed with yellow scales.
In front it is a bull, behind, a dragon,
Turning and twisting in impatient fury.
It bellows till the very shores do tremble.
The sky is struck with horror at the sight.
The earth in terror quakes; breath of the beast
Poisons the air. The very wave that brought it
Runs back in fear. All fly, forgetting courage
Which cannot help — and in a nearby temple
Take refuge — all but brave Hippolytus.
A hero's worthy son, he stays his horses,
Seizes his darts, and rushing forward, hurls
A missile with sure aim, and wounds the beast
Deep in the flank. It springs, raging with pain,
Right to the horses' feet, and roaring, falls,
Writhes in the dust, shows them his fiery throat,
And covers them with flame and smoke and blood.
Fear lends them wings; deaf to his own voice for once,
Heeding no curb, the horses race away.
Their master tires himself in futile efforts.

Each courser's bit is read with blood and foam.
Some say a god, in all this wild disorder,
Is seen, pricking their dusty flanks with goads.
They rush to jagged rocks, urged by this terror.
The axle crashes, and the hardy youth
Sees his car broken, shattered into bits.
He himself falls, entangled in the reins. —
Forgive my grief. That cruel sight will be
For me, the source of never-ending tears.
I saw thy luckless son — I saw him, Sire,
Dragged by those horses that his hands had fed.
He could not stop their fierce career — his cries
But added to their terror. All his body
Was soon a mass of wounds. Our anguished cries
Filled the whole plain. At length the horses slackened.
They stopped close by the ancient tombs which mark
The place where lie the ashes of his fathers.
I ran there panting, and behind me came
His guard, along a track fresh stained with blood,
Reddening all the rocks; locks of his hair
Hung dripping in all the briers — gory triumphs!
I came and called him. Stretching out his hand,
He opened dying eyes, soon to be close.
"The gods have robbed me of a guiltless life."
I heard him say, "Take care of sad Aricia,
When I am dead. Friend, if my father mourn
When he shall know his son's unhappy fate —
One accused falsely — then, to give me peace,
Tell him to treat his captive tenderly,
And to restore —" The hero's breath had failed,
And in my arms there lay a mangled body —
A thing most piteous, the bleeding spoil
Of Heaven's wrath — his father could not know him.
And then Aricia,
Flying from you, cam timidly to take him
To be her husband, there, before the gods.
And coming close, she saw the grass, all reeking,
All bloody red, and (sad for a lover's eyes!)

> She saw him, lying there, disfigured, pale —
> And for a time she knew not her misfortune.
> She did no know the hero she adores.
> She looked and asked, "Where is Hippolytus?"
> Only too sure, at last, that he was lying
> Before her there, with sad eyes, silently
> Reproaching Heaven, she groaned, and shuddering
> Fell fainting, all but lifeless, at his feet.
> Ismene, all in tears, knelt down beside her,
> And called her back to life, a life of nothing
> But sense of pain. And I to whom the light
> Is only darkness, now, come to discharge
> The duty he imposed on me: to tell you
> His last desire — a melancholy task.

Troezen: a city in the Peloponesus, the setting of the play **Mycenae**: another ancient city of the Peloponesus

53

GENESIUS, REHEARSING THE PART OF A MARTYR, WINS CHRIST

(c1607-1608) LOPE DE VEGA, Acting Is Believing, *tr. Michael McGaha, Act 3, Sc. 3*

St. Genesius, the patron saint of actors, was a Roman actor who, according to legend, while performing a farce mimicking Christian ceremony, suddenly coverted to Christianity and began preaching before the Emperor Dioclesian, for which lapse he was immediately executed. Lope de Vega converted this legend into a drama that gives equal weight to the ascension of Dioclesian, an impoverished soldier, to the Imperial throne, and to the miracle of Genesius' embrace of

Christianity and his martyrdom.

In de Vega's play, Genesius, a renowned actor, is ordered by the Emperor to perform a play about Christians; he chooses one in his repertory with which his company of actors is familiar. But in the process of putting the play back on its feet, Genesius loses the distinction between the actor's role and his real, and new, self.

The process begins when he is rehearsing alone. As both leading actor and playwright, he is intent on doing a convincing performance of a Christian for the Emperor, and so "to convince them that I am that very Christian," he conscientiously adds new elements to the role: a bit of a talk with Christ, perhaps, even with his mother Mary, a cry to the saints, even a little iconoclasm toward the pagan statues those Christians hate. Pleased with these contemplated inserts, ambition grows larger: he'll imitate the martyr's being tortured and at the same time, add—what the Christians report as happening—seeing the heavens open and then communicating with a dead martyr up there. Then warming to it more, he improvises dialogue: tests hurling curses at Caesar during his torment. Still in the guise of an actor pleased with his invention, he goes one step further, and crosses the barrier between play-acting and reality: out of his mouth unbidden comes the conclusion of his play-acting prayer, "Give me baptism, Lord."

And the heavens in fact do open (in stage terms, to be sure: music, a reveal, a portrait of the Holy Family with martyrs attending). Shocked at what he himself has inadvertently provoked, he nevertheless still keeps his invention in the context of rehearsal, and so tries the prayer again. But this time, he is answered by the voice of Christ.

Still holding on to the context of play-acting, he determines to be baptised "even if [my] performance as a Christian is just an act," but by logical steps, from accepting baptism to accepting the idea of "following [Christ] from now on," he has begun the process of divesting himself of role-playing and becoming the role.

In the play, the process of Genesius' transformation continues until, as a martyr impaled on the cross, he delivers a last sermon to the people of Rome, explaining how he has divested himself of the human comedy, and is now playing in the real, the divine comedy instead. But the play as a whole, beyond even the saga of Genesius himself, uses theatre as a contracted metaphor for the idea, as in Calderon de la Barca [see I, #54], of divestment, *desengano,* sharing the idea of the world as illusory.

> **GENESIUS**
>
> I'd better think about this character Caesar is so interested in. He wants to see a Christian who is steadfast in his faith. What shall I do to convince them that I am that very Christian when they lead me off to be tortured? How shall I move, what kind of facial expression, what gestures shall I use to win their praise? Shall I talk with Christ? Yes. And what about Mary? Yes, her too, for I understand she was his mother, and I think I can write that scene really well! Just like them, I'll cry out to the saints, who shed their blood here, for help! I'll furiously knock down the idols they hate. I'll just make believe that I'm being cruelly tortured and that I see the firmament open, for that's what they all say, and that some previous martyr is talking to me, or that I'm talking to him. Oh, what a clever idea, what a great scene! I'll call Caesar cruel, right to his very face. "You dog, you bloody tyrant!" Oh, this is good! I'm really getting mad! "You're hurting only yourself by torturing me, for God is pleased with me. You ferocious beast, don't think that your iron and fire nor even the most atrocious martyrdom will make me blindly worship your gods!" I sound terrific when I shout! Now I should look up to heaven and call upon the saints, as if I'm waiting for this fierce torture to make me one of them. "Holy martyrs, pray to Christ, in whose Passion you found the strength to bear less fearful tortures, that he may give me courage. And since you said yourself that I cannot come to you unless I be baptized, give me baptism, Lord."
>
> *(As music plays, doors open high up on the stage, revealing a painting of Mary, Christ in the arms of God the*

Father, and some martyrs on steps leading up to the
throne of God)

Why did I ask to be baptized? I didn't write anything about baptism
in the original version of this play. And how is it that I heard such joyous and harmonious sounds in the heavens? But I must be
mistaken…As for asking to be baptized, what better way could I find
to imitate the Christian who longs to be saved? All right then, I'll say
it again: "Oh, saints, ask God for this favor, for I want to be a saint
too. Help me to win heaven!" What a lot of nonsense I'm saying, and
all because I want to give a convincing performance as a Christian for
Caesar.

"You will not play this role in vain, Genesius, for you will be saved."

(The doors close on the painting)

Heaven help me! What's going on? Who spoke to me? It must have
been one of my actors, who saw me from the wings rehearsing this
scene. How well he answered me! It really sounded like a heavenly
voice. He said that I'll be saved. In order to do that, oh Christ, I'll
have to be baptized. Genesius, even if your performance as a Christian
is just an act, I suspect that Christians really do go to heaven. I suspect
I should believe that that voice which reached my very soul was
Christ, since it has touched and moved me so. They say that Christ
descended from heaven and took on human flesh in the womb of a
Virgin, joining his sovereign greatness to our humility, and that this
mortal part of him suffered a shameful death for the sake of
men…and opened the gates of heaven, which sin had closed. But if
the only way to get to the place where he now dwells in glory is to
adore him and receive the holy water of baptism,…why should I be
surprised that his name penetrated my senses so powerfully?

And they say that there's a hell for those who refuse to follow him!
Then it's no wonder that a Christian would die for Christ! Yes, God
did speak to me and showed me who He is! Oh, Christ! You spoke to
me through an angel! Oh, Christ, since you are God, you'll lead me to
you, for I shall follow you from now on!

54

SEGISMUND, AFTER LIFELONG CAPTIVITY, YEARNS TO KNOW FREEDOM

(1636) CALDERON DE LA BARCA, Life Is a Dream, *tr. Roy Campbell*, Act 1

One of the most persistent questions that haunted Europe throughout the 17th century had to do with the insubstantiality, the mutability of the real world: the world as theatre (Corneille's *The Comic Illusion*), the world as magic illusion (Shakespeare's *The Tempest*), the world as dream (Calderon's *Life Is a Dream*). One 20th century reversion to Post-Reformation Catholicism, Claudel's twelve-hour tetralogy *The Satin Slipper*, pronounces in its last line, when all its principal characters have been reduced either to death or beggary, "the captive souls are free." What they are free of is the illusion of the world, having undergone—the essential concept governing this particularly Spanish reading—*desengaño*, "disenchantment," or rather, *un*-enchantment: the stripping away of worldly illusion to have revealed what is permanent and immutable in existence.

The Prince Segismund, in Calderon's drama, is the Hamlet of Spanish literature. His spiritual journey is understood in the context of Catholic theology as the *desengaño* of the world as dream, making possible the triumph of his free will over the illusory captivity of a fateful predestination.

His father Basilio, the King of Poland, was apprised before Segismund's birth that his son would usurp his throne and rule as a tyrant. To forestall the prophecy, he has had his son imprisoned in a tower from birth, where he lives in a state of moral ignorance. But inevitably, his instruction comes from nature itself, in which he discovers examples of the freedom he has been cruelly denied. His first utterance in the play is a lamentation, a forlorn prayer, for the same freedom he sees granted to fish, birds, beasts and brooks. The yearning that runs through the speech is his longing to know "What greater crime, apart from being born, / Can thus have earned my greater chastisement?" The burden of guilt he carries has for him no explanation, no origin, and he is moved to know what, over and above the shared guilt of having been born, is his alone. (His later, outraged discovery [see I, #55] that the crime was not his leads to a burst of violence that almost fulfills his father's prophecy.)

His lamentation is formally structured: it follows one of the patterns of Spanish Baroque poetry; parallel images, one after the other, gathered into summary closure. The poem's refrain, "And I...must have less liberty?" gives powerful cumulative emotional effect to the speech.

SEGISMUND
Unhappy me!
Oh, miserable me! You heavens above,
I try to think what crime I've done against you
By being born. Although to have been born,
I know, is an offence, and with just cause
I bear the rigours of your punishment:
Since to be born is man's worst crime. But yet
I long to know (to clarify my doubts)
What greater crime, apart from being born,
Can thus have earned my greater chastisement.
Aren't others born like me? And yet they seem
To boast a freedom that I've never known.

The bird is born, and in the hues of beauty
Clothed with its plumes, yet scarce has it become
A feathered posy—or a flower with wings—
When through ethereal halls it cuts its way,
Refusing the kind shelter of its nest.
And I, who have more soul than any bird,
Must have less liberty?

The beast is born, and with its hide bright-painted,
In lovely tints, has scarce become a spangled
And starry constellation (thanks to the skilful
Brush of the Painter) than its earthly needs
Teach it the cruelty to prowl and kill,
The monster of its labyrinth of flowers.
Yet I, with better instincts than a beast,
Must have less liberty?

The fish is born, the birth of spawn and slime,
That does not even live by breathing air.
No sooner does it feel itself a skiff
Of silver scales upon the wave than swiftly
It roves about in all directions taking
The measure of immensity as far
As its cold blood's capacity allows.
Yet I, with greater freedom of the will,
Must have less liberty?

The brook is born, and like a snake unwinds
Among the flowers. No sooner, silver serpent,
Does it break through the blooms than it regales
And thanks them with its music for their kindness,
Which opens to its course the majesty
Of the wide plain. Yet I, with far more life,
Must have less liberty?

This fills me with such passion, I become
Like the volcano Etna, and could tear
Pieces of my own heart out of my breast!
What law, justice, or reason can decree
That man alone should never know the joys
And be alone excepted from the rights
God grants a fish, a bird, a beast, a brook?

skiff: a small one-person boat **the volcano Etna**: in Sicily

55

SEGISMUND, EMBRACING LIFE AS A DREAM, RUMINATES ON ITS FINAL VALUE

(1636) CALDERON DE LA BARCA, Life Is a Dream, *tr. Roy Campbell, Act 3*

"Let us seek that which endures" is Segismund's final conclusion and commitment [see I, #54]. The route by which he arrives at it is, in summary, as follows: King Basil, ready to offer succession to his throne to a nephew, but unwilling to banish his son's claim without further test, has Segismund drugged and brought sleeping to the palace. He's awakened, is persuaded his past life was merely a dream, and is offered the homage owing to a royal prince. But dream or not, the shock of the change, and his outrage at having been deprived all his life of his rightful place, enrage him, and he responds with savagery: killing a servant, assaulting court ladies, attacking his cousin the presumed heir, even threatening his father's life. The King is persuaded of the accuracy of the prophecy, and Segismund is again drugged and returned to his prison. Waking, he is in a quandary. Three conclusions are possible: one, that he dreamed the extraordinary episode in the palace; another, that it had actually occurred; a third, that he is dreaming now. He resolves his quandary by meditation that slowly, painfully, tracks through his disorienting doubt.

1) Was the episode in the glittering palace a dream? Rosaura, a witness, recalls the event as he does, and so its reality is assured. 2) Still, can it be taken as true, when his life of imprisonment, before and after that episode, if real in its own right, puts the reality of the palace episode terribly in doubt. (How can the life of this chained prisoner be one with the life of that lofty Prince?) 3) So slender is the borderline between the two conditions that they call into question the truth or falsity, reality or dream, of what one knows, or thinks one knows, as

"experience." 4) If copy and original can be thought of as so near to one another, then all that glittering world, all that "grandeur, power, majesty and pomp" must "evaporate," that is, be consigned to a dream-state, in which it may provide pleasure, but is, of necessity, mutable. 5) By the same token, this very moment, this present state, may be a dream. Very well, then let's use this dream-state for the best use our dream-states offer: pleasure. For example, let's use Rosaura, who is at the moment groveling at my feet, for a bit of strenuous dream-pleasure while the dream lasts. But 6) consider: why settle for a moment's pleasure—mere "vainglory and a dream?" Why, if it is mere phantasy, lose for its sake "true glory?" By extension, 7) all past "vainglories," all heroic glories and vain pleasures, might well be only dreams. If so, what are they in fact but a "lovely flame" of pleasure that will inevitably turn to dust and ashes. Conclusion 8): Such vanity, such pointlessness rejected, leaves one with a more worthwhile goal: the enduring, which has no admixture of spurious pleasure or vain glory.

What drives this mental journey toward *desengano* is Segismund's desperate longing to find his way out of the thicket of doubt and confusion into which the disorienting ambiguity of his journey has thrown him. He tosses argumentative alternatives aside like so many vexatious obstacles in the path of his climb until he's cleared a sufficient passage to win clarity. The speech depicts the drama of intellectual discovery on a par with the sequence of realizations through which Hamlet struggles in "To be or not to be." Unlike Hamlet's, this one finds its positive closure.

> SEGISMUND
> Heavens! If it is true I'm dreaming,
> Suspend my memory, for in a dream
> So many things could not occur. Great heavens!
> If I could only come free of them all!
> Or never think of any! Who ever felt

Such grievous doubts? If I but dreamed that triumph
In which I found myself, how can this woman
Refer me to such sure and certain facts?
Then all of it was true and not a dream.
But if it be the truth, why does my past life
Call it a dream? This breeds the same confusion.
Are dreams and glories so alike, that fictions
Are held for truths, realities for lies?
Is there so little difference in them both
That one should question whether what one sees
And tastes is true or false? What? Is the copy
So near to the original that doubt
Exists between them? Then if that is so,
And grandeur, power, majesty, and pomp,
Must all evaporate like shades at morning,
Let's profit by it, this time, to enjoy
That which we only can enjoy in dreams.
Rosaura's in my power: my soul adores her beauty.
Let's take the chance. Let love break every law
On which she has relied in coming here
And kneeling, trustful, prostrate at my feet.
This is a dream. If so, dream pleasures now
Since they must turn to sorrows in the end!
But with my own opinions, I begin
Once again to convince myself. Let's think.
If it is but vainglory and a dream,
Who for mere human vainglory would lose
True glory? What past blessing is not merely
A dream? Who has known heroic glories,
That deep within himself, as he recalls them,
Has never doubted that they might be dreams?
But if this all should end in disenchantment,
Seeing that pleasure is a lovely flame
That's soon converted into dust and ashes
By any wind that blows, then let us seek
That which endures in thrifty, lasting fame
In which no pleasures sleep, nor grandeurs dream.

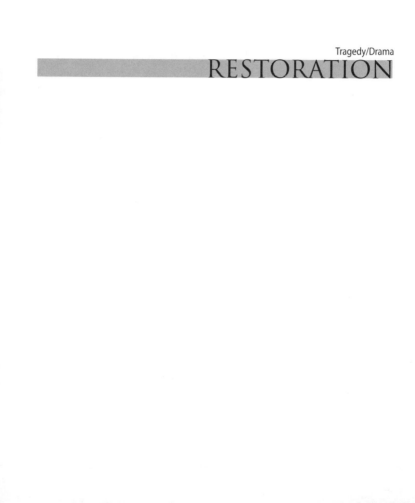

Tragedy/Drama

RESTORATION

56

ESSEX, ABJECT, BEGS THE QUEEN FOR RETURN TO FAVOR UNTIL SHE LEAVES WITH NO REPLY
(1681) JOHN BANKS, The Unhappy Favorite, or, The Earl of Essex, *Act 2, Sc. 1*

The Unhappy Favorite was, after *Hamlet* and *Macbeth,* the most popular play in England for its first 30 years of life. For good reason. The rhetoric, never admired in its own time nor now, still crackles with theatrical energy, and rises and falls with a musical cadence matching its emotional tides. Banks was one of the playwrights who engaged in gently disassembling the lofty scaffolding of Heroic Tragedy, and bringing dramatic sentiment within the range of more modest and more common feeling. Love in its more heartfelt modes, friendship, pity—what were called the "softer" passions, hence, "she-tragedies"—were displacing the male-oriented Heroic Tragedies with their "Honor"-driven, battlefield-beset, male heroes.

In *The Unhappy Favorite,* the volatile, fiery-tempered Essex, suffering from a sense of unrequited devotion to his Queen, is pitted against the Queen's conflicted passions. She loves Essex in the she-tragedy mode—as a "woman"—but is obliged to maintain her royal authority—the public figure torn by unrevealable private emotion. Essex, returned from his command in Ireland under suspicion of sedition, torn by Elizabeth's apparent ingratitude for his feeling and for his service, humbles himself before her to plead "my wronged and wounded innocence."

What he does not hear is the Queen's pained, carefully hidden response: "he melts; it flows, and drowns my heart with pity." But fearing for her "fame" ("If I stay longer, I shall tell him so"), she abruptly leaves, without responding to his pleas but only commanding that the "traitor" be removed from her sight.

Essex, whose plea was heartfelt, is dumbfounded by her response. Without Elizabeth's support, he sees his political destruction staring him in the face.

(Essex kneels.)

ESSEX

Long live the mightiest, most adored of queens,
The brightest power on earth that Heaven e'er formed;
Awed and amazed the trembling Essex kneels,
Essex that stood the dreadful voice of cannons,
Hid in a darker field of smoke and fire
Than that where Cyclops blow the forge, and sweat
Beneath the mighty hill, whilst bullets round me
Flew like the bolts of heaven when shot with thunder,
And lost their fury on my shield and corslet;
And stood these dangers unconcerned and dauntless.
But you, the most majestic, brightest form
That ever ruled on earth, have caught my soul,
Surprised its virtues all with dread and wonder;
My humble eyes durst scarcely look up to you,
Your dazzling mien and sight so fill the place,
And every part celestial rays adorn.

'Tis said I have been guilty—
I dare not rise, but crawl thus on the earth,
Till I have leave to kiss your sacred robe,
And clear before the justest, best of queens,
My wronged and wounded innocence.

What, not a word! a look! not one blessed look!
Turn, turn your cruel brow, and kill me with
A frown; it is a quick and surer way
To rid you of your Essex
Than banishment, than fetters, swords, or axes.—

What, not that neither! Then I plainly see
My fate, the malice of my enemies
Triumphant in their joyful faces; Burleigh,
With a glad coward's smile, that knows h'as got

Advantage o'er his valiant foe, and Rawleigh's proud
To see his dreaded Essex kneel so long,
Essex that stood in his great mistress' favour
Like a huge oak, the loftiest of the wood,
Whilst they no higher could attain to be
Than humble suckers nourished by my root,
And like the ivy twined their flatt'ring arms
About my waist, and lived but by my smiles—

Still am I shunned as if I wore destruction.—*(Rises.)*
Here, here my faithful and my valiant friends,
Dearest companions of the fate of Essex,
Behold this bosom studded o'er with scars,
This marble breast that has so often held,
Like a fierce battlement against the foes
Of England's Queen, that made a hundred beaches
Here, pierce it straight, and through this wild of wounds
Be sure to reach my heart, this loyal heart,
That sits consulting 'midst a thousand spirits
All at command, all faithful to my Queen.

(Exeunt Queen and her attendants, manet Essex solus)
She's gone, and darted fury as she went—
Cruellest of queens!
Not heard! Not hear your soldier speak one word!
Essex that once was all day listened to;
Essex that like a cherub held thy throne,
Whilst thou didst dress me with thy wealthy favours,
Cheered me with smiles, and decked me round with glories;
Nor was thy crown scarce worshipped on thy head
Without me by thy side; but now art deaf
As adders, winds, or the remorseless seas,
Deaf as thy cunning sex's ears to those
That make unwelcome love.—
Then does my wrack come rolling on a-pace.

Cyclops, Greek mythology: the one-eyed armorer of Zeus **corslet**: a corset of body armor **mien**: bearing or aspect, as showing character, feeling, etc. **suckers**: leeches, parasites **adder**: a viper **wrack**: wreck

57

ESSEX IMPORTUNES SOUTHAMPTON TO PLEAD HIS CAUSE TO THE QUEEN

(1681) JOHN BANKS, The Unhappy Favorite, or, The Earl of Essex, *Act 2, Sc. 1*

After the lash of Elizabeth's rebuke [see I, #56], Essex is confronted by his two greatest enemies at court, Burleigh and Rawleigh, who come with a devastating message from the Queen. All Essex's titles, honors and commands are taken from him, and he is to be sequestered under house arrest. What, they ask, is his response, for the Queen is waiting for it. Both he and his only remaining supporter and friend at court, Southampton, hurl venomous response at these courtiers, these, in Essex's words, "creeping things," and left to themselves, Essex appeals to Southampton, as a last resort, to plead once again to the Queen to give him audience for his defense.

It is not just desperation to be cleared, but more the shock of the Queen's seeming ingratitude that moves Essex to beg Southampton to recapitulate for the Queen his former services, his former position, her former favors heaped on him, to fix in her mind the image and worth of the man she is dismissing so cruelly. It is the sort of plea that would have been anathema to the hero of a Heroic Tragedy, whose *amour propre* would forbid such abject rehearsal of his merits in order to beg for favor. In She-tragedy, it is fitting; men and women are moved to tears, and move spectators to tears, by recitations of the pity or favor owed them. It is a favorite recital—the force and purity of the emotion that propels it is its more than sufficient self-justification. With the advent of She-tragedy, emotion itself moves high in the scale of virtues.

ESSEX

Go thou,
My brave Southampton, follow to the Queen,
And quickly ere my cruel foes are heard,
Tell her that thus her faithful Essex says:
This star she decked me with; and all these honours else,
In one blessed hour, when scarce my tender years
Had reached the age of man, she heaped upon me,
As if the sun, that sows the seeds of gems
And golden mines, had showered upon my head,
And dressed me like the bridegroom of her favour.
This thou beheld'st, and nations wondered at;
The world had not a favourite so great,
So loved as I.

Thou canst remember too (for all she said was signal)
That at the happy time she did invest
Her Essex with this robe of shining glories,
She bade me prize 'em as I would my life,
Defend 'em as I would her crown and person:
Then a rich sword she put into my hand,
And wished me Caesar's fortune; so she graced me.

Go thou Southampton, for thou art my friend,
And such a friend's an angel in distress;
Now the false globe that flattered me is gone
Thou art to me more wealth, more recompense
Than all the world was then.—Entreat the Queen
To bless me with a moment's sight,
And I will lay her relics humbly down,
As travelling pilgrims do before the shrines
Of saints they went a thousand leagues to visit,
And her bright virgin honours all untainted,
Her sword not spoiled with rust, but wet with blood,
All nations' blood that disobeyed my Queen;
This staff that disciplined her kingdoms once,
And triumphed o'er an hundred victories;

> And if she will be pleased to take it, say
> My life, the life of once her darling Essex.
> Fly, my Lord, and let my hopes repose
> On the kind zeal Southampton has to serve.

the star she decked me with: the star worn by Knights of the Garter **globe**: his circle of "friends"

58
ESSEX, IN ANGUISH, DESPAIRS OF RISING AGAIN TO FAVOR
(1681) JOHN BANKS, The Unhappy Favorite, or, The Earl of Essex, *Act 3, Sc. 1*

When Southampton leaves, Essex gives way altogether to despair: "Here I'm sure that I can fall no further." [see I, #56, 57] Contradicting his glimmer of hope when he begs Southampton to approach the queen, he recognizes that his fall is already accomplished. It is a speech that, remarkably, anticipates the Romantic heroes of the 19th century, whose emotionally volatile euphoria is matched by the dole of their paranoia. It's understandable that the most popular play in Banks's time was *Hamlet*.

After rehearsing the "greatness" of his time of glory, when he outdid the dawn (Aurora) in popular appeal, when his splendor was envied by the sun itself, he, a tall-built pyramid, was as though in an instant struck by lightning and "dashed from the heavens." Now confronting doomsday, he acts out the metaphor of his doom: dropping to the ground, he lies, flat on his back, demonstrating the impossibility of his falling further. Self-pity becomes a staple of these "softened" tragedies, but pity sufficiently anguished was, and can still be, happily embraced by the spectator.

ESSEX

Where art thou, Essex! where are now thy glories!
Thy summer's garlands, and thy winter's laurels,
The early songs that ev'ry morning waked thee,
Thy halls and chambers thronged with multitudes
More than the temples of the Persian god,
To worship thy uprising; and when I appeared,
The blushing Empress of the East, Aurora,
Gladded the world not half so much as I.
Yesterday's sun saw his great rival thus,
The spiteful planet saw me thus adored;
And as some tall-built pyramid, whose height
And golden top confronts him in his sky,
He tumbles down with lightning in his rage,
So on a sudden has he snatched my garlands,
And with a cloud impaled my gaudy head,
Struck me with thunder, dashed me from the heavens,
And oh! 'tis doomsday now, and darkness all with me.
Here I'll lie down—Earth will receive her son.
Take pattern all by me, you that hunt glory,
You that do climb the rounds of high ambition;
Yet when y'ave reached, and mounted to the top,
Here you must come by just degrees at last,
If not fall headlong down at once like me—
Here I'll abide close to my loving centre:
For here I'm sure that I can fall no further.

Empress of the east, Aurora: the dawn **impaled**: surrounded **centre**: i.e., the earth

59

ESSEX, ENRAGED BEYOND CONTROL, LASHES OUT AT THE QUEEN FOR HER INGRATITUDE

(1681) JOHN BANKS, The Unhappy Favorite, or, The Earl of Essex, *Act 3, Sc. 1*

The Countess of Rutland, secretly married to Essex, pleads his cause before the Queen [see I, #56, 57, and 58]. She does this so movingly that the Queen, on the strength of Rutland's arguments ready to countenance Essex's presence, is in torment once again, realizing that Rutland is her secret rival for the love of Essex. And when he arrives, the Queen, once again divided in her feelings, is as ready to send him to the Tower as to forgive him.

His plea, though, is calculated more for the Tower than for forgiveness. He argues the rightness of his former decisions in Ireland: not to attack the rebels, to conciliate the rebel Tyrone, to delay answering or returning to England at the Queen's command, as signs, all of them, of his devotion to his duty and loyalty to the Queen. But capping all is his response to the outrage of being accused of treason. The fire of his attack at the very word, added with his throwing down at the Queen's feet his emblems of office and insultingly turning his back on her as if to leave, enrages the Queen. She steps toward him and slaps him hard across the face, thus doubling his rage. The danger of the moment is intense, and climactic. Essex, almost beyond himself, puts his hand on his sword. Favorite moment of the tragedy: will he, the tempestuous hero, exceed all bounds, and destroy himself? He does not, but he is destroyed already. But the *amour propre* guarded so jealously by the heroes of Heroic Tragedy descends now on the hero of this softer tragedy, on the principle that the values of the latter go just so far, but can't obliterate, without shame, those of the former. Essex, in tempestuous response, dooms himself.

ESSEX

Behold, your Essex kneels to clear himself
Before his Queen, and now receive his doom.
Well, well, you cruel fates! well have you found
The way to shock the basis of a temper,
That all our malice else could ne'er invent,
And you, my Queen, to break your soldier's heart.
Thunder and earthquakes, prodigies on land
I've borne, devouring tempests on the seas,
And all the horrid strokes beside
That Nature e'er invented; yet to me
Your scorn is more.—Here take this traitor,
Since you will have me so; throw me to dungeons,
Lash me with iron rods, fast bound in chains,
And like a fiend in darkness let me roar:
It is the nobler justice of the two.
My parleying with the enemy?

Is that alleged against me for a fault,
Put in your royal breast by some that are
My false accusers for a crime? Just Heaven!
How easy 'tis to make a great man fall,
'Tis wise, 'tis Turkish policy in courts.
For treating!

Am I not yet your general, and was
I not so there by virtue of this staff?
I thought your Majesty had given me power,
And my commission had been absolute
To treat, to fight, give pardons, or disband:
So much and vast was my authority,
That you were pleased to say as mirth to others,
I was the first of English kings that reigned
In Ireland.

The reason why
I led not forth the army to the north,
And fought not with Tyrone, was that my men

Were half consumed with fluxes and diseases,
And those that lived, so weakened and unfit,
That they could scarce defend them from the vultures
That took 'em for the carrion of an army.

'Tis too plain
My life's conspired, my glories all betrayed:
That vulture Cecil there with hungry nostrils
Waits for my blood, and Rawleigh for my charge,
Like birds of prey that seek out fighting fields,
And know when battle's near: nay, and my Queen
Has passed her vote, I fear, to my destruction.
Now banish him that planted strength about you,
Covered this island with my spreading laurels,
Whilst your safe subjects slept beneath their shade.
Give 'em to courtiers, sycophants and cowards
That sell the land for peace and children's portions,
Whilst I retreat to Afric in some desert,
Sleep in a den and herd with valiant brutes,
And serve the King of Beasts; there's more reward,
More justice there than in all Christian courts:
The lion spared the man that freed him from
The toil, but England's Queen abhors her Essex.

You said that I was bold, but now who blames
My rage? Had I been rough as storms and tempests,
Rash as Cethegus, mad as Ajax was,
Yet this has rammed more powder in my breast,
And blown a magazine of fury up.—
A traitor! Yes, for serving you so well;
For making England like the Roman Empire
In great Augustus' time, renowned in peace
At home and war abroad; enriching you
With spoils both of the wealthy sea and land,
More than your Thames does bring you in an age,
And setting up your fame to such a height
That it appears the column of the world
For tumbling down the proud rebellious earls,

Northumberland and Westmorland, which caused
The cutting both their heads off with an axe
That saved the crown on yours.—This Essex did,
And I'll remove the traitor from your sight.

> *(Essex offers to go. The Queen comes up to him and gives him a box on the ear.)*

Ha! Furies, death and hell! a blow!
Has Essex had a blow!—*(Lays hand on his sword.)* Hold, stop my arm,
Some god!—Who is't has given it me? The Queen!
Y'are my Queen; that charms me. But, by all
The subtlety and woman in your sex,
I swear that you had been a man you durst not,
Nay, your bold father Harry durst not this
Have done.—Why say I him? not all the Harrys,
Nor Alexander's self were he alive,
Should boast of such a deed on Essex done
Without revenge.

> *(Exeunt Queen, etc. Manent Essex and Southampton.)*

By heaven! my cheek has set on fire my soul,
And the disgrace sticks closer to my heart,
Than did the son of old Antipater's,
Which cost the life of his proud master.—Stand off,
Beware you lay not hands upon my ruin,
I have a load would sink a legion that
Should offer but to save me.

Let us retire,
And shun this barbarous place.
Abhor all courts if thou art brave and wise,
For then thou never shalt be sure to rise;
Think not by doing well a fame to get,
But be a villain, and thou shalt be great.
Here virtue stands by't self, or not at all,
Fools have foundations, only brave men fall;

But if ill fate and thy own merits bring
Thee once to be a favourite to a king,
It is a curse that follows loyalty:
Cursed in thy merits, more in thy degree,
In all the sport of chance its chiefest aim,
Mankind's the *hunt*, a favourite is the *game*.

The Earl of **Tyrone** in Ireland: a military expedition under Essex was sent against him which failed when Essex made a truce with Tyrone **fluxes**: dysentery William **Cecil** Lord Burghley: lord high treasurer and principal minister under Elizabeth **Rawleigh**: Sir Walter Raleigh, founder of the Virginia colony in America, a court favorite of Elizabeth's whose position was challenged by Essex **Cethegus**: one of Catiline's associates in Rome, who was deputed to murder Cicero **Thames...age**: all foreign imports were brought into the capital on ships through the ports on the Thames **Northumberland, Westmoreland**: two Catholic Earls who headed a rebellion against Elizabeth on behalf of Mary, Queen of Scots, Essex was three years old at the time **father Harry**: Henry VIII **Alexander** the Great **Antipater**: one of Alexander's generals suspected of poisoning him

60

THE BLACK PRINCE OROONOKO, ENSLAVED BY THE ENGLISH PLANTERS IN SURINAM, SCORNS THEM AND THEIR CHRISTIANITY
(1695) THOMAS SOUTHERNE, Oroonoko, *Act 1, Sc. 2*

Oroonoko is an African prince who, with his royal father, trafficked in slaves with an English ship's captain, a man of questionable business morality. Predictably, Oroonoko is betrayed by the Englishman and is himself captured and sold into slavery to English planters in the West Indies. In Southerne's portrayal, Oroonoko is not at all like the American Indian "Noble Savage" of European fantasy, but an African Prince who in sentiments, manners and self-presentation could easily pass for equivalent English gentleman. He has a character and style unknown to history, but familiar to Restoration Whig fantasy. As a paragon of Valor, Virtue, and Good Manners, he becomes in this guise a prophetic voice for what are later to be, in the 18th century, ideals of universal human dignity wrapped in the overriding ideal of personal liberty. Give me liberty, his tragic story says, anticipating, or give me death.

As may not have been usual among British plantation owners in the West Indies, Oroonoko's native royal bearing is recognized and honored by his new owners. Their courtesy is reciprocated by Oroonoko, but not until they hear this utterance after he arrives in a column of newly acquired slaves, in chains. Oroonoko addresses his betrayer, the ship's captain, and the religion by which the lying captain swore his businessman's honor, with a dignified contempt that instantly commands the respect and deference of his new owners. A likely story.

> **OROONOKO**
> *(To Captain Driver)* So, sir, you have kept your word with me. You are
> A better Christian than to keep it with a heathen.
> Be a Christian still:
> If you have any god that teaches you
> To break your word, I need not curse you more:
> Let him cheat you, as you are false to me.
>
> *(Embracing his friends.)*
> You faithful followers of my better fortune!
> *(To fellow-slaves)* We have been soldiers in the field;
> Now we are fellow-slaves. This last farewell.
> Be sure of one thing that will comfort us,
> Whatever world we next are thrown upon,
> Cannot be worse than this.

(All slaves go off, but Oroonoko.)
(To Captain Driver) Live still in fear; it is the villain's curse,
And will revenge my chains: fear even me,
Who have no power to hurt thee. Nature abhors,
And drives thee out from the society
And commerce of mankind, for breach of faith.
Men live and prosper but in mutual trust,
A confidence of one another's truth:
That thou hast violated. I have done.
I know my fortune, and submit to it.

(To his new and compassionate master Blanford)
Be satisfied,
I am above the rank of common slaves.
Let that content you. The Christian there that knows me,
For his own sake will not discover more.

(All leave, but Oroonoko and Blanford)
I am unfortunate, but not ashamed
Of being so. No, let the guilty blush,
The white man that betrayed me: honest black
Disdains to change its colour. I am ready:
Where must I go? Dispose me as you please.
I am not well acquainted with my fortune,
But must learn to know it better: so I know, you say:
Degrees make all things easy.
The slavish habit best becomes me now.
Hard fare, and whips, and chains may overpower
The frailer flesh, and bow my body down.
But there's another, nobler part of me
Out of your reach, which you can never tame.
Do what you will with me.

XVIII CENTURY ENGLISH/GERMAN

61

BARNWELL EXECUTES A MURDER AGAINST HIS WILL
(1731) GEORGE LILLO, The London Merchant, *Act 3, Sc. 3*

In the strictest sense, one would suppose that *The London Merchant* is not what it has always been called—a bourgeois tragedy—but a proletarian one, since its protagonist, the initially virtuous apprentice George Barnwell, falls into temptation, is seduced into committing theft and murder, and finally suffers execution. But the recounting of this fall from virtue is written entirely from a bourgeois perspective— the first of many to come in the 18th and 19th centuries—all uniformly sentimentally compassionate toward their lower class victims, but along with their compassion, sternly cautionary. *The London Merchant,* the first of the genre of tragedies devoted to cautioning the lower classes, is also a hymn to the newly surging middle class and its newly flaunted values. And enfolded within it is an apprehensive sermon to its employees to keep their hands out of the till and their libidos out of the reach of destabilizing temptation.

Lest tragedy's dignity suffer from descending too enthusiastically into society's underclass, its unfortunate protagonist's internal life had to be elevated to a level of psychological and rhetorical respectability, and it reached, however incongruously, for poetic sentence. Whether it succeeded or not, it is traditional tragedy's levels of poetic intensity that Lillo is emulating in his plot and in his prose, the same ambition that is to haunt, and more often than not cripple, later bourgeois tragedies written to warn. The model Lillo is using is Shakespeare, and the tragedy he is emulating is *Macbeth.* Young Barnwell walks in the footsteps of Macbeth's fall from virtue, subject to the temptation not of ambition but of lust. He struggles as does Macbeth with the torment of observing with abhorrence his own plunge into criminality. But unlike Macbeth, who declines into a sort of moral inanition, Barnwell rises to more and more strenuous flights of moral fervor, becoming, according to the formula that is to become familiar to cautionary melodrama, both pious sermonizer and criminal transgressor.

Young Barnwell, a loyal and trustworthy apprentice to the merchant Thorowgood, is seduced by Millwood, a woman who, once cruelly deceived by men, now preys on them for her sustenance and for the pleasure of perpetrating their downfall. Step by step, she urges a pliant Barnwell first to steal from his master, then to murder his beloved Uncle. Barnwell, horrified by his deeds, is nevertheless helpless to resist. On the night of his planned murder of his Uncle, he waits, in darkness, for his arrival. Instead of, "Is this a dagger which I see before me?" and the several starts and frights of Macbeth waiting to murder Duncan, Barnwell endures terror, and then a wavering resolve, and then self-disgust, but finally, resolution.

What is striking about the rhetorical "high sentence" of The London Merchant is that even in its most flamboyant moments, it continues to have emotional and psychological validity. That is true of the "villainous" Millwood whose bitter self-justification rings as true now as it certainly did then. And it is true of Barnwell's torment before the murder of his uncle and of his ungovernable remorse afterwards. For both Millwood and Barnwell, the text is imitative, but the suffering is real.

> **BARNWELL**
> A dismal gloom obscures the face of day; either the sun has slipped behind a cloud, or journeys down the west of heaven with more than common speed, to avoid the sight of what I'm doomed to act. Since I set forth on this accursed design, where'er I tread, methinks, the solid earth trembles beneath my feet. Yonder limpid stream, whose hoary fall has made a natural cascade, as I passed by, in doleful accents

seemed to murmur 'Murder.' The earth, the air, and water, seemed concerned—but that's not strange; the world is punished, and nature feels a shock when Providence permits a good man's fall! Just heaven! Then what should I be?—for him that was my father's only brother, and since his death has been to me a father, who took me up an infant, and an orphan; reared me with tenderest care, and still indulged me with most paternal fondness. Yet here I stand avowed his destined murderer. I stiffen with horror at my own impiety. 'Tis yet unperformed. What if I quit my bloody purpose, and fly the place! *(Going, then stops.)* But whither, oh whither, shall I fly? My master's once friendly doors are ever shut against me; and without money Millwood will never see me more, and life is not to be endured without her. She's got such firm possession of my heart, and governs there with such despotic sway—ay, there's the cause of all my sin and sorrow! 'Tis more than love; 'tis the fever of the soul and madness of desire. In vain does nature, reason, conscience, all oppose it; the impetuous passion bears down all before it, and drives me on to lust, to theft, and murder. O conscience! feeble guide to virtue, thou only show'st us when we go astray, but wantest power to stop us in our course.—Ha, in yonder shady walk I see my uncle. He's alone. Now for my disguise! *(Plucks out a visor.)* This is his hour of private meditation. Thus daily he prepares his soul for heaven—whilst I—but what have I to do with heaven? Ha! No struggles, conscience!

Hence, hence, remorse, and ev'ry thought that's good:
The storm that lust began must end in blood.

> *(Puts on the visor, draws a pistol. Throwing down the pistol)*

Oh, 'tis impossible! A man so near me!
Nay, then there's no retreat.

> *(Plucks a poniard from his bosom, and stabs him.)*

62

BARNWELL SUFFERS AGONIES OF REMORSE
AFTER MURDERING HIS UNCLE

(1731) GEORGE LILLO, The London Merchant, *Act 3, Sc. 7*

[see I, #61]

(BARNWELL throws off his mask, runs to him, and, kneeling by him, raises and chafes him.)

BARNWELL

Expiring saint! O murdered, martyred uncle! Lift up your dying eyes, and view your nephew in your murderer! Oh, do not look so tenderly upon me! Let indignation lighten from your eyes, and blast me ere you die!—By heaven, he weeps in pity of my woes. Tears,—tears, for blood! The murdered, in the agonies of death, weeps for his murderer.—Oh, Speak your pious purpose—pronounce my pardon then—and take me with you!—He would, but cannot.—Oh, why, with such fond affection, do you press my murdering hand?—What! will you kiss me?

(Barnwell kisses his uncle, who groans and dies.)

Life, that hovered on his lips but till he had sealed my pardon, in that kiss expired. He's gone forever—and oh! I follow. *(Swoons away upon his uncle's dead body.)*—Do I still live to press the suffering bosom of the earth? Do I still breathe, and taint with my infectious breath the wholesome air? Let heaven from its high throne, in justice or in mercy, now look down on that dear murdered saint and me the murderer, and, if his vengeance spares, let pity strike and end my wretched being!—Murder the worst of crimes, and parricide the worst of murders, and this the worst of parricides! Cain, who stands on record from the birth of time, and must to its last final period, as accursed, slew a brother favored above him. Detested Nero by another's hand dispatched a mother that he feared and hated. But I, with my own hand, have murdered a brother, mother, father, and a friend most loving and beloved. This execrable act of mine's without a parallel. Oh, may it ever stand alone—the last of murders, as it is the worst!

Nero…mother: Nero ordered the murder of his mother Agrippina

63

SPIEGELBERG, AFTER A FOOL EXPLOIT WITH STUDENTS, PROMOTES PLAN FOR AN 'IMMORTAL' EXPLOIT

(1782) FRIEDRICH SCHILLER, The Robbers, *ad. L. Katz, Act 1, Sc. 1*

University students in a tavern in Leipzig have dressed up as monks, set off the town's churchbells, and tied up two Professors and two Doctors, whom they march on all fours to the tavern's outhouse. In solemn procession, they carry a dog on a litter—for whose death the mock monks hold the academics guilty—and force them to consecrate the outhouse as the gravesite of Judith, the mongrel of their student leader, Karl Moor. Finishing the ceremony, the monks pour libations over the academics with "wine we'd already drunk."

Spiegelberg, the most frenetic of Moor's followers, is ecstatic: the lunatic exploit came off. He's inspired to go further, to cap the merely mad with the ultimately demented. He urges Karl Moor to lead them all to a madman's glory, and in a kind of frenzied ecstasy, outlines his scheme.

The *sturm und drang* generation of the 1770s and 1780s in Germany was in some ways—not all—comparable to the 1960s and 1970s generation in the U.S. and Europe. Its rebelliousness was as profoundly unleashed culturally and intellectually, but ended politically as superficially. Both movements "staged" their outrage at academic and literary rigidity and bourgeois respectability. But both moved back to acceptable orthodoxies in literature, mores and politics.

The seeds of *orthodoxy* in the *sturm und drang* moment were inherent in the movement itself. Schiller's *The Robbers,* the great example of the movement's moral idealism, is also the perfect illustration of its self-destruct. It is Karl Moor, the young scion of nobility, while a student at the university, who becomes the great symbol of the movement's rage against conformity, and who leads his fellow students into a life of robbery and murder as—in the logic of helplessly frustrated alienation—moral protest. But from the beginning, a sharp distinction is implied between the titanically raging morality of Karl Moor and the vulgar, suspect deviltry of Spiegelberg, who, as the play's later action carefully delineates, is the movement's subversive spirit, the spirit of negation. Spiegelberg undermines the lofty initial intent of the band by goading it more and more into pointless criminality, until, recognized as the spirit of treachery itself, he is murdered by his fellow robbers.

After several years of terrorist exploits, Karl Moor recognizes that he himself, in action as opposed to initial intent, has become the equivalent of Spiegelberg, and turning his back on his band, voluntarily surrenders himself to authority. The division between the two of them, though, is implicit in this first scene. Karl does not lead his followers into rebellion, but is pulled into leadership by Spiegelberg, whose temptation is momentarily halted when he recognizes a barrier he's in no position to contend with: Karl's devoted love for his Amelia.

Spiegelberg begins by giving Moor a bit of adulation for the outhouse exploit—"Now you're singing in the right key!"—and then urges him to join in flight "up, up, up, to the temple of immortal fame!"

> **SPIEGELBERG**
> Spiegelberg, you're blessed! You found a madman great enough to thumb his nose at all the quacks in Leipzig and fart at the stupid times we live in! Now you're singing in the right key. Like the heroes of old. Ah, Karl Moor, you've brought back the spirit of the great Hermann, the immortal Siegfried, to our miserable times! Ah, the way of the world, Karl! For the next hundred years, the citizens will worship at your outhouse shrine, but tomorrow morning, the law will piss on it!

Listen. Suppose, brother—just suppose—remember, for your ears
only!—a religious thought that's haunted me for years, and—now,
here—I've found the hero born to my purpose!—Drink, brother,
drink! What do you say—Oh, God, it's precious!—What do you say,
we give out that we're Jews, and that we're crusading to Palestine and
founding the New Jerusalem? No, listen, it's cunning, it's worthy of us!
We send a manifesto to the four corners of the earth, summoning
everyone who eats no pig to join with us in Palestine. And there I
prove by holy documents that Solomon was my great-grandfather, and
so on. Then, a victory, on some battlefield, anywhere, and then we
drive the Turks out of Asia, and hew cedars in Lebanon like my saint-
ed ancestor Solomon did, and build ships, and meanwhile—

I begin to think you mistrust me.—What happened to the Moor of
two minutes ago? You mean to bury your genius in this stinkhole? Let
all your talents go to waste? You think your little pranks in Leipzig are
the *ne plus ultra* of genius? Moor, let me show you the great world—
Paris, London! London, where they knock you to the ground if you
insult one of its citizens by calling him an honest man! We'll have a
holiday practicing all the great arts! Moor, it will open your eyes—to
learn how signatures are forged, how dice are loaded, how locks are
picked, how safes are blown to kingdom come!—All that, you can
learn from Spiegelberg! You'll see wonders, your head will spin like a
top!—It's clarifying, clarifying!—Thoughts, plans, fermenting in my
brain! Oh, this damned lethargy that's kept me chained to a rock! No
more! I'm awake now, and flying! I can see now, for the first time,
what I am and what I'm destined to become!

Spiegelberg, they'll say, you're a magician! Look: I stand before the
King. What a pity he says—to me!—what a pity you weren't a general; you could have chased the whole Austrian army out of here
through a buttonhole! And doctors crying, moaning: Spiegelberg, why
oh why didn't you study medicine; you could have discovered the ultimate cure for the clap! From one end of Germany to the other, the
word will be: Spiegelberg! So down into the *merde* with all of you,

cowards, reptiles, while Spiegelberg spreads his wings and sails up, up, up to the temple of immortal fame! Moor, you were made for the work! Then why…

Ah! Your Amelia! Ah, then Moor too is chained to the *merde* and to the rock.

Hermann (17 BC - AD 21): regarded as the earliest hero of German nationalism who defeated the Romans in AD 9, causing permanent Roman retreat from their province of Germania **Siegfried**, hero of the *Nibelungenlied,* the German national epic **the Turks…**: the Turkish (Ottoman) Empire was the most powerful in Central Asia at the time *ne plus ultra*, Lat: the best, the top, the ultimate *merde*, Fr: shit

64

FRANZ CONTEMPLATES PLANS FOR BETRAYAL AND MURDER OF FATHER AND BROTHER

(1782) FRIEDRICH SCHILLER, The Robbers, *ad. L. Katz, Act 1, Sc. 2*

In the castle of Old Moor, Karl's younger twin Franz reads a letter to his father, one ostensibly from the authorities, describing Karl's wild, even criminal life in Leipzig [see I, #63]. The letter is Franz's forgery, part of a campaign to have his father disown Karl as his son. Old Moor, broken-hearted but persuaded, authorizes Franz to notify his brother, "But Franz—don't drive him to despair!" Left alone, Franz reviews his motives, his plans for the future, his contempt for his father and hatred for his brother.

Franz is Schiller's amalgamation of Shakespeare's Richard III (physically and morally warped) and Lear's conscienceless son Edmund ("Thou, Nature, art my goddess!") As a character, he looms as large in his remorseless villainy as does Karl in his passionate moral yearning, both in fact reaching the dimensions of figures in Elizabethan tragedy (traditionally, the roles in performance—each in itself a *tour de force*—are played by the same actor.) In this soliloquy, Franz debates with himself: given the limitlessness of his criminal intent, what are his justifications? One after another, he ticks off the catalogue of the usual, humdrum, civilized restraints—the crimes one must not commit against Nature, the fears that should rankle conscience, the sacred ties of blood, the sanctity of paternity, the obligations of familial love—and puts them all down to "superstition." His rule is duplicity ("love," he calls it) and force, the only effective means, the only justifications.

His style, though, is different from his credo. Like Edmund's, like Richard III's, there is a light, good-humored touch to his tolerance of his own arguments, to his pretense that they are the norms of reason. And, like Richard, not until the last moments of the play does he lose entirely his usual rhetorical pitch: an easy, self-pleased lightness of tone punctuated almost every other word by a dagger-like thrust of venom.

FRANZ

(Alone) Be easy, old fool! You'll never press your darling son to your bosom again. I've put a gulf between you and him as wide as the gulf between heaven and hell.—Get rid of the letter, Franz, burn it, or that prying old man will recognize your handwriting. And so, the son is disposed of, and so, Franz—the way is clear. Grief should soon get rid of the old man too.—Ah, Franz, unnatural Franz, tearing a loving son from his father's arms, nudging an old man into heaven before his time—crimes, crimes against nature, old mother, old whore. What do I owe to her? She could have dragged me first out of the womb. Why not the first? Why not the only one? And why, with this face, and this body, drag me out at all? Nature, old misery, old whore, kneaded together all the refuse of the world, baked it in her oven, and got me, filth of the world. Who gave her the right to deny me, and give everything to Karl? Did he flatter her before he was born? Or did I offend her before I existed? Why hate me and love him before we were conceived?

No, Franz, you do the old whore an injustice. She gave us all, in the beginning, the gift of invention, set us naked and helpless on the shore of the world, and said: You'll swim if you have the wit to figure it out, but if your wit is dull and lumpish, you'll sink. She gave me that and nothing else: the wit to use my wits. Our natural rights are equal: claim against claim, strength against strength, and the strongest claims the right. The only limit of the law is the limit of our strength.

So—courage, Franz! The man who is afraid of nothing is as powerful as the man who is feared by all. It's now the fashion to wear buckles on your underwear to loosen or tighten their fit at will. I'll do the same for my conscience, buckle it *a la mode*, and the fatter I grow, the looser I'll buckle. I've heard a lot of twaddle about ties of the blood— enough to make a sane man mad. He's your father—ah, your father!—he gave you life, he's your flesh and blood, and so he's holy to you! Stupid deduction! Think, Franz, how did he beget you? Out of love for you? How could he have known you before you existed? Was he thinking of you during the begetting? Did he know how you would look, and be? If he did, he'd better not let on, or there'll be retribution. Should you be grateful to him because you came out a man? As little as you should blame him if you came out a woman. And so what is sacred about paternity? Is it the deed itself out of which you grew? The deed was the animal's, not the father's. Or is it the result of the deed, which comes of itself, out of that old whore Nature's necessity, and which that loving father would just as soon dispense with, if it weren't so costly in flesh and blood. Then what do I owe him for his love? And what is his love but his vanity—the same as the artist's who admires his own work no matter how hideous it might be. And there, Franz, is the whole superstition, wrapped up in a mystical veil to torture and frighten superstitious sons. No more of that, Franz! To work—with no fear and no shame! You'll root out everything that stands in the way of your becoming master of this house. Because master I must be—and what can't be won by love must be won—how does Nature do it?—by force.

65

SPIEGELBERG EXHORTS STUDENTS
TO BECOME A ROBBER BAND

(1782) FRIEDRICH SCHILLER, The Robbers, *ad. L. Katz, Act 1, Sc. 3*

The function of Spiegelberg in Schiller's ideology becomes even clearer [see I, #63] when he exhorts the students who had fun with the outhouse joke to cut all their ties with conventional life and become a band of robbers. Earlier, Karl, responding to Spiegelberg's crazy notion of "giving out that we're Jews" to reconquer the Holy land, laughed it off: "I understand! You want to make foreskins a dead fashion, just because the surgeon had to slice yours off" (presumably for the clap), to which Spiegelberg replied: "Child, mine was snipped in the cradle, long before I had to bring it pimpled to the surgeon."

Spiegelberg is a Jew. His contrast with Karl could hardly be greater, and the contrast Schiller is making hardly more familiar: Karl is a scion of the nobility, and is imagined, even in Spiegelberg's rhetoric, as descending from the paragon of German heroes, Hermann, who in myth saved the identity of the German race from being smothered by Roman hordes. Exhorting the abashed students to take the plunge into a life of crime, the salvation Spiegelberg dangles before them, if they would merely drop their allegiance to mediocrity, is the immortality of hanging from the gallows like "the greatest of all of us," the one who died similarly suspended. Spiegelberg is not only subversive, he's sacrilegious. But his rush of energy and dazzling paradox carries the naive ones along, and so begins the demonstration of part of the play's thesis: that the passionate motives of rebellion lose their moral lustre because of their criminal acts, but those acts are inevitably defined not by the virtuous at its helm, but by the devils at its fringe. Schiller's *sturm und drang*, in other words, has it both ways: the rebellion of the alienated is virtuous in aim, but inevitably subverted by the vicious. How it also subverts itself is Karl's story [see I, #66].

SPIEGELBERG

(Sneering) Keep you out of jail this morning! Oh, God! Is that all your miserable soul can long for? I tell you, Spiegelberg can make you heroes, princes, gods, if you have the courage to follow him! Courage is all you need—I'll provide the brains. Courage, I say! Schweitzer, Roller, Schufterle! *(Solemnly)* If there's still a drop of blood of the old heroes of Germany flowing in your veins, then—come! Follow me! To the forests of Bohemia, where we'll pull together a band of robbers, and—What's the matter? Is all the blood of the Valsungs drained out of your veins already? You're not the first devils who have shit in the shadow of the gallows. Do you want to rot in jail till the day of Judgment? Or earn your bread singing beggar's songs in the streets and alleys of all the towns in Germany? Or sign up as volunteers and serve time-in-advance in purgatory under a bloodhound of a sergeant who thinks he has to earn his pay by crippling you? That's the catalogue; those are your choices. Or, we could all put our heads together, and with all our university wisdom, we could, well, get out an anthology, or an almanac, or something, and maybe write play reviews and sell them to the press for a penny a line. Or possibly turn Methodist, and hold prayer meetings once a week, and pass the hat for pennies.

Worms! My plan will exalt you! You'll have glory—and be immortal into the bargain! Oh, sweet immortality! Immortality! Even mounting to heaven on a rope, and hanging close to the angels forever while the vultures come to pay you court. Glory! Yes, glory! Every miserable peasant on the road who sees you swinging in the wind and rotting away overhead mutters to himself: 'that man had the brains to live a full life;' then he kicks his own behind for the miserable nothing of his own days, and crosses himself, remembering the greatest of all of us who was nailed to the gallows, and whose fame lives for hundreds and thousands of years! But your kings and councillors of the last hundreds and thousands of years—how many of them are remembered, except by those drudges who fill up their histories with names that nobody remembers or wants to remember—so they can pad their pages and get extra pennies from their publishers.

And do you think you'll be less honest as a highwayman than you are as a starving student? I'll tell you what's honest. To waylay rich misers on the road and relieve them of half their cares; to fling their gold into general circulation; to help socially conscious men with the equitable distribution of property; and to do in the weak and the sick and the helpless and so save Providence the bother of sending war, famine, pestilence and doctors to do the job in their clumsy way. That's what I call honest! Ah, but then, my friends, to be able to sit down to dinner every day, and say to yourself: this I won by my own cunning, my own labors, my own long watchings through the night, my own lion's courage!

And so—we consign our souls to the devil! Yes? Ecstasy, ecstasy! Up, come, we're off!

Bohemia: a region in Central Europe that today falls mainly in the Czech Republic **Valsungs**: warrior women in the *Nibelungenlied* who brought dead heroes from the battlefield to Valhalla **university wisdom**: Leipzig, the setting of the play, is famous for its university

66
KARL RETURNS THE CAPTIVE PRIEST TO TOWNSMEN WITH MESSAGE: "MY HOLY CALLING IS VENGEANCE"
(1782) FRIEDRICH SCHILLER, The Robbers, *ad. L. Katz, Act 2, Sc. 2*

It is months since Karl's robber band began its guerilla operations in the forests of Bohemia. During one exploit, one of their number is caught and about to be hanged. To rescue him, the band fires the town, blows up its powder shed killing more than 80 townspeople, and gets the prisoner off safely. In response, 1,000 townsmen arm themselves, and the band finds itself surrounded and potentially doomed.

A priest arrives at the camp to offer terms: if the band surrenders without bloodshed, the punishment of the men will be commuted from hanging to merely being broken on the wheel. Karl restrains his men's response—they're happily ready to throttle the priest—and instead offers the priest a message to take back to the town.

Karl's message has since had wider significance. Beyond the play itself, its credo has become the credo of rebellion against the brutalities of church and state power and their suffocating hypocrisies over the last two centuries. Its watchwords are retribution and vengeance, and its rage, like Karl's, is unabating. What is extraordinary about Karl's message, and rage, is that they have automatically and accurately universalized themselves, and unabatingly keep alive, with whatever inevitable self-contradiction, the inherent moral passion that urged them into life in the first place. It is the one moment in the play when the revolutionist's - or terrorist's - moral passion for his cause is expressed with unalloyed conviction. When the battle promised to the Priest is over, and when Karl is faced with its tally of 300 enemy dead to one of his men, that he is forced to stare directly at the anomaly of his commitment [see I, #67].

> **KARL**
>
> Listen to me, holy man! There's a band of men here, whose Captain I am, and there's not one among them who's learned to dance away from the music of a fight, and out there stand a thousand men grown old and grey under the weight of their muskets. You'll bring back this message to them from Karl Moor, Captain of the incendiaries.—It's true that I've burned and plundered the church of St. Dominic, and flung firebrands into your bigoted city, and brought down the powder-shed on the heads of devout Christians. But that's not all—I've done more.
>
> *(He holds out his right hand)*
>
> You see these rings, one on each finger? Tell those merciful town fathers with their power of life and death what you're about to see and hear. This ruby I took from the finger of a minister whom I left dead

at his Prince's feet when he was out hunting. He was a man of the people who flattered his way to his Prince's elbow, and the ladder he used was the ruin of his neighbors. This diamond I took from a minister of finance, who sold titles and place to the highest bidder but drove loyal old soldiers from his door. This agate I wear in honor of one of your own cloth, whom I strangled with my bare hands after he wept from his pulpit over the waning power of the Inquisition. I could tell you more stories of my rings, but I repent for the words I've already wasted on you.

You hear him? Did you hear his sigh? There he is, your holy priest, imploring fire from heaven to come down and destroy the world's sinners, pronouncing judgments with a shrug of the shoulder, and sending men to eternal damnation with a Christian 'Alas!' How is it possible for a man to be so blind? A hundred eyes to spy out the sins of his brothers, but none to spy out his own! They preach love of one's neighbor while they curse the old and the blind and drive them from their door. They rack their brains wondering how the world could give birth to a Judas, while the best of them would betray the Holy Trinity for one—not even thirty—pieces of silver. All of you, apes and mockers of God! Kneeling before the cross without shame and scourging your backs and mortifying your flesh, and thinking that these pitiful tricks can fool the God that you in the same breath call all-wise and all-seeing. The God who sees through your hearts would rage against the One who made you, if he weren't one and the same God who created both you and the monsters of the Nile!—Take him away! Get him out of my sight! Tell your forbearing masters that what I've done I'll no doubt read one day in the book of heaven, and before Him alone, I'll shed tears of remorse. But with his miserable ministers on earth, I'll waste no more words. Tell your masters that my merciful trade is retribution, and my holy calling is vengeance.

(He turns his back on him)

agate: semiprecious stone, variegated quartz

67

KARL, REMEMBERING HIS INNOCENCE, YEARNS: "MAKE ME A CHILD AGAIN"
(1782) FRIEDRICH SCHILLER, The Robbers, *ad. L. Katz, Act 2, Sc. 2*

The battle promised to the townsfolk [see I, #66] is over, and Karl Moor and his men, numb, return to their camp and drop to the ground in exhaustion. Once again, Karl asks for the tally: 300 dead of their enemy the townsmen, as against Roller, the one man of their own who died. Supine, and altogether vulnerable physically and psychologically, Karl's reverie drifts toward purity, toward what is purest—the Sun, and so inevitably to its opposite, what is cursed, what is damned. It is perhaps the most profound moment in Karl's journey—the moment when the man alienated from his hated society recognizes that he is equally alienated from his own retributive acts. "Give me back my innocence," he prays. "Then all my days will be sweet." At this nadir of belief in his original mission, he reconciles himself to the only commitment left that can still accord with his moral sensibility: an eternal commitment to the men for whose doomed lives he is responsible. "I will never abandon you," he swears to them.

But even this commitment he will later be guilty of violating, and once again out of a sense of moral propriety, when in the end he turns his back on the band's criminal life, and surrenders to a poor man "who can claim the reward." The tragic irony of the moral anomaly inherent in any act of retribution persists to the end.

KARL
Ach! I must rest.

(He drops to the ground. The men do the same)
I'm numb from head to foot. And my mouth is as dry as a sandpit. I'd ask one of you to fetch some water, but you're all of you as tired as I am. It was a warm day's work!

(He sits up)
My dear Roller! We beat back that whole army of pious Christians, and you were the only one we lost. My Roller died a noble death.—If he had died in any cause but this, there'd be a marble monument set over his grave.—Well, this grave will have to do. How many of the holy pious did we kill? About three hundred? Three hundred for one.

Look. The sun's going down behind those hills. It's a glorious sunset. Like a hero going to his death.—Once that sun was worshipped. By me. When I was a boy, I used to dream of living like the Sun-God. And dying like him. That was childish, wasn't it? There was a time— Do you know, when I was very young, I couldn't fall asleep at night if I'd forgotten to say my prayers.

That was very young. Very young.—But I'd like to be that child again. The earth was beautiful then. The whole world was glorious. It is still. Beautiful, yes. Those fields over there, everything on them grown so lush and so tall, everything ripe for harvest. And the branches of those trees almost breaking with the weight of their fruit. So perfect a spring day! Every living thing warm and red in the rays of the setting sun. As though every living thing's joined in one family, with one Father over them.—But Karl Moor's not among them, and the Father's disowned him. He's not in the ranks of the blessed, and breathes nothing from all the blessings of heaven but the torments of the damned.—Ill? Oh yes. In my soul. Because I'm chained to a life of murder and theft, hanging over the abyss, and wondering whether it's best to live out this miserable life, or go at once into eternal damnation.

The sight of the grave, I suppose. And the thought that Roller's lying in it. For my cause. He died for my sin.

Is there something we can do? There is. Make me a child again. Give me back my innocence. Then all my days will be sweet, and the look of that sunset wonderful, and loving.—If I could be born again as a beggar, or a laborer who sweats away his life in the field, I'd work till the blood poured out of my body, and I'd know the joy again of one night's sleep without guilt, and one waking day without a feeling of hatred for my own soul.

(He looks up at his men)

Every one of you has a price now on his head. Earned in my cause.

(He gets up)

We're brothers in earnest! And I swear to you, I'll never abandon you. I swear it on Roller's grave.

XIX CENTURY ENGLISH/FRENCH

68
MANFRED CONTEMPLATES SUICIDE
(1817) GEORGE GORDON BYRON, Manfred, *Act 1, Sc. 2*

Manfred is an example of what in England was called "closet drama," that is, drama that was by general agreement unendurable on stage, and so rejected as often as possible for production. Not that it was necessarily "undramatic;" most closet drama learned its theatrical lessons from concurrent and enormously popular melodrama, and was generally as extravagant and laughable in its action as melodrama itself. But in a different way, it was out of its time in England: it featured poetic rhetoric and philosophic intellection.

Neither was a novelty in English tradition. Elizabethans like Jonson and Marlowe and Chapman unabashedly wrote lengthy cogitations into their plays with a weight and complexity of the kind that Byron and Shelley in the early 19th century emulated in their "closet dramas." But the level of popular drama had so shifted that, in theatrical terms, their cogitations on stage, no more nor less ambitious than those of Goethe's and Schiller's concurrent dramas in Germany, had become effectively irrelevant. In Manfred, at least, Byron gave up the claim to theatrical viability altogether, and called his play a Dramatic Poem. Nevertheless, the sheer intensity of Manfred's rhetoric and the uninhibited, unmodulated scale of his emotions makes it understandable that in Europe, though not in his native land, "Byronism" became a synonym for the darkest and wildest reaches of romantic suffering.

What was he suffering? His time—the closing-in of repressive rule throughout Europe, the creeping mediocrity of the bourgeois century, the failure of the hopes generated by the early days of the French Revolution—and secretly, in himself, an unspecified, unnamable sense of guilt. "Byronism" defined not a helpless passivity but a raging anguish of despair, and the final proof of its authenticity had to be suicide. In Manfred, the despair is not particular nor defined by story incident; it is metaphysical, and takes the soul's sickness as a given.

Like Marlowe's Faustus, Manfred has already had dealings with the supernatural, and it has "abandoned" him. In the midst of the overwhelming landscape of the Swiss mountains, he feels separated from the beauty and grandeur of nature: it "shin'st not on my heart;" and looking down toward the torrential streams raging far below, he confronts his To be or not to be: the imperative to jump, the imperative to remain alive. And again like Faustus, he prays for altered states to escape not, as in Faustus's case, the damnation of Hell, but the damnation of living: to be a bodiless sound, a "breathing harmony," instead of this "blighted trunk" of a decaying tree. And hearing the crash of an avalanche, he laments, "Why stood I not beneath it?" And he reels, sick at heart, overwhelmed by an onrushing snowstorm, ready to fall.

Subsequently [in I, #69], his "pang" finds a voice—a voice not Byron's or Manfred's alone—the confession of the wholly separated, wholly alienated, man who hates his connection with humanity itself with which he feels no commonalty of being, and takes refuge not only in solitude, but in exploring and fingering "the caves of death," in the forbidden "sciences," in emulating and entering into the life of the torrent, the wave, the lightning. But then, once having experienced the true horror of solitude—that it is "peopled with the Furies"—he becomes wild to escape it, praying for madness, for death (once again denied by some restraining force), for obliterating fantasy—in a word, for forgetfulness. Once more he turns to "the superhuman art," but this time, he longs to call up the "immortal spirits" for only one reason: to subject him to any torture at any hour, "so it be the last."

"Byronism," so riddled with despair and guilt, so living with unnamable torments, so longing for oblivion, found echoes throughout European literature, most profoundly in Russia, where Dostoyevsky explored the psychology and moral dimensions of the "Byronic" in his greatest novels.

(The Mountain of the Jungfrau.—Time, Morning.—
MANFRED alone upon the Cliffs.)

MANFRED
The spirits I have raised abandon me,
The spells which I have studied baffle me,
The remedy I reck'd of tortured me;
I lean no more on superhuman aid;
It hath no power upon the past, and for
The future, till the past be gulf'd in darkness,
It is not of my search.—My mother Earth!
And thou fresh breaking Day, and you, ye Mountains,
Why are ye beautiful? I cannot love ye.
And thou, the bright eye of the universe,
That openest over all, and unto all
Art a delight—thou shin'st not on my heart.
And you, ye crags, upon whose extreme edge
I stand, and on the torrent's brink beneath
Behold the tall pines dwindled as to shrubs
In dizziness of distance when a leap,
A stir, a motion, even a breath, would bring
My breast upon its rocky bosom's bed
To rest for ever—wherefore do I pause?
I feel the impulse—yet I do not plunge;
I see the peril—yet do not recede;
And my brain reels—and yet my foot is firm:
There is a power upon me which withholds,
And makes it my fatality to live,—
If it be life to wear within myself
This barrenness of spirit, and to be
My own soul's sepulchre, for I have ceased
To justify my deeds unto myself—
The last infirmity of evil.

(An eagle passes.)

Ay, thou winged and cloud-cleaving minister,
Whose happy flight is highest into heaven,
Well may'st thou swoop so near me—I should be
Thy prey, and gorge thine eaglets; thou art gone
Where the eye cannot follow thee; but thine

Yet pierces downward, onward, or above,
With a pervading vision.—Beautiful!
How beautiful is all this visible world!
How glorious in its action and itself!
But we, who name ourselves its sovereigns, we,
Half dust, half deity, alike unfit
To sink or soar, with our mix'd essence make
A conflict of its elements, and breathe
The breath of degradation and of pride,
Contending with low wants and lofty will,
Till our mortality predominates,
And men are—what they name not to themselves,
And trust not to each other.

Oh, that I were
The viewless spirit of a lovely sound,
A living voice, a breathing harmony,
A bodiless enjoyment—born and dying
With the blest tone which made me!
To be thus—
Grey-hair'd with anguish, like these blasted pines,
Wrecks of a single winter, barkless, branchless,
A blighted trunk upon a cursed root,
Which but supplies a feeling to decay—
And to be thus, eternally but thus,
Having been otherwise! Now furrow'd o'er
With wrinkles, plough'd by moments,—not by years;—
And hours—all tortured into ages—hours
Which I outlive!—Ye toppling crags of ice!
Ye avalanches, whom a breath draws down
In mountainous o'erwhelming, come and crush me!
I hear ye momently above, beneath,
Crash with a frequent conflict; but ye pass,
And only fall on things that still would live;
On the young flourishing forest, or the hut
And hamlet of the harmless villager.

The mists boil up around the glaciers; clouds
Rise curling fast beneath me, white and sulphury,

Like foam from the roused ocean of deep Hell,
Whose every wave breaks on a living shore,
Heap'd with the damn'd like pebbles.—I am giddy.

Mountains have fallen,
Leaving a gap in the clouds, and with the shock
Rocking their Alpine brethren; filling up
The ripe green valleys with destruction's splinters;
Damming the rivers with a sudden dash,
Which crush'd the waters into mist, and made
Their fountains find another channel—thus,
Thus, in its old age, did Mount Rosenberg—
Why stood I not beneath it? Such would have been for me a fitting
tomb;
My bones had then been quiet in their depth;
I am most sick at heart—
I am all feebleness—the mountains whirl
Spinning around me—I grow blind—

SD **Jungfrau**: mtn of the Jungfrau (Virgin) is in the Swiss Alps **Mount
Rosenberg**: a peak in the Swiss Alps

69

MANFRED CONFESSES HIS GUILT AND DESPAIR
(1817) GEORGE GORDON BYRON, Manfred, *Act 2, Sc. 2*

[see I, #68]

MANFRED
My pang shall find a voice. From my youth upwards
My spirit walk'd not with the souls of men,
Nor look'd upon the earth with human eyes;
The thirst of their ambition was not mine,
The aim of their existence was not mine;

My joys, my griefs, my passions, and my powers,
Made me a stranger; though I wore the form,
I had no sympathy with breathing flesh,
Nor midst the creatures of clay that girded me,
And with the thoughts of men,
I held but slight communion; but instead,
My joy was in the Wilderness,—to breathe
The difficult air of the iced mountain's top,
or to plunge
Into the torrent, and to roll along
On the swift whirl of the new breaking wave
or catch
The dazzling lightnings till my eyes grew dim;
These were my pastimes, and to be alone;
For if the beings, of whom I was one,—
Hating to be so,—cross'd me in my path,
I felt myself degraded back to them,
And was all clay again. And then I dived,
In my lone wanderings, to the caves of death,
Searching its cause in its effect; and drew
From wither'd bones, and skulls, and heap'd up dust,
Conclusions most forbidden. Then I pass'd
The nights of years in sciences untaught,

And with my knowledge grew
The thirst of knowledge, and the power and joy
Of this most bright intelligence, until—

Oh! I but thus prolong my words,
Boasting these idle attributes, because
As I approach the core of my heart's grief—
But to my task.
My solitude is solitude no more,
But peopled with the Furies;—I have gnash'd
My teeth in darkness till returning morn,
Then cursed myself till sunset;—I have pray'd
For madness as a blessing—'tis denied me.

I have affronted death—but in the war
Of elements the waters shrunk from me,
And fatal things pass'd harmless; the cold hand
Of an all-pitiless demon held me back,
Back by a single hair, which would not break.
In fantasy, imagination, all
The affluence of my soul—which one day was
A Croesus in creation—I plunged deep,
But, like an ebbing wave, it dash'd me back

Into the gulf of my unfathom'd thought.
I plunged amidst mankind—Forgetfulness
I sought in all, save where 'tis to be found,
And that I have to learn; my sciences,
My long-pursued and superhuman art,
Is mortal here: I dwell in my despair—
And live—and live for ever.
Immortal spirit, aid me!
To do this thy power
Must wake the dead, or lay me low with them.
Do so—in any shape—in any hour—
With any torture—so it be the last.

Croesus, Cresus: a Roman of legendary wealth

70

SAILOR WILLIAM, LEGALLY BUT NOT MORALLY GUILTY, DEFENDS HIMSELF AT HIS TRIAL BEFORE THE ADMIRALTY

(1829) DOUGLAS JERROLD, Black-Ey'd Susan, *Act 3, Sc. 2*

I write," said Pixerecourt, the father of 19th century melodrama, "for those who cannot read." He might have added that he wrote for characters who could barely talk. That its stage characters don't talk like normal humanity is in dramatic tradition no novelty—they never did or do—but in melodrama there is an unbroken principle that governs the artifice of its stage talk. Certainly without knowing it, melodrama returned to Western drama's earliest notion of character differentiation in which characters are wholly delineated by four features: sex, age, social function and moral bent (e.g., an old man who is a merchant and who is greedy, or a young woman who is a captive slave and who is kindly). Within these bluntly defining characteristics, early British melodrama did with characters as it did with plot: fell back on basics, and did so with rigid consistency. To keep characters crystal clear, each were compelled, in their every word of dialogue and their every moral gesture, to iterate and reiterate their definition.

William in *Black-Ey'd Susan* is a young man who is a sailor and who has a pure heart. He does not utter a sentence without flagging his profession or perform a deed that does not spring from a pure heart. In his dialogue, he is a walking nautical encyclopedia; in his action, he is a pattern of young male sailor-virtue. Melodrama holds to this template of characterization with a purity that allows for no admixture: he is a sailor and nothing else, he is virtuous at heart and nothing else. And in the single direction of that predicated moral predisposition, every feeling, ideal, urge, and belief of type are exhibited in their perfection, without nuance or addition. This is both the absurdity and the appeal of melodrama, now as much as then, in exhibiting for us perfect variants of the commonly-held fictions of human character.

Sailor William has come home to port; he is the unconditionally heart-felt, loving husband of Black-Ey'd Susan. He is also the unconditionally heart-felt, loyal, wholly willing, wholly submissive subject of his ship's Captain, the British Navy, King, Country, and all their laws. At dockside, what should he see but a man in uniform molesting Susan with bestial sexual advances. With not a moment's hesitation, William pulls out his cuirass, whacks the man on the back, and thinking he's killed him, his glance tells him—it's his ship's Captain.

At his trial, he doesn't suppose for a moment that mitigating circumstances—incredibly persuasive though they might be—can alter his being sentenced to death for striking an officer. He has heard his shipmates testify to his character, but in his response to his judges, he quickly puts their character-references aside as irrelevant, and begs of his judges, altogether submissively, that though they must condemn the sailor, "to respect the husband." On what grounds? Reasons of the heart: recalling "the wives you honor and the children you love." Aside from that, Sailor William has no quarrel with his impending sentence of death.

> **WILLIAM**
>
> Your honours, I feel as if I were in irons, or seized to the grating, to stand here and listen—like the landlord's daughter of the Nelson—to nothing but yarns about sarvice and character. My actions, your honours, are kept in the log book aloft—if, when that's over-hauled, I'm not found a trim seaman, why, it's only throwing salt to the fishes to patter here.
>
> In a moment, your honours. Damn it, my top-lights are rather misty. I have been three years at sea, and had never looked upon or heard from my wife—as sweet a little craft as was ever launched. I had come

ashore, and I was as lively as a petterel in a storm; I found Susan—that's my wife, your honours—all her gilt taken by the land-sharks; but yet all taut, with a face as red and rosy as the king's head on the side of a fire bucket. Well, your honours, when we were as merry as a ship's crew on a pay-day, there comes an order to go on board. I left Susan, and went with the rest of the liberty men to ax leave of the first lieutenant. I hadn't been gone the turning of an hour-glass, when I heard Susan giving signals of distress. I out with my cutlass, made all sail, and came up to my craft. I found her battling with a pirate—I never looked at his figure-head, never stopped—would any of your honours? long live you and your wives say I! Would any of your honours have rowed alongside as if you'd been going aboard a royal yacht? No, you wouldn't; for the gilt swabs on the shoulders can't alter the heart that swells beneath. You would have done as I did—and what did I? Why, I cut him down like a piece of old junk; had he been the first lord of the Admiralty, I had done it!

(Overcome with emotion.)

All I wish, whilst you pass sentence, is that your honours, whilst it is your duty to condemn the sailor, may, as having wives you honour and children you love, respect the husband. All my cable is run out—I'm brought to.

top-lights: signal lights on top of the mast **cutlass**: a short, heavy, slightly curved sword used at sea at the time **the gilt swabs on the shoulders**: officer's insignia worn on the shoulders

71

SAILOR WILLIAM, CONDEMNED, PREPARES TO MEET HIS DEATH
(1829) DOUGLAS JERROLD, Black-Ey'd Susan, *Act 3, Sc. 4*

Sailor William, in irons, is waiting to be summoned on deck for hanging [see I, #70]. His Lieutenant motions him to the open chest holding his life's belongings, inviting him to make disposition of them before his end. And, compassionate friend that he is, his Lieutenant urges William to be "a brave fellow, and fear not death."

William's response gives us genuine insight into the machinery of the ideal underclass hero of early melodrama. The articles of faith appropriate to his age, sex, social function and moral bent [see I, #70], are these: (1) that in the King's service he's lived with death as part of duty and has no fear of it; (2) that he is uncomplainingly and abjectly submissive to the echelons of authority above him, and also to the laws with which they govern him; (3) that he is proud, and fervently so, of such total deference, regarding his self-abnegation as the very badge, the very height, of the low man's honor; (4) that his greatest pride and happiness is in his perfect fit in the niche called "Sailor;" (4) that his perfect submission to power and law, and his perfect fulfillment of the functions and tasks and pieties of Sailorhood, are observed and rewarded in Heaven.

With death approaching, he has only one sorrow: that in the presence of his shipmates and the neighbors of his hometown, he will die swinging from the neck like a common criminal, although, notably, he has no complaint against the irony of the law that will put him there.

But it is the ceremony of the distribution of his gifts—in effect, his legacy—that raises the fate and feeling of William to high dignity, and we discover, in just such scenes as these, in which melodrama's wronged heroes and heroines give quiet voice to their uncomplaining acceptance of fortune, that melodrama aspires, however awkwardly, to gain for its undeserving victims something beyond pity—a measure of genuine tragic respect, even awe.

(As to William's fate, not to worry. A letter appears just in time confirming William's navy discharge before the date of his punishable act. It is brought by the Ship's Captain himself, rushing out of his sickbed, to rescue the sailor whom he had wronged, and who had been his ship's pride.)

WILLIAM

Death! No—since I first trod the king's oak, he has been about me—I have slept near him, watched near him—he has looked upon my face, and saw I shrunk not—in the storm I have heeded him not—in the fury of the battle I've thought not of him. Had I been mowed down by ball or cutlass, my shipmates, as they had thrown me to the sharks, would have given me a parting look of friendship, and over their grog have said I did my duty—this, your honour, would not have been death, but lying-up in ordinary. But to be swayed up like a wet jib to dry—the whole fleet—nay the folks of Deal, people that knew me, used to pat me on the head when a boy—all these looking at me. Oh! thank heaven, my mother's dead.

I know you won't despise the gift because it comes from one who walked the forecastle—here's my box, keep it for poor Will's sake. You and I, your honour, have laid yard-arm and yard-arm with many a foe—let us hope we shall come gunwale to gunwale in another climate.

(Gives him box—to MARINE OFFICER)

Your honour's hand—Blue Peter's flying—the vessel of life has her anchor a-trip, and must soon get under way for the ocean of eternity. Your honour will have to march me to the launching-place—you won't give a ship a bad name because she went awkwardly off the stocks? Take this, your honour,

(Opens watch.)
this paper was cut by Susan's fingers before we left the Downs; take it, your honour, I can't look at it. Master Quid, take this for my sake.

(Gives chain and seals, among which is a bullet.)
You see that bullet; preserve that more than the gold—that ball was received by Harry Trunnion in my defence. I was disarmed, and the Frenchman was about to fire, when Harry threw himself before me, and received that bullet in his breast. I took it flattened from his dead body—have worn it about me—it has served to remind me that Harry suffered for my sake, and that it was my duty, when chance might serve, to do the like for another.

Lieutenant, you see this locket. *(Points to locket at his neck.)* It is Susan's hair—when I'm in dock, don't let it be touched. I know you won't: you have been most kind to me, Lieutenant, and if those who go aloft may know what passes on the high sea, I shall yet look down upon you in the middle watch, and bless you.

72

MORDAUNT ACCUSES LADY MABEL OF "THE DEEPEST CRIME"
(1842) J. WESTLAND MARSTON, The Patrician's Daughter, *Act 3, Sc. 2*

Mourdant, a man of considerable address but without a title, is invited to the home of Lord Early, where he falls in love with his daughter, Lady Mabel. But in the seat of aristocracy, the divide between blue blood and plebeian is vast, and Lady Mabel, although she responds to his love, suppresses her feeling when it is falsely suggested to her that Mourdant's suit is tainted with sordid, lower class motive. When he is contemptuously rejected, his humiliation moves him to an outburst of denunciation of Lady Mabel's duplicity (although she had never stooped to confessing her love for him, its silent signs were proof enough). But the nature, and the verbiage, of his outburst were novel at the time, and were a part of the playwright's radical attempt at innovation.

The idea was to elevate a contemporary domestic thesis drama by adding the dignity of verse. It seemed peculiarly fitting for this particular drama, since it dealt not only with the traditional punctilio involved in the delicate sensibility of lovers not professing their love, but with the special punctilio belonging to class division and class behavior. By the time the play was written, aristocracy was rapidly losing its grasp of, and its relevance to, the real springs of power, and was driven to making more and more capital of its mere appurtenances and mystique. Its battle for privilege was increasingly fought in the social rather than in the political or economic arena; the less aristocratic plumage meant in reality, the more fervently it was cultivated. The play, addressed to the upper-class audience that continued to turn its back on popular theatre, is draped in the same plumage. Its text, its subject, its manner, its characters' behavior, are all terribly lofty, and so realize Marston's goal of, in effect, patrician drama, but at the same time, at its cost, loses connection with everyday language as spoken even by lordlings.

But Mordaunt's outburst is meant to shock the sensibilities of his listeners; his intention is to blast them with the passion of his truth, the reality, never before spoken in their circle, of his accusation. And so to a degree, his speech, passionately poetic as it is, in context earns its language.

But in addition to its poetic passion, his text is also remarkably sensitive in its articulation of the precise sin of which Lady Mabel is guilty. The portrait he is drawing of her is of a Diana-like Goddess "gliding" with "feet as light" over lovers' hearts, and "with eye as radiant and with brow as smooth," not deigning to notice the crime she is committing in her delicate trampling over inflamed hearts. It's a crime that passes unnoticed, is untracable, is unpunishable, but so casually awakening a love even to madness, and so blithely crushing it, "paraliz[ing] the expectant mind," is truly the deepest crime.

Marston allows the plebeian Mordaunt the most articulate, the most deeply felt, and even the most elegant language among these lofty ones.

MORDAUNT
Stay! Before we part, I have a word or two
For Lady Mabel's ear. *(MABEL returns)* I know right well
The world has no tribunal to avenge
An injury like mine; you may allure
The human heart to love, warm it with smiles,
To aspirations of a dream-like bliss,
From which to wake is madness;
And that very heart, brought to this pass,
You may spurn from your path, pass on in jest,
And the crowd will jest with you; you may glide,
With eye as radiant, and with brow as smooth,
And feet as light, through your charmed worshippers,
As though the angel's pen had failed to trace
The record of your crime; and every night,
Lulled by soft flatteries, you may calmly sleep
As do the innocent; but it is crime,
Deep crime, that you commit. Had you, for sport,
Trampled upon the earth a favorite rose,
Pride of the garden, or in wantonness
Cast in the sea a jewel not your own,
All men had held you guilty of offence.

And is it then not sin
To crush those flowers of life, our freshest hopes,
With all the incipient beauty in the bud,
Which knows no second growth? to cast our faith
In human kind, the only amulet
By which the soul walks fearless through the world,
Into those floods of memoried bitterness,
Whose awful depths no diver dares explore?
To paralyze the expectant mind, while yet

On the world's threshold, and existence' self
To drain of all save its inert endurance?
To do this unprovoked, I ask it of you,
Is it not sin? To the unsleeping eye of Him
Who sees all aims, and knows the wrongs
No laws, save his, redress, I make appeal
To judge between us. There's an hour will come
Not of revenge, but of righteous retribution.

73

ROBERT BRIERLY, IN PRISON, GRIEVES FOR THE SUFFERING HE IS CAUSING HIS FAITHFUL WIFE MAY

(1863) TOM TAYLOR, The Ticket-of-Leave Man, *Act 4*

By the middle of the 19th century, all the prayers for judgment and relief from the miseries and injustices that melodrama's virtuous victims consistently channeled toward Heaven [see I, #70] were being channeled more precisely toward their social, economic, and political origins for correction. "Ticket-of-leave man" means "man on parole." Brierly, though innocent, was unwittingly caught in a forgery scam, and spent four years in prison, from which he emerged—as only, melodrama taught, inner virtue can bring about—positively strengthened in decency, honesty, and reliability. During his time in prison, the love between himself and May, a poor girl to whom he had shown compassion during his last day of freedom, grew, and on the day of his release, while seeing her in her lodgings, is fortunate enough to find, through her, a respectable job with a respectable employer, a Mr. Gibson. Six months later, on the very day of his planned marriage to May, he is recognized by one of the true culprits of the original crime, denounced to his boss as a ticket-of-leave man, and dismissed.

As with other mid-century melodramas, the story is inherently a protest against a deep-rooted social wrong. Yet it is still in line with melodrama's earlier fixation on the injustice of condemning the appearance of evil while being blind to the victim's inner good. This is Brierly's continuing and inevitable plight: he is turned away everywhere until, winning a last chance, he is once again betrayed by the same culprits who had been hounding him from one job to another in order that, destitute, he could be useful to them once again.

So personalized, it might seem that the villainy lies with the villains alone. Hardly so; it is the universal turnoff against parolees—even by the rough laborers with whom Brierly hopes to share his last promised employment—that is the social deviltry behind the personal one. Brierly, his courage drained, recognizes that he's cornered, and looks to flight, enlistment, suicide, anything that is self-obliterating, as options. (Interesting that enlistment, which in the early days of melodrama was a virtue in itself, is now on a par with suicide.) But note: even in despair, the code of sensibility remains alive. What pains him most is the misfortune he's brought on his beloved. (And what pains her most is that he is for so slight a reason as her pain, pained.)

> **BRIERLY**
> Yes, the old anchor is my last chance—I've tried every road to an honest livelihood, and one after another they are barred in my face. Everywhere that dreadful word, jail-bird, seems to be breathed in the air about me—sometimes in a letter, sometimes in a hint, sometimes a copy of the newspaper with my trial, and then it is the same story— sorry to part with me—no complaint to make—but can't keep a ticket-of-leave man. Who can it be that hunts me down this way? Hawkshaw spared me. I've done no man a wrong—poor fellows like me should have no enemies. I wouldn't care for myself, but my poor lass, my brave, true-hearted May; I'm dragging her down along with me. Ah! here she is.

> *(MAY EDWARDS comes in, poorly dressed. She has a*
> *can, and some food in a bundle.)*

Thank thee, darling—I'm not hungry. Thou'st been out after work all
the day—eat thyself—thou need'st strength most. Thou has had
courage for both of us. Every blow that has fallen, every door that has
been shut between me and an honest livelihood, every time that clean
hands have been drawn away from mine, and respectable faces turned
aside as I came near them, I've come to thee for comfort and love and
hope, and I've found them till now. But I've brought thee to sorrow
and want and shame. Till I came back to thee thou hadst friends,
work and comforts. But since Mr. Gibson turned us off, the plight
that has followed me has reached thee too, the bravest, honestest,
brightest lass that ever doubled a man's joys, and halved his burdens.
Oh! it's too bad—it kills the heart out of me—it makes me mad. May,
lass, I sometimes think I had better let it all go—run—'list—make a
hole in the water, anything that would rid thee of me; thou could'st
make thy way alone.

74

AUBREY TANQUERAY ALERTS HIS FRIENDS: HIS NEW
WIFE MAY NOT MEET WITH THEIR SET'S APPROVAL
(1893) ARTHUR WING PINERO, The Second Mrs. Tanqueray, *Act 1*

Your wives," explains Tanqueray, "may not—like—the lady I'm
going to marry." His message is in the hiatus, his significant
pause. For more than a century or so in British social life, a distinctive
style of sending messages was developing almost counter to the style
social messages had formerly deployed. It had been the pleasure of
rational 18th century social rhetoric to make fully articulate and
unmistakably clear its private meanings, conversation emulating the
standards of public address. And noticeably, the very boldness and
forthrightness of its assertion registered a large measure of courage and

personal integrity in being so delivered. Why was this possible or even desirable? Because the moral posture of discourse—anybody's—signified a challenge inviting a reply of the same forthrightness, the same full articulation. It was generally the pleasure of 18th century discourse, and its delight, to pitch its sentences like swordthrusts, not intending pain, but anticipating thrust and parry in response. Statement was either exactly asserted or over-asserted. *"Thus* I refute Berkeley," said Samuel Johnson, kicking a stone, and so obliterating Berkeley's cavil about cause and effect. Then, meaning surfaced; by the late 19th century, it hid.

What had happened to articulation that it took such total umbrage? How did saying nothing or less than nothing become the preferred mode of conveying meaning? How did it come about that the 18th century-like sentences of Bernard Shaw or Oscar Wilde became, in the context of the turn of the century, blusteringly refreshing or shockingly belligerent?

It was because the consciousness of what was in fact being said, the actual assumptions and understandings being thoroughly shared in conversational silence, were morally embarrassing or even shameful to the very people who were signifying them by not uttering them. A morality had developed in the course of the 19th century that became the touchstone of ordinary, everyday proper thought. But the practicalities of what class and privilege were living by were remote from its own moral sermons. The gap could be narrow or wide, depending, but it was inevitably there. And so the face-saving way of talking to one's peers was with an implied nod and an implied wink, to which the response, far from challenge, was implied but silent accord.

Aubrey Tanqueray leaving out the point of his statement says it all to his friends, and they like him take for granted the bedrock of practical assumptions over which the hiatus passed in silence, yet were fully understood. The total about-face in educated discourse in British upper-strata life came about by way of a mutual acknowledgement not to acknowledge its implicit mendacity.

The intention of Aubrey's speech is to give his friends the necessary permission not to surrender rock-solid class prejudice for the lesser good of Christian egalitarianism.

> **AUBREY**
>
> Look here; I want you to understand me. You know a marriage often cools friendships. What's the usual course of things? A man's engagement is given out, he is congratulated, complimented upon his choice; the church is filled with troops of friends, and he goes away happily to a chorus of good wishes. He comes back, sets up house in town or country, and thinks to resume the old associations, the old companionships. My dear Frank, my dear good doctor, it's very seldom that it can be done. Generally, a worm has begun to eat its way into those hearty, unreserved, prenuptial friendships; a damnable constraint sets in and acts like a wasting disease; and so, believe me, in nine cases out of ten a man's marriage severs for him more close ties than it forms.
>
> I know what you're going to say, Frank. I hope so, too. In the meantime let's face dangers. I've reminded you of the *usual* course of things, but my marriage isn't even the conventional sort of marriage likely to satisfy society. Well, your wives may not—like—the lady I'm going to marry. Yes, yes, let us anticipate it. And let us make up our minds to have no slow bleeding-to-death of our friendship. We'll end a pleasant chapter here to-night, and after to-night start afresh. When my wife and I settle down at Willowmere it's possible that we shall all come together. But if this isn't to be, for Heaven's sake let us recognize that it is simply because it can't be, and not wear hypocritical faces and suffer and be wretched.
>
> The lady, my dear Frank, belongs to the next chapter, and in that, her name is Mrs. Aubrey Tanqueray. Then, in an old-fashioned way, I propose a toast. I give you 'The Next Chapter!'

75

LORENZACCIO DELIBERATES: "AM I SATAN?"

(1834) ALFRED DE MUSSET, Lorenzaccio, *tr. L. Katz, Act 3, Sc. 3*

orenzaccio, so particular to its time and so universally resonant in
its implications, must be dwelled on at some length. Lorenzaccio
means "Lorenzo the Monster." He was so christened by the
Florentines for his services to their ducal tyrant Alessandro dei Medici,
who, after his absolute power over his city was guaranteed by the Holy
Roman Emperor, indulged in the worst excesses of political tyranny,
including theft of estates and casual recourse to murder and abandoned, altogether unchecked libertinism. When the leading families
of Florence under the Republic realized that the Republic was, under
Alessandro, effectively destroyed and that "they were reduced to equal-
ity with the Florentine citizens they had regarded as their inferiors,
their rage," says one historian, "was indescribable."

The hated Lorenzo dei Medici, Alessandro's distant cousin, was his
companion, his accomplice, his procurer, his fellow voluptuary. But in
Musset's tragedy, the behavior and reputation of Lorenzo hide a complexity of motives that elides the grossest villainy with the loftiest
idealism. The paradox, as described in terms of 16th century Florence,
and when understood in Lorenzo's/Musset's terms, offers deadly
insight into what had happened to Romanticism's political idealism
over the course of the decades since the French Revolution until the
time of the repressive political world of the 1830's.

The two greatest chroniclers in 19th century drama of this demise
of political faith were the French Musset in *Lorenzaccio* and his exact
contemporary, the German Buchner in *Danton's Death* (the two
tragedies were written a year apart.) All four—the playwrights Musset
and Buchner, their historical inventions, Lorenzo and Danton—
underwent the same agonizing loss of their sustaining credo, the
impossibility of sustaining it ending in their disillusion with political

gestures of any kind, and their embrace of a desperate negativity that was closer to mourning than to outright submission. [For Danton's resolution, see II, #61].

Lorenzo (like the revolutionary idealist Buchner, who in his pamphlet, *The Hessian Courier*, called the peasants in his province to rebellion) had in his earlier innocence determined to sabotage the tyrant Alessandro and restore republican government to Florence. His strategy: to bore from within, to become the accomplice of the hated tyrant, to win his complete confidence, and with that accomplished, to assassinate him. His justification? The Republican cause, the people's cause, the cause of Liberty. But so close to the core of power, Lorenzo, like Danton, makes debilitating discoveries. Every act, every gesture, generates a chain of consequences, and once so generated, the actor himself becomes to a degree the witness/victim more than the generating agent of that chain of events. In Lorenzo's case, the acts he's performed for and along with Alessandro have radically changed who he is. But changed him in a double sense: first, they've awakened in him Alessandro's own appetites; he has now, at the least, an unquenchable thirst for wine, women and song. He loves, in effect, his corruption; it's now him. Second, and more punishing, he's learned humanity's bottom nature. "The hand," Lorenzo explains, "that has once raised the veil that hides the truth can never let it fall again," not since "humanity lifted her underclothes and exposed to me her monstrous nudity." And here, one must be careful not to confuse Musset's response to that "monstrous nudity" with Hamlet's or Lear's sense of it as nauseating corruption. The evidence is the same, but for Musset, it is not nauseating; it is simply so, it is what humanity is, and invites from him no jeremiads. But what, then, is it, and why is that knowledge paralyzing to political idealism's hopes? Here we reach the ultimately determining factor in political idealism's failure at the time. Over and above "appetites" of Alessandro's kind, "Humanity's veil" lifted exhibits a trunkful of irreducible inanities and irrelevancies to politically moral behavior. "I've known men as they really are, and it's made me wonder who I'm striving for," concludes Lorenzo. What are these inanities and irrelevancies? "Citizens" filter events through myths, games and superstitions (as in Wallenstein's "cradle" creeds in II, #53), which eternally fill their minds, repositioning events into dreamlike contexts (Musset parodies some of them in Act 5, Sc. 5). They convert events (such as Lorenzo's assassination of the tyrant) quickly into historical drama, putting them outside, and irrelevant to, daily living. And when they make themselves actors (with the practical encouragement of rewards and favors) within that mythic historical drama, their action (the mob's assassination in turn of Lorenzo) diverts altogether the possibility of pursuing the direction of his original intent.

The case, then, of Lorenzo, is overwhelmingly, tragically complex. His view now of moral action is that it is essentially meaningless, and of himself, that he's become irredeemably evil, satanic, for no purpose. But the naive intention he had in the first place—a political assassination as a gesture toward liberty—still, and alone, holds vestigial justification for his existence, though it's become meaningless for him. Even more damning for him is his foregone conclusion: after his gesture will be made, the chances that it will be understood as a patriotic gesture toward liberation, or that it will initiate such a movement, is almost nil. The very Republicans, the very populace, for whom the gesture is presumably made, will convert it at once into a historic/mythic or a simply criminal act, and the course of events, and of history, will not only diverge from it, but be instigated by it toward paths entirely irrelevant to it.

All this is, in fact, what happens as a result of Lorenzo's act. The Florentine government quickly repositions itself, elects a new ducal head, offers huge bounty for the murder of Alessandro's assassin, destroys in numbers suspected Republicans, who, among them, also produce political opportunists in exile, and either rally or cow the remaining populace into continued, uninterrupted submissiveness.

And all this is, again, precisely what Lorenzo anticipates. Before his murderous act, he has a long session with a remarkably upright member of the Republican opposition to Alessandro's rule, Philip Strozzi, the head of one of the most prominent and formerly powerful families in Florence. He believes still, as Lorenzo is no longer capable of believing, in the cause of freedom, and judges all men in black and white. And he has supposed, as Lorenzo has always reassured him and also once believed, that his alliance with Alessandro was political stealth, unwavering and uncorrupted in its intent. The colloquy between them is like one between the first generation of Romantics who thrilled to the early slogans of the French Revolution ("Bliss was it then to be alive," wrote Wordsworth, "and to be young was very heaven") and this third generation of Romantics, or rather Anti-Romantics, who had witnessed the disintegration of those hopes and had suffered, on the one hand, the spectacle of their repression, and on the other, their cynical co-option into official rhetorical fantasy. Lorenzo tries to explain to Philip Strozzi, who is unwilling to lose his uncorrupted faith, the realities of his education in coming face to face with the "monstrous nudity." The issue at hand is practical. Lorenzo is intent on preserving old Strozzi from taking up his rusty ideological sword in a renewed brave fight against tyranny, and to leave what remains of that fight to Lorenzo alone, and to his futile and yet still inherently meaningful, and in a sense memorial, gesture.

> LORENZO
>
> Am I Satan? God in Heaven, I remember the first girl I ever seduced. In all decency, I should have wept with her, and I would have, if she hadn't begun to laugh. And I remember when I first took on the role of a modern Brutus, disguised in the uniform of the vast brotherhood of vice, I felt like a small boy in the armor of a great giant. I thought that corruption was a visible stigma, and that only monsters bore the signs of it written across their brows. So I began by proclaiming that all my twenty years of virtue before this time were nothing but a suffocating mask. And then, Philip, I saw life for the first time, and looked at people face to face, and they were all the same. All their masks fell before my

eyes, and humanity lifted her underclothes and showed me, as one of her own, her monstrous nudity. I saw men as they are, and I wondered, "For whom am I striving?" When I wandered the streets of Florence, with my shadow beside me. I looked around me, looked for the faces that could give me courage, and I asked myself, "When I've done the terrible deed, will this one, or this one, profit by it?" I saw the Republicans in their studies, and visited their shops. I watched, I listened, I eavesdropped on the conversations of the people, I took note of how tyranny affected them, and I went to their patriotic banquets where I drank the wine out of which came their noble, lofty speeches of revolution. I've swallowed, between kisses, the most virtuous and the most tender of tears. And always I was watching for humanity to show a visible sign of honesty in it's face — like a lover scrutinising the face of his bride-to-be anticipating their wedding day.

I know you see me as a despiser of men. But that's unjust. I know perfectly well that there are good men, but what cause are they serving, what are they doing, what are they accomplishing? What good is a troubled conscience if the arm is dead? There are ways of seeing everything as good. A dog, for example, is a faithful friend, the most loyal, the most loving. But the tongue that licks his master's hand with such devotion smells of rot from his neighbor's refuse, where he's been happily wallowing in mounds of corruption.

I was virtuous once, Philip. But the hand that once lifted the veil of truth can never let it fall again. It remains aloft, always lifted higher and higher above the head of a man, until his eyes are sealed shut forever by the merciful angel of death.

Marcus Junius **Brutus** (85? - 42 BC): the Republican who with Cassius led the conspiracy to assassinate Julius Caesar

76

LORENZACCIO REHEARSES HIS PROCEDURE FOR MURDERING ALESSANDRO

(1834) ALFRED DE MUSSET, Lorenzaccio, *tr. L. Katz, Act 4, Sc. 9*

In his mind Lorenzo runs through the plan he's to put into execution for the assassination of the tyrant Alessandro dei Medici [see I,
#75]. But his mind is a darting one; he leaps from one consideration
to another, their order following the random flow of his nervous exci-
tation. And so his soliloquy is neither in the classical nor the
Shakespearean mode—ordered, logical, coherent consideration of a
set subject (To be or not to be, on-the-one-hand-on-the-other
hand)—but an anarchic pattern of self-interruptions, each thought
intruding in mid-flight on another, each in a different frame of reference; his assassination agenda; his recurring pang of conscience about
his sister Catherine's losing her virginity in the process (she's the decoy
that's to entice Alessandro into Lorenzo's house and bedroom); his
mother's dying of shame; his listening for the hour to strike; his making mental rearrangements of the murder protocol—whether in a
lighted or unlighted bedroom, whether with his victim sitting, lying
or standing, whether to stab from front or back; his contempt for the
impotent Republican factions that talk forever but never act; his
worry about Alessandro's having thought up another underclothes
armor like the chain-mail Lorenzo himself had to steal away before
this night; his rendering Alessandro's sword useless by tying it up in its
own belt; whether in the interim during this hour's wait, to stop at the
tavern for a drink, or to just sit down on the street-bench out of
fatigue

He imagines meeting Alessandro in the tavern: "Evening,
mignon," Alessandro might say. "Why don't you drink a glass with
[Alessandro's possible companion, his spy] Giomo?" Then he quotes
another question Alessandro might ask: Is Lorenzo's bedroom "quiet

and secluded [for uninterrupted fornication]? Can anything be heard in the neighboring rooms?" Lorenzo chuckles over this one because for days, or longer, he's had mock fencing sessions in his bedroom with his assistant in the murder, Scoronconcolo. During these practices they would yell bloody murder so that if Alessandro screamed during his assassination, the neighbors would suppose there was another "fencing session" going on, and pay it no mind. And then— a magnificent note introduced by Musset, which deserves extended comment*—Lorenzo notices in the light drifting out of the portico of a nearby church, something entirely irrelevant to his preoccupation: some workmen carving a crucifix.

Finally, Lorenzo, the critical moment for the murder having arrived, is suddenly seized by an odd, not to say impossibly imbecilic, response: complete relief. He's ready to dance, to hop about like a bird. He calls out as though to his tyrant master Alessandro, using their mock term of endearment for one another ("mignon," meaning anything from "my dear little one" to "my whore"), and in very high good humor sings out: Tra la la, get dressed in your best for your night of virgin debauchery, but let me warn you…!

Responses of altogether unhinged imbecilic irrelevance, which in Elizabethan/Jacobean drama signified madness, in these grim 19th century Romantic/Anti-Romantics, signified—in the face of the norm, the rational—the grimly fitting.

---

*In the intrusion of the vision of workmen carving a crucifix, Musset introduces a device memorable in, among others, Shakespeare's King Lear and Kafka's The Trial: the sudden shriveling of the dramatic/emotional space of the central event when it is placed into the context of the infinitely larger space of the world's unnoticing, normal, daily routines. That central dramatic moment, in relation to the world outside its frame, is instantaneously redefined as, however huge in itself, also tiny. The recognition of the enormity of a scene's tragic grip, and simultaneously of its nothing impact when distanced by the rest of life, is shown in this subtle, ironic self-diminishment to enormous effect in several remarkable moments in literature.

In King Lear, when Gloucester's son Edgar is forestalling his blind father's attempt at suicide, he pretends to have brought him to the edge of a high cliff. He indicates the frightening height of the non-existent cliff by describing the fishermen doing their daily chores so far below that they seem to be dots on the shore's edge. In The Trial, when Joseph K is being escorted to the city park where he is to be executed, he glances up for a moment at an apartment building, and sees the lighted windows of the workingmen's flats who before dawn are getting ready to leave for their day's jobs. For a moment, dramatic intensification gives way to its corrective attenuation.

(A square at night. Enter LORENZO.)

LORENZO

I'll tell him it's because of her modesty, and I'll douse the light. It
happens every day. A virgin bride makes her husband promise to
do it in the dark before she'll walk into the nuptial chamber. And
Catherine is understood to be a virgin. Poor child! If she's not,
who is? The shock of this could kill my mother. It might. So be
it. Patience! An hour to go; the clock's just struck. But if you're
anxious to? — No, why should you be? — Shall I take it away? I
could leave a candle. The first time a woman yields, it's very simple. — Come in and get warm. Oh, Lord, it's just a young girl's
notion. — How could anyone suppose this is all set up for a murder? They'll be stunned, everyone, even Philip,

(The moon rises.)

Pale moon, there you are! If the Republicans had any guts, after
tonight, there'd be a revolution in the city tomorrow. But Pierre is
a nothing, only ambitious. The Rucellai are the only ones worth
anything. Oh their words, their words, their everlasting words! If
there's a God in heaven, he must be laughing himself to — well.
It's funny. It is really funny. These incapacitated talkers! These
great warriors against the already-dead; these terrifying battering-
rams against wide-open doors! Oh, you armless, helpless men! —
No, no, I won't take away the light. I'll go straight for his heart
Yes, good, he'll see himself being murdered. Blood of Christ,
won't all the good citizens be staring out of their windows tomorrow! Unless he's wearing chain mail under his shirt. That
miserable inventor of chain mail! Wrestling with God or the Devil
is nothing compared to making a hole through those bits of iron
locked so tight together by the filthy hands of that filthy armorer.
— I'll come in after him. He'll lay his sword down there — or
maybe there, yes, on the sofa. Then I'll tangle his belt around the
hilt of his sword, that's no problem. Then — if he would lie
down, that would be perfect. Lying, sitting or standing? No, sit
ting, oh yes. And then, first, I'll walk out. Scoronconcolo is
waiting in the study. We come in together. But I don't want him
to have his back toward me. No, I want to come at him face to
face. — Quiet . Peace. — It's time, the clock is striking. I'll stop
off at a tavern. I hardly noticed, but I'm shivering with cold. I'll

order a bottle of wine. No, no, I won't drink. Anyway, the taverns
are all closed. Where the devil should I go? — Is she a good girl?
Yes, she really is. But in her nightgown? No, not likely. Poor
Catherine! It would be sad if my mother died because of this. But
if I had told her my plan, would it have done any good? Instead
of consoling her, she would have been screaming, "Crime!
Crime!" till her last breath. Why am I still on my feet? I'm ready
to drop.

(*He sits*)

Sitting under the chestnut tree, so long ago, with Philip's beautiful daughter! Her white hands! How many days have I spent
sitting under trees? So much at peace. That beautiful landscape at
Cafaggiuolo. Concierge's daughter, lovely Jeannette, spreading her
linens to dry on the grass, and the goats trampling all over them.
Jeannette chasing them. The white goat with the long slender feet
always came back.

(*A clock strikes*)

I most goit's time. — Evening, mignon. Come, have a drink with
Giomo! Ah, that's good wine! — Imagine if he took it into his
head to ask, "Is your room isolated, quiet?. Can your neighbors
bear anything?" That's been well taken care of, no, the neighbors
wont be alarmed. It would be particularly funny if he asked that.
— I was wrong about the hour, it's only half past. What's that
light from under the church porch? Men working there, hewing
stones. It takes a lot of grit to cul and chisel like that. Ah, they're
making a crucifix, and they're going at it with such zeal! God! I
hope the stone thing jumps up and grabs them by the throat and
— What's happening to me? I have an incredible urge to dance! If
I let myself go, I'd hop like a sparrow over all that plaster and fly
over all those wooden beams. Ah. mignon! Put on your brand
new gloves and your very best clothes. Sing tra-la-la, and look
your very finest for your beautiful, beautiful bride! But I tell you
this in your ear: look out, look out for her little shiny knife!

(*He runs off.*)

Rucellai: Republican nobles in opposition to the tyrant Alessandro di Medici

77

TRIGAEUS, ON HIS WAY TO HEAVEN, BEGS HIS MOUNTED BEETLE NOT TO NOTICE SHIT IN THE WORLD BELOW

(421 BC) ARISTOPHANES, Peace, *ad. L. Katz*

Trigaeus wants peace. He's given up on getting it through ordinary channels, and so he's resolved to go to Zeus in heaven to put an end to the war. He's tried to make the trip once before: built ladders to heaven, but fell and ended with a fractured skull. His new idea is this: to fatten up a dung beetle, get him to spread his wings, and by such transportation fly to heaven on the beetle's back. The problem is, the dung beetle not only lives on shit, but loves it—the very smell of it steers him in its direction.

So Trigaeus, once in flight, begs the Athenian audience to control itself for three days, neither fart nor shit, or the beetle will zoom directly toward the smell and toss him.

The speech is going on during Trigaeus' flight. Trembling, he tries to keep the beetle's nose tilted up toward heaven, but there are dangers below. Flying over a cesspool, the beetle gets tempted. Then a man is taking a shit in the street near the whorehouses. Then—worst possibility—Trigaeus himself, with so much wind raised around him in flight, is afraid he'll shit himself in fright, and warns the machinist controlling the crane (to which the beetle assembly is attached backstage) to be steady, or he'll be beetle food himself.

Aristophanes' hairbrained mode of comedy did not survive Western classical tradition, but stayed alive in its underbelly, surfacing in *commedia dell'arte*, in *Ubu Roi*, in Dario Fo, and other brilliant examples.

TRIGAEUS

Gently, gently, easy, beetle! Don't start off so cocky, and don't be
so sure of your prowess! Work up a little sweat first. Flap your
wings a lot to loosen up your joints. And don't, whatever you do,
fart, I beg you, don't, or I'd just as soon you stayed at home in the
stable. — Silence, silence, everybody! We're taking otr

I'm doing this for the good of all the Greeks, so no discouraging
talk, no skeptics, and all you Athenians out there, keep very still,
and shut down all your drains and outhouses, and most important of all, put a cork up all your assholes, so this beetle and I can
make it up to Zeus with no accidents. It can be done, oh yes. I
know it from Aesop's Fables, where only the beetle could fly up to
heaven, where it took revenge on the eagle and broke its eggs?
Remember? — So goodbye! Goodbye! Remember, Athenians, no
farting or shitting for three days, none, or this beetle will nosedive
straight for the shit, it's his food, he can't help it, and we'd go
down, and I'd land flat on my — let's not even think about it. —
Now, beetle, my little Pegasus, nose straight up in the air, no
looking down, no smelling — oh my God, what are you doing?
— Cesspools! Easy, easy, no, don't look down, up, up, up in the
air, stretch those wings, we're heading straight for the palace of
Zeus, with those ears pricked up, and that golden bridle jingling,
straight, straight to the heavens, and — what? — NO! You down
there! What are you doing? He's taking a crap in the Piraeus, right
near the whorehouses! Do you want me to die, do you want to
kill me? *Bury* it, bury your shit, cover it up with a great big
mound of earth, and plant — plant thyme all over it, and lots of
perfume, all over, cover it. If I crash, if I die, your town pays. It's a
five talent fine — and that'll be thanks to your stupid ass.

A-ah!! — What are you laughing at, you idiot propman! You
scared the life out of me! Watch what you're doing with that
machine! I think I'm going to — I got so scared I might — I
think I'm going to shit food for the beetle, and then, oh my god!
— Ah, ah, thank the gods! There it is, the halls of Zeus! We're

here! Open the doors, open the —

Ah, Hermes!

(The beetle lands.)

Pegasus: the mythological winged horse **brothels of Piraeus**: the red-light district of Pirrhea, the port of Athens, indicates the direction in which Trigaeus is flying **talent**: currency in ancient Greece; five talents is quite a lot of money

Comedy
ITALIAN RENAISSANCE

78

CALLIMACO REPORTS ON HIS PERFECT NIGHT WITH LUCREZIA

(c1515-20) MACHIAVELLI, Mandragola, *tr. Kenneth and Laura Richards, Act 5, Sc. 4*

Pragmatic Machiavelli constructed an efficient plot that goes straight to its mark: a young man, Callimaco, falling in love with the portrait of a Florentine lady married to an old fool of a husband, flies back from Paris to win her. Reckoning the obstacles to winning her bed—that she is married, that she has a stupid but suspicious husband, and that she is virtuous—he enlists the aid of first his servant, then a parasite, then the husband himself, then her confessor, and finally her mother. All of them contribute handily to the trick—a pretense that the mandrake root, an aphrodisiac which on its first use kills, but used thereafter would guarantee the husband blessed renewal of potency and a son, the trick which puts Callimaco into her bed, and into her love. Each potential confederate's resistance to this iniquity is handily overcome by direct and blatant appeal to self-interest.

The cool assumption of this principle that so perfectly oils the wheels of the plot and rides Callimaco to his success is only slightly qualified in this summing-up speech in which Callimaco confesses to a slight pang of conscience operating until three o'clock in the morning. But the principle is thoroughly reconfirmed by him and—as he reports in Lucrezia's response—by her as well, surrendering as she does virtuous principle for eternally rewarding policy.

CALLIMACO

As I've already told you, my dear Ligurio, I didn't begin to be happy till past three o'clock this morning, because, though I *had* had a lot of pleasure, I hadn't really enjoyed it. But then I revealed to her who I was, and made her appreciate the love I bore her, and went on to tell her how easily—because of her husband's simplemindedness—we should be able to live together in happiness without the slightest scandal. I finished by promising her that whenever it pleased God to translate her husband I should take her as my wife. She thought this over and having, among other things, tasted the difference between my performance and Nicia's between, that is, the kisses of a young lover and those of an old husband, she said to me, after heaving several sighs: "Since your guile, my husband's folly, the simple-mindedness of my mother, and the wickedness of my father-confessor have led me to do what I should never have done of my own free will, I will judge it to be Heaven that willed it so, and I cannot find it in myself to refuse what Heaven wishes me to accept. In consequence, I take you for my lord, my master, and my guide. You are my father, my defender, my love and sovereign good, and what my husband wanted on *one* night I want him to have forever. So make friends with him, and go to church this morning, and then come and have dinner with us. You shall come and go as you please, and we shall be able to meet at any time without arousing the least suspicion."

When I heard these words I was ravished by their sweetness. I couldn't tell her more than a fraction of what I wished to say in reply. I'm the happiest and most contented man that ever walked this earth, and if neither Death nor Time take my happiness from me, the saints themselves shall call me blessed!

Let's go into the church.

79

MARCA DETAILS SOBERLY HOW HE AND HIS COMPANIONS CHEATED THE LANDLORD OUT OF A BANQUET

(c1581) GIORDANO BRUNO, Il Candelaio, *tr, J. R. Hale, Act 3, Sc. 8*

The great Bruno, philosopher, skeptic and martyr, once lapsed into the writing of comedy. In *Il Candelaio,* his efforts breached the limits of the genre. Plots stumble over plots, and each, with no regard for forward motion, is halted dead in its tracks by passages such as this one—lengthy non-sequiturs ranging from editorials to anecdotes, which, apart from Bruno's depraved scenes of pure farce, constitute the wisdom, the wit, the essentially profligate, Rabelaisian flavor of the play. Since the comedy assumes the proportions and the leisure of a novel, a single passage of dialogue might pass for a finished short story, a finished pseudo-philosophical essay, a finished sermon or dia-tribe. Marca's is a short story; his intent in telling it is used up in the telling; it is not forging forward; it is not advancing the plot; on the contrary, it is hindering it.

Marca is tertiary among the play's nineteen characters, the hench-man of a secondary character, Sanguino, who is pretending to be, and is disguised as, a constable complexly involved in duping the three fools whose undoing makes up the play's three interlocked main plots. The slightness of Marca's significance in the plots enjoins no restric-tion on the prominence of his monologues.

MARCA
Well, then, yesterday evening, at the Cerriglio inn, we had a good meal and then we sent out the landlord to get some nuts and sweets and raisins and things, you know, to nibble at, because he didn't have any in the house. Well, when we couldn't think what to ask for next, one of the lads staged a fainting fit, and when the landlord ran up

with the vinegar, I said "Aren't you ashamed, you shabby little man! Go and bring orange brandy, malmsey, and juniper bitters." The landlord started muttering I don't know what under his breath and then yelled out, "Devil take it, do you think you're dukes and marquises? Are you the sort to throw money away like this? What's to happen about the bill? I don't know. It's not right to ask for things like that in an ordinary public house." "Scoundrel," said I, "rascal, thief, do you think you have scum like yourself to deal with? Don't try to be smart, you shameless turd, you twisty liar," said I. Then, very fine, we got up from the table and grabbed ourselves a spit each, one of those ten-foot-long one, you know, with the meat stuck on them, and the landlord got hold of a great pike, and two of the servants had a couple of rusty swords. There were six of us, and our spits were longer than the pike, but we thought we'd pick up dish covers and use them as shields and some of us put pots on our heads to serve as helmets and fully armed, we backed out, defending ourselves down the stairs toward the door, though we kept pretending to attack.

When the landlord saw how bold we were and yet how we mysteriously seemed to give ground all the time, instead of triumphing over us, he began to have suspicions, and lowering his pike he called off the servants, as he didn't want to start a real quarrel. And he said to us. "Gentle sirs, forgive me, I've no desire to offend you, on my honor. Pay me and go in peace!"

"And you want to kill us, traitor," said I; and with this we were outside the door. Then he realized that we weren't going to fall for his compliments and bowing and scraping, and took up his pike again and called up the servants and his sons and his wife. There was a fine racket. The landlord shouted, "Pay me! Pay me!" The others yelled, "Rogues! Rascals! Dirty thieves!" But for all that no one ran at us because the darkness was on our side. Still, not wanting to come up against the innkeeperly wrath, the fury of mine host, we took refuge in a room at the Carmelites', and we still, in fact, owe them three days' rent.

malmsey: a strong, sweet wine originally made in Greece, now in Madeira
juniper bitters: a liquor made from bitter herbs, particularly juniper berries
Carmelites: Roman Catholic cloistered order for women

80

SANGUINO TAKES PRIVATE COMFORT IN HIS PARABLE OF HOW THE TRICKED CAN BECOME THE TRICKSTER

(c1581) GIORDANO BRUNO, Il Candelaio, *tr., J. R. Hale, Act 2, Sc. 4*

Sanguino, an adventurer who wanders into the plot from elsewhere, becomes its key: he will subsequently disguise himself as a constable and bring about, in the guise of authorized punishment, the duping and divesting of coin and even of clothing, of the play's three prime fools [see I, #79]. Here, he is justifying to the bawd Vittoria his motive for playing a trick on the miser Bonifacio, one of the prime fools. But his justification is a bit roundabout: a long parable, very much in the vein of Aesop, about animals behaving with the imperfection of humans, demonstrating how much and with what malevolence he will get back at Bonifacio, who has already with malevolence gotten back at him.

Its ultimate purpose, to be sure, informs his telling of the parable, but Bruno's intellect and his understanding of the relation between saying and reason for saying is undermined if the parable is delivered with its "motivational" function intrusively visible and intrusively uppermost. Sanguino, with the rhetorical bravado of all of Bruno's dupers—whether as knowing as Sanguino or as self-duped as Bonifacio—is exhibiting his "presentational" self-assurance, his abiding certainty of the centrality of his person to the scheme of things, his spreading of his wings over the surface of allotted time—that kind of ease of delivery. And for the sake of the telling, more than for the sake of the reason for the telling. The wit of Bruno is as evident in his posture *toward* his characters—his uniform sneer at their self-aggrandisement, their self-display in, as here, their verbal largesse—as in the follies of their conduct.

SANGUINO

Once upon a time the lion and the donkey kept company, and going on a journey together, agreed that when they came to a river they would help each other over, first the donkey carrying the lion, then the lion helping the donkey. Making for Rome, then, and there being neither bridge nor boat at the river Garigliano, the donkey took the lion on his back, and as he swam toward the other bank, the lion, for fear of slipping off, dug his claws deeper and deeper into the donkey's skin till they reached the poor creature's very bones. But the poor wretch, making a virtue of necessity, went on as best he could without a word. All he did, when they came to dry land, was to twitch his coat a little and rub his back two or three times in the warm sand, and on they went. A week later, when they came back, it was the lion's turn to carry the donkey, who, to stop sliding into the water, took the scruff of the lion's neck in his teeth, and as that wasn't enough to hold him firm, he pushed his instrument, or rather his—well, you understand me—into the—let's call it the vacant space under the lion's tail so that for the lion it was worse than a woman in labor, and he cried out, "Ow! Ouch! Ouch! Eee-ouch! Traitor!" To which the donkey replied, with a straight face and dignified tone, "Patience, my brother, you know this is the only hook I've got to hang on by." So the lion had to put up with it till he got to the other side. The moral? *Omnio rero vecissitudo este,* in turn the tricked becomes the trickster, and no one is such a donkey as not to turn the tables when the chance comes. A few days ago, Bonifacio was upset by a trick I played on him: today, just as I thought he'd forgotten it, he has treated me worse than the donkey did the lion, and I'm not going to leave it at that.

omnio rero vecissitudo este, Lat: all things are subject to change

81

BERNARDO EXPLAINS TO HIS LOVE THE VIRTUE OF FORGETTING ABOUT HONOR

(c1581) GIORDANO BRUNO, Il Candelaio, *tr. J. R. Hale, Act 5, Sc. 11*

B ernardo, a painter hired by the old miser Bonifacio to do his por-trait, is more enraptured by Bonifacio's beautiful young wife than by his commission [see I, #79]. To win her, he methodically traps the old man in a maze of plot entanglements—disguising the old man as himself and his wife as the courtesan the old man desires, disguising a clutch of rogues as constables who along with his wife catch the old man at the critical moment of seduction, and then accusing the old man of slanderously impersonating himself. With the old miser under "arrest" and away, Bernardo finally gets to work on the beautiful Carubina.

But Bruno's skepticism colors his dialogue as much as it does his speculative treatises. Not a word Bernardo says has any bearing on his meaning, which is under and to one side of the words. Nor are his words intended as persuasions at face-value of Carubina, who, he assumes, understands the nature of this kind of discourse. The hyper-bole of his language is thoroughly corrected by the directness of his tone and look which say, concurrently, "You *are* following, no?" As it happens, she does, and although answering his suspect rapture and equally suspect arguments with virtuous objections, she wanders off, at scene's end, with Bernardo, the two in untroubled accord.

BERNARDO

To serve you, my love, I would throw myself over a thousand precipices. And now my fortune and good luck—and please the gods may you confirm it—have brought me so close to you. I beg, by the devotion I feel and have always felt, that you will have pity on a heart that has been so deeply wounded by your divine eyes. I love you; I adore you. If heaven had only granted you to me instead of this ungrateful and stupid man who doesn't appreciate the miracle of your beauty, my breast would never have held a spark of love for anyone but you, who live there now.

Sweet goddess, if you have ever felt the flame of love—and what noble, generous, and affectionate heart has not?—don't take what I say amiss; don't believe, don't entertain the thought for a single moment, that it's because I don't value your honor—I would shed my blood a thousand times for it—that I ask you this: to quench the passion that consumes me and which I cannot believe will lessen even with death.

Life of my life, you know what constitutes honor and dishonor, I am sure. Honor is only reputation, what people think of one. As long as they think you honorable, you are. Honor is the good opinion other people have of us; while that continues, so does our honor. It is not what we are or what we do that makes us honored or dishonored, but just what people think of us, how we stand in their eyes.

Hope of my life. Don't let heaven have made you lovely in vain, for though it has been lavish of beauty and grace, it has been mean as well, in not marrying you to a man who could appreciate them, and cruel to me, for making me distracted by them and die a thousand deaths each day. You should mind more about keeping me alive, my love, than about losing some fragment of your honor. I will gladly kill myself—if grief doesn't do it for me—should cruel fortune deny what is dearer to me than life, and which I have almost within my grasp. Oh, life of this distracted soul, your honor won't suffer if you deign to save my life, but it will, if I die because of your cruelty.

82

SCARAMURE WANTS WHORES AND WHORE-MONGERS ENTIRELY ABSOLVED OF REPROACH

(c1581) GIORDANO BRUNO, Il Candelaio, *tr. J. R. Hale, Act 5, Sc. 18*

Scaramure, having earlier taken on the role of alchemist/magician to cheat the miser Bonifacio out of his money, is now in league with Sanguino, who is currently disguised as a Captain of the Watch, and is holding Bonifacio on the charge, among other charges, of consorting with a prostitute. (As it happens, his own wife who was then so disguised—see I, #81.) Since the old fool still possesses, miraculously, eight guineas, the clothes he's wearing, and his rings, there's more roguery still to be done by the two rogues. And so while Sanguino plays the adamant man of law refusing to give legal ground, Scaramure plays the compassionate defender-in-court of the culprit, and addresses before 'His Honor' one charge of culpability at a time—first, that of whoremonger. In arguing his defense, Scaramure takes the normal privilege of a Bruno character—unobstructed verbal effluence, adding knowingly to the misery of Bonifacio, who all through his defender's lengthy defense is desperate to go to the bathroom.

Scaramure's argument follows the laws of logic characteristic of Italian Renaissance classical comedy [see I, #79]—that morality can be as persuasive upside down as right side up. The techniques of persuasion are here, of course, considerably elaborated and distended, but still follow precept, example, proof accomplished, and still continue to demonstrate the inherent message of the skeptical Brunos and Machiavellis, that church and legal argument can comfortably accomodate any immediate need of the sufficiently urbane.

SCARAMURE

Your Honor knows that in Italy it is not as in certain countries to the
north where they make prostitution a crime, either because of the cold
there, or too much religious zeal, or because of the sordid avarice of
the officers of justice. Here in Naples, for instance, or in Rome or
Venice, founts and mirrors of every sort of nobility as they are to the
whole world, not only are whores, or courtesans, as we say, permitted,
not only are they tolerated by the civil and municipal law, but brothels
are founded, just like convents.

In Rome, because the whores were scattered all over the city, in 1569
His Holiness ordered them all to be brought together on pain of being
whipped, and gave them a street to themselves which was locked off at
night.

I say nothing of Venice, where by the magnanimity and liberality of
the most illustrious Republic—think what you like of certain Mr.
Head-in-the-airs who have themselves castrated for tuppence to
improve their voices—whores are exempted of all penalties; they are
even better off than ordinary citizens, though there are so many—for
the greater and finer the city the more they are—that if they did pay a
small tax, there would be enough to fill a second treasury almost as
full as the first. There is no doubt that if the Senate wished to stoop to
doing as others do, it could make the city a good deal richer than it is,
but because the text says "by the sweat of your brow" and not "by the
sweat of—" well, it has refrained from doing it. What is more, their
courtesans are highly respected, as you can see from the recent law
that prevents, under heavy penalty, any person, base or noble, whatever his condition, from daring to reproach or insult them. And that has
never been done for any other sort of women.

I conclude that the true greatness of Italy resides in these three cities,
for among all the others, even the greatest is far behind the least of
these. So we see that prostitutes in Naples, Venice, and Rome, *ideste* in
all Italy, are allowed, nay, encouraged, to have their own statutes, laws,
taxes, and other privileges. And so, in consequence, those who go to

prostitutes should not be hounded or punished by the law—and not only that; the law should assiduously refrain from troubling, persecuting, or arresting those who frequent ladies of honor, for our rulers think it to be a barbarous thing to take the lust that a man of reputation and standing might have in his heart and brand it on his forehead.

In conclusion, I point out to Your Honor that Master Bonifacio's intemperance was caused by a woman, who, be she respectable or a whore, should not be the cause whereby a man of position and breeding should be exposed as a jailbird, *etcetera*, which could lead others to be greatly compromised into the bargain. I think I have said enough to appraise Your Honor, as a man of the world, how the matter stands.

ideste, Lat: that is

Comedy

ELIZABETHAN/JACOBEAN

83

SLITGUT TAKES NOTE OF SEVERAL PASSENGERS CRAWLING OUT OF THE THAMES AFTER SHIPWRECK

(1604) MARSTON, CHAPMAN and JONSON, *Eastward, Ho!*, *Act 4, Sc. 1*

On the very day when several suspect characters have set off on the Thames in a boat destined for the colony of Virginia in America, Slitgut, an apprentice to a butcher, has to climb up a pole ("this…tree…all fruit and no leaves") set above the river to attach a sign-post advertising his master's shop.

1) This spot above the Thames is known as Cuckold's Haven, and as 'homage' to its name, London butchers hoist above it their traditional emblem, a pair of ox horns. The young stripling Slitgut disclaims personal connection with the emblem or the place, 'for there are none but married men cuckolds.'

2) But the higher he climbs, the more he feels a wild storm, a positive tempest blowing, and worries that his ox horn will be blown out of his hand, then notes that the Thames is churning, as uncontrolled as a wild horse—"the bit is out of her mouth"—that any passengers "on her back now" are in serious danger.

3) Still, storm or no, he manages to get the ox horn posted facing London Bridge—the right exposure to do most good—and that task done, settles down on the pole to watch the Thames "in her desperate lunacy."

4) And sure enough, he sees a boat wrecked, and a passenger afloat, being washed toward Cuckold's Haven. When the man is just below, Slitgut hollers encouragement to him, and then instructions: Stand up, you're in shallow water. But the poor man in his nightcap loses footing, falls back in the water, flailing. He gets his footing again, and finally makes it to the shore—an old man in a fix a younger man wouldn't welcome.

5) The old man safe, another floating passenger comes into view further upstream, close to St. Katharine's Home for Fallen Women. In woman's clothing, she has the advantage of their billowing, and they appear to support her above water until—a wave! She might be drowning! But she escapes the wave, "swims like a mermaid" to shore, and is rescued by a boy who lowers a ladder into the water. Because she's beautiful, reasons Slitgut, "the billows durst not devour her."

Slitgut has little reason to know it, but it was a sort of ship of fools that was making its way in the storm up the Thames toward America, and stopped in their journey by shipwreck before they were even out of London. And the shipwrecked passengers might have preferred the relief of being drowned to the shame they are to suffer at being saved. Slitgut, perched on his pole, utterly unaware that he is the observer and chronicler of this climactic event of the comedy, provides in effect a long-shot camera view of the scene, as ignorant of its import as if he were in fact a camera: a brilliant device invented by three brilliant comic playwrights for staging an unstageable but necessary scene.

> *(Enter Slitgut, with a pair of ox horns, discovering*
> *Cuckold's Haven above.)*

SLITGUT

All hail, fair haven of married men only, for there are none but married men cuckolds! For my part, I presume not to arrive here, but in my master's behalf (a poor butcher of Eastcheap) who sends me to set up (in honor of Saint Luke) these necessary ensigns of his homage. And up I got this morning, thus early, to get up to the top of this famous tree, that is all fruit and no leaves, to advance this crest of my master's occupation.

Up then; heaven and Saint Luke bless me, that I be not blown into the Thames as I climb, with this furious tempest. 'S light, I think the Devil be abroad, in likeness of a storm, to rob me of my horns! Hark how he roars! Lord, what a coil the Thames keeps! She bears some injust burthen, I believe, that she kicks and curvets thus to cast it.

Heaven bless all honest passengers that are upon her back now; for the bit is out of the mouth, I see, and she will run away with 'em!

So, so, I think I have made it look the right way; it runs against London Bridge, as it were, even full butt. And now let me discover, from this lofty prospect, what pranks the rude Thames plays in her desperate lunacy.

O me, here's a boat has been cast away hard by! Alas, alas, see one of her passengers labouring for his life to land at this haven here! Pray heaven he may recover it! His next land is even just under me; hold out yet a little, whatsoever thou art; pray, and take a good heart to thee. 'Tis a man; take a man's heart to thee; yet a little further, get up o' they legs, man; now 't is shallow enough. So, so, so! Alas, he's down again! Hold thy wind, father; 't is a man in a nightcap. So! Now he's got up again; now he's past the worst; yet, thanks be to heaven, he comes toward me pretty and strongly. Poor man, how weak he is! The weak water has rushed away his strength. What young planet reigns now, trow, that old men are so foolish? What a desperate young swagger would have been abroad such a weather as this upon the water?

Ay me, see another remnant of this unfortunate shipwrack, or some other! A woman, i' faith, a woman! Though it be almost at St. Katharine's, I discern it to be a woman, for all her body is above the water, and her clothes swim about her most handsomely. O, they bear her up most bravely! Has not a woman reason to love the taking up of her clothes the better while she lives, for this? Alas, how busy the rude Thames is about her! A pox o' that wave! It will drown her, i' faith, 't will drown her! Cry God mercy, she has scaped it, I thank heaven she has scaped it! O how she swims like a mermaid! Some vigilant body look out and save her. That's well said; just where the priest fell in, there's one sets down a ladder, and goes to take her up. God's blessing o' thy heart, boy! Now take her up in thy arms and to bed with her. She's up, she's up! She's a beautiful woman, I warrant her, the billows durst not devour her.

coil: disturbance **curvets**: twists **butt**: end, goal; and so, final position **trow**: pray

84

MOSCA EJECTS VOLPONE'S WOULD-BE HEIRS
(1606) BEN JONSON, Volpone, *Act 5, Sc. 1*

Volpone the Venetian Magnifico loves gold as much as life itself, and with his servant Mosca conceives of a way of adding to his treasure with little more effort than by lying in bed. He gives out that he is dying, and all the avaricious, eager to be remembered as his heirs, flock with gifts — some of gold, some of treasured services, one man of his wife. The procession continues until Volpone, to cap his malicious pleasure, spreads the news that he is dead, having Mosca pretend to be his only reputed heir. While hidden, Volpone enjoys the spectacle of each of them discovering from Mosca the "true" heir, and in the teeth of their chagrin, observes their being mercilessly mocked and thrown out by Mosca.

Mosca performs his duty impeccably with one panting suitor after the other, reminding each one in turn of what their avarice offered in exchange for wealth. Lady Wouldbe, the bribe of her body for Mosca's intercession; Corvino, the offer to Volpone of his wife; Corbaccio, the disinheriting of his son and proposing Mosca's poisoning Volpone; Voltore the advocate, corrupting justice on Volpone's behalf.

The trick works perfectly, to Volpone's delight, but subsequently, Mosca's works better. The pretended "will" Mosca holds declares him Volpone's heir, and Volpone, like the other dupes, is thrown out and left a beggar. Both, in their ensuing struggle, undo one another, and both in the end win nothing but a thoroughly deserved justice.

> MOSCA
> Madam! pray you fairly quit my house.
> Nay, raise no tempest with your looks; but hark you,
> Remember what your ladyship offered me
> To put you in an heir; go to, think on't;

And what you said e'en your best madams did
For maintenance, and why not you? Enough.
Go home, and use the poor Sir Poll, your knight, well,
For fear I tell some riddles. Go, be melancholic.

(Exit Lady Wouldbe.)

Lord! Will not you take your dispatch hence yet?
Methinks of all you should have been th'example.
Why should you stay here? With what thought? What promise?
Hear you, do not you know I know you an ass,
And that you would most fain have been a wittol
If fortune would have let you? That you are
A declared cuckold, on good terms? This pearl,
You'll say, was yours? Right. This diamond?
I'll not deny't, but thank you. Much here else?
It may be so. Why, think that these good works
May help to hide your bad. I'll not betray you;
Although you be but extraordinary,
And have it only in title, it sufficeth.
Go home, be melancholic, too, or mad.

(Exit Corvino.)

Sir. Stop your mouth,
Or I shall draw the only tooth is left.
Are not you he, that filthy, covetous wretch,
With the three legs, that here, in hope of prey,
Have, any time this three year, snuffed about
With your most grov'ling nose; and would have hired
Me to the pois'ning of my patron, sir?
Are you not he that have today in court
Professed the disinheriting of your son?
Perjured yourself? Go home, and die, and stink;
If you but croak a syllable, all comes out.
Away, and call your porters!

(Exit Corbaccio.)

Go, go, stink.
Why, who are you?
What! Who did send for you? O, cry you mercy,
Reverend sir! Good faith, I am grieved for you,
That any chance of mine should thus defeat
Your—I must needs say—most deserving travails.
But I protest, sir, it was cast upon me,
And I could almost wish to be without it,
But that the will o'th'dead must be observed.
Marry, my job is that you need it not;
You have a gift, sir—thank your education—
Will never let you want, while there are men
And malice to breed causes. Would I had
But half the like, for all my fortune, sir.
If I have any suits—as I do hope,
Things being so easy and direct, I shall not—
I will make bold with your obstreperous aid,
Conceive me, for your fee, sir. In meantime,
You that have so much law, I know ha' the conscience
Not to be covetous of what is mine.
Good sir, I thank you for my plate; 'twill help
To set up a young man. Good faith, you look
As you were costive; best go home, and purge, sir.

(exit Voltore.)

wittol: a cuckold who knows and tolerates his wife's infidelity **three legs**: a reference to Corbaccio's walking-stick **travails**, Fr: labors **causes**: lawsuits **costive**: constipated

85

NOVICE RALPH INSPIRES BUMBLING MEN TO BATTLE AND GLORY

(1607) BEAUMONT AND FLETCHER, *The Knight of the Burning Pestle, Act 5, Sc. 2*

A play is about to begin at Blackfriars. The Prologue is interrupted by a Citizen in the audience who wants not this sort of play but one about London shopkeepers. The Actor explains their play is ready and they have no other. But the Citizen's Wife has a remedy: Ralph our apprentice, she volunteers, is a fine actor and will play such a play. He's costumed, and interspersing the scenes that the company is playing, Ralph the Grocer's apprentice, with the encouragement of the Citizen Grocer and his Wife in the audience, interjects his own Don Quixote-ish character into the action. He's a Knight, and for the honor of his trade, his shield bears the sign of a Burning Pestle. With two other apprentices, he sets out, a Knight-errant or Grocer-errant, properly accompanied, as in heroic romance, with a squire and a dwarf, and after many adventures, etc.

Wanting a battle scene somewhere in the action, the Citizen's Wife calls on Ralph to provide it, with an army of pewterers and poulterers, shopkeepers and apprentices, and Ralph, rising to the warlike occasion, musters, drills and rallies his citizen army.

RALPH

You want a nose, and you a stone.—Sergeant, take a note on't, for I mean to stop it in the pay.—Remove and march! (*They march.*) Soft and fair, gentlemen, soft and fair! Double your files! As you were! Faces about! Now, you with the sodden face, keep in there! Look to your match, sirrah; it will be in your fellow's flask anon! So; make a crescent now! Advance your pikes! Stand and give ear!—Gentlemen, countrymen, friends, and my fellow soldiers, I have brought you this day from the shops of security and the counters of content to measure out in these furious fields honor by the eye and prowess by the pound. Let it not, O, let it not, I say, be told hereafter, the noble issue of the city fainted; but bear yourselves in this fair action like men, valiant men, and free men! Fear not the face of the enemy, nor the noise of the guns, for, believe me, brethren, the rude rumbling of a brewer's car is far more terrible, of which you have a daily experience; neither let the stink of powder offend you, since a more valiant stink is nightly with you. To a resolved mind his home is everywhere. I speak not this to take away the hope of your return, for you shall see (I do not doubt), and that very shortly, your loving wives again and your sweet children, whose care doth bear you company in baskets. Remember, then, whose cause you have in hand, and, like a sort of true-born scavengers, scour me this famous realm of enemies. I have no more to say but this: stand to your tacklings, lads, and show to the world you can as well brandish a sword as shake an apron. Saint George, and on, my hearts!

stone: flint **make a crescent**: stand in curved formation **pike**: an infantry weapon with a long shaft and a pointed metal head **ell**: measure of length equal to 45 in. **rumbling of a brewer's car**: over cobblestones **sort**: a crew **tackling**: gear, tackle

86

RALPH, WITH A FORKED ARROW THROUGH HIS HEAD, RECITES HIS DYING SPEECH

(1607) BEAUMONT AND FLETCHER, The Knight of the Burning Pestle, *Act 5, Sc. 3*

The story of the true play now over [see I, #85], the Citizen demands that interloper Ralph's play have a true ending as well. "Ralph," calls the Citizen to his apprentice offstage, "come away quickly, and die, boy!" Ralph obliges.

Fatally wounded, presumably, on a battlefield, he stumbles onstage with an arrow through his head, but nevertheless, he is almost as long in dying as he was in living. In the language of high romance, he reviews his exploits which, like Don Quixote's, become idyllically elevated in the telling. His Dulcinea was the shoemaker's daughter Susan. For her sake he "followed feats of arms" through Waltham's neighborhood—renamed Waltham Desert—invaded Barbaroso's barber shop, and "rescued" his clients from his shaving knife and reducing baths, and scorned the love of the Princess of Moldavia. After once again clerking in the grocer's shop, he "battled with Death" in Moorfields after "Death" came into his shop and had the temerity to throw a pound of pepper in his face. For his trouble, he came out of the Moorfields scrape with an arrow through his head. Bidding farewell to his fellow apprentices, he mourns the leaving of their pranks, and dies.

(Enter Ralph, with a forked arrow through his head.)

RAFE

When I was mortal, this my costive corpse
Did lap up figs and raisins in the Strand,
Where, sitting, I espied a lovely dame,
Whose master wrought with lingel and with awl,
And underground he vamped many a boot.
Straight did her love prick forth me, tender sprig,
To follow feats of arms in warlike wise
Through Waltham Desert, where I did perform
Many achievements, and did lay on ground
Huge Barbaroso, that insulting giant,
And all his captives soon set at liberty.
Then honor pricked me from my native soil
Into Moldavia, where I gained the love
Of Pompiona, his beloved daughter,
But yet proved constant to the black-thumbed maid,
Susan, and scorned Pompiona's love;
But all these things I Ralph did undertake
Only for my beloved Susan's sake.
Then coming home, and sitting in my shop
With apron blue, Death came into my stall
To cheapen *aqua vitae*, but ere I
Could take the bottle down and fill a taste,
Death caught a pound of pepper in his hand,
And sprinkled all my face and body o'er,
And in an instant vanished away.
Then I took up my bow and shaft in hand,
And walked into Moorfields to cool myself,
But there grim cruel Death met me again,
And shot his forked arrow through my head.
And now I faint. Therefore be warned by me,
My fellows every one, of forked heads!
Farewell, all you good boys in merry London!
Ne'er shall we more upon Shrove Tuesday meet,

and pluck down houses of iniquity.—
My pain increaseth—I shall never more
Hold open, whilst another pumps both legs,
Not daub a satin gown with rotten eggs;
Set up a stake, O, never more I shall!
I die! Fly, fly, my soul, to Grocers' Hall!
O, O, O, etc.

costive: constipated **lingel**: waxed thread **awl**: a shoemaker's tool for piercing holes in leather **vamp**: to patch up, repair a shoe **prick forth**: goad, incite **Moldavia**: a province in NE Romania **cheapen**: bargain for *aqua vitae*, Lat: liquor, as brandy or whiskey **pluck…iniquity**: a traditional liberty of the apprentices on Shrove Tuesday **daub**: to smear, dirty **set up a stake** for attaching a bull or bear for baiting; or conceivably, "setting a stake" for burning a victim (an improbable prank)

Comedy

RESTORATION

87

BAYES THE POET EXPLAINS HIS STRATEGY FOR MAKING PLAYS

(1671) GEORGE VILLIERS, DUKE OF BUCKINGHAM, The Rehearsal, *Act 1, Sc. 1*

Intelligent audiences were having problems with the most touted play-genre of the moment: Heroic Tragedy. It had the authority and support of the most respected poet of his time, John Dryden, its chief proponent and chief purveyor. But when subjected to common sense, it betrayed a few characteristic weaknesses: the fixed and endless "debates between love and honor, the tedious points of casuisty, the bombastic language and far-fetched comparisons, the lack of probability in the motivation and catastrophe." In a word, its unlikelihood. In 1671, the Duke of Buckingham (George Villiers) and a covey of friends—about six—noticing the plays (as they catalogue in their burlesque of them) were simply a round of "fighting, loving, sleeping, rhyming, dying, dancing, singing, crying; and everything but thinking and sense," immortalized Heroic Tragedy's absurdities in *The Rehearsal.*

The play is not only a lampoon of the Heroic play, but of Dryden himself. He is fictionalized as Bayes, and in its first production, the enormously popular Lacy, celebrated for farce and low comedy, mimicked Dryden's manner, speech, and dress to a T. It was a devastating send-up, and included in its mockery not only Dryden's work but about seventeen other Heroic Tragedies. Updated revisions during the years of the burlesque's popularity added even more works.

At play's opening, two gentlemen are complaining about Heroic Play nonsense when Mr. Bayes "crosses o'er the stage." They collar him, and insist on his enlightening them on the meaning of his current play. He at once sidesteps that chore, for the suspected reason that he has no idea. But he does inadvertently pull out his book of "drama commonplaces," and (in possibly the most cutting putdown of all) reveals what the burlesque takes to be a dramaturgical handbook of standard Dryden practice: plagiarism by other names—what we would politely call "adaptation."

The parody of Bayes goes no further in the first scene than his recitation of the easy rules by which his plays are written. In the following scenes, the plays themselves, as written and performed, become the prime target.

BAYES

Your most obsequious and most observant very servant, sir. Sir, it is not within my small capacity to do favors, but receive 'em, especially from a person that does wear the honorable title you are pleased to impose, sir, upon this.

Sweet sir, your servant. A favor, now? Aye, sir. What is't? To tell the meaning of my last play? How, sir, the meaning! Do you mean the plot? Faith, sir, the intrigo's now quite out of my head: but I have a new one in my pocket, that I may say is a virgin; 't has never yet been blown upon. I must tell you one thing, 'tis all new wit; and though I say it, a better than my last; and you know well enough how that took. In fine, it shall read, and write, and act, and plot and show— aye, and pit, box and gallery, 'y glad, with any play in Europe. This morning is its last rehearsal, in their habits and all that, as it is to be acted; and if you and your friend will do it but the honor to see it in its virgin attire, though, perhaps, it may blush, I shall not be ashamed to discover its nakedness unto you.

(Puts his hand in his pocket)

I think it is in this pocket. Yes, here is it.—No, cry you mercy! this is my book of drama commonplaces, the mother of many other plays. What's that? Why, sir, some certain helps that we men of art have found it convenient to make use of. And I do here aver that no man yet the sun e'er shone upon has parts sufficient to furnish out a stage except it were by the help of these my rules. What are those rules? Why, sir, my first rule is the rule of transversion, or changing verse into prose, or prose into verse, alternative as you please. Nothing so easy when understood. I take a book in my hand, either at home or elsewhere, for that's all one—if there be any wit in't, as there is no book but has some, I transverse it: that is, if it be prose, put it into verse (but that takes up some time); and if it be verse, put it into prose. What do with it then? Make it my own. 'Tis so changed that no man can know it. My next rule is the rule of record, by way of table-book. Pray observe. As thus, I come into a coffee house, or some other place where witty men resort. I make as if I minded nothing (do you mark?), but as soon as any one speaks, pop! I slap it down, and make that, too, my own. Rule for invention? Yes, sir, that's my third rule that I have here in my pocket.

Why, sir, when I have anything to invent, I never trouble my head about it, as other men do; but presently turn over this book, and there I have, at one view, all that Perseus, Montaigne, Seneca's tragedies, Horace, Juvenal, Claudian, Pliny, Plutarch's *Lives*, and the rest, have ever thought upon this subject; and so, in a trice, by leaving out a few words or putting in others of my own, the business is done.

Sirs, if you make the least scruple of the efficacy of these my rules, do but come to the play-house and you shall judge of 'em by the effects.

(Exeunt)

pit, box, and gallery: the three-tiered seating in the theatre (ground level, boxes above and high balcony) **transversion…**: a hit at Dryden's use of the same materials in prose and verse, as explained in the text **table-book**: pocket notebook **coffee house**: the most popular meeting place in London at the time **this book**: a popular anthology of quotations **Perseus**: Greek mythology, the hero who cut off the Gorgon Medusa's head **Montaigne** (1533-92): French philosopher and essayist **Seneca, Horace, Juvenal, Claudian, Pliny**: Roman writers **Plutarch**: Greek biographer

88

BAYES SEEKS ADVICE ON
PRESENTING HIS PROLOGUE

(1671) GEORGE VILLIERS, DUKE OF BUCKINGHAM, *The Rehearsal*, *Act 1, Sc. 2*

B ayes [see I, #87], before rehearsal begins, has one more query for the gentlemen he's invited to watch the dress rehearsal of the play: of the two interchangeable texts he's prepared: which would serve best for Prologue, and which for Epilogue? With a nod, apparently, toward Aristotle, one appeals to the audience's Pity (the one divulged in this selection), the other to its Fear (played by two characters called Thunder and Lightning). (For the Heroic Play, Dryden added another criterion to Aristotle's two: Admiration—not only of the Hero but of the stunning incidents and the loud verse.)

The first, depending on Pity, invites a drama of its own: the Poet enters wearing a black veil with a hangman behind him, threatening the audience with the options of either applauding before the play begins or witnessing the hangman chop off the Poet's head. As to the question of whether the audience might elect not to applaud, Bayes is nonplussed, and sputters. Recovering, he explains the guarantees that they will. There's the play's "design," which he will distribute in print to the audience in advance, and there are "the two or three dozen of my friends ready in the pit." Both would be proof against the "calumniating" critics.

Bayes is a character whose mad logic holds him captive. Both in these selections and throughout the play, he is aggressively driven as though by reason, and is immune to it.

BAYES

Now, gentlemen, I would fain ask your opinion of one thing. I have made a prologue and an epilogue which may both serve for either (that is, the prologue for the epilogue, or the epilogue for the prologue)—do you mark? Nay, they may both serve too, 'y gad, for any other play as well as this. And I would fain ask your judgements now, which of them would do best for the prologue. For you must know there is, in nature, but two ways of making very good prologues. The one is by civility, by insinuation, good language, and all that, to—a— in a manner, steal your plaudit from the courtesy of the auditors: the other, by making use of some certain personal things, which may keep a hank upon such censuring persons as cannot otherways, a gad, in nature, be hindered from being too free with their tongues. To which end my first prologue is, that I come out in a long black veil, and a great, huge hangman behind me, with a furred cap and his sword drawn; and there tell 'em plainly that if, out of good nature, they will not like my play, 'y gad, I'll e'en kneel down, and he shall cut my head off. Whereupon they all clapping—a—

But suppose they don't you say? Suppose! You may suppose what you please, I have nothing to do with your suppose, sir; no, nor am not at all mortified at it—not at all, sir; 'y gad not one jot, sir. "Suppose," quoth a!-ha! ha! ha! If I writ, sir, to please the country, I should have followed the old plain way; but I write for some persons of quality and peculiar friends of mine, that understand what flame and power in writing is; and they do me the right, sir, to approve of what I do.

I'm sure the design's good: that cannot be denied. And then, for lan-guage, 'y gad, I defy 'em all, in nature, to mend it. Besides, sir, I have printed above a hundred sheets of paper, to insinuate the plot into the boxes: and, withal, have appointed two or three dozen of my friends to be ready in the pit, who, I'm sure, will clap, and so the rest, you know, must follow. I therefore would choose this to be the prologue. For, if I could engage 'em to clap before they see the play, you know 'twould be so much the better, because then they were engaged: for let a man write never so well, there are, now-a-days, a sort of persons they call critics, that, 'y gad, have no more wit in them than so many hobby-horses; but they'll laugh you, sir, and find fault, and censure things that, 'y gad, I'm sure they are not able to do themselves—a sort of envious persons that emulate the glories of persons of parts, and think to build their fame by calumniating of persons that, 'y gad, to my knowledge, of all persons in the world are, in nature, the persons that do as much despise all that as—a—In fine, I'll say no more of 'em.

Why, I'll tell you, sir, sincerely, and *bona fide*, were it not for the sake of some ingenious persons and choice female spirits that have a value for me, I would see 'em all hanged, 'y gad, before I would e'er more set pen to paper; but let 'em live in ignorance like ingrates.

prologue and epilogue: for the writing of which Dryden was famous **plaudit**: applause **hank**: a restraining hold, influence **insinuate the plot into the boxes**: refers to the printed papers Dryden had distributed to the audience explaining that his play *The Indian Emperor* was a sequel to *The Indian Queen* **choice female spirits**: a hit at the protection given Dryden by Lady Castlemaine

89
RHODOPHIL LAMENTS THE MISFORTUNE OF MARRIAGE, AND PLANS CONSOLATION WITH A YET-TO-BE-WON MISTRESS
(1672) JOHN DRYDEN, Marriage-a-la-Mode, *Act 1, Sc. 1*

Dryden, the Restoration playwright who was one of the first to adopt the new mode of permissive laxity in comedy, promises his audience in the Prologue to *Marriage-a-la-Mode* the courtesy of treating them to "a room, and a couch within" later in the play, so that "however the play fall short," they'll be obliged for the scene of sexual license so promised. He's not as good as his word, but in dialogue and plot, he's at least close enough to be mildly titillating. And to dress his comic characters—in the prose-comedy half of an otherwise poetic-Heroic play—in the free-wheeling derelictions that go along with anticipation of a "room, with a couch within."

Rhodophil, a Captain of the King's Guard in Sicily (a stand-in location for Charles II's London), meets his old companion Palamede on "the walk" (in London, it was the walk in St. James' Park, where mutual display and mutual ogling between the sexes took care of the late afternoon, the blank stretch after dinner and before the theatre). There Rhodophil confides to his friend his present misery: he's married. It's a cardinal principle of Restoration comedy that marriage, however it begins in rapture, settles into bondage. It's a companion to the principle expressed when Palamede confided to his friend that he's returned from travel "by command of an old rich father." Rhodophil at once assumed that, ah yes, with "the hopes of burying him." It's in this spirit of moral probity that Rhodophil mourns the fact of his marriage; it would put him out of fashion not to mourn over it. His speech, then, is a sigh of sorrow laced with a sense of fashionable propriety. He's not so much devastated as correct; he's, as Restoration comic heroes imagine themselves to be, *comme il faut.*

The solution, of course, is a mistress. Rhodophil has already fixed on one, but hasn't yet won her. It's naturally Dryden's pleasure to make plot arrangements for his potential mistress to be, unknown to either of them, his friend Palamede's potential wife.

> **RHODOPHIL**
> Alas, dear Palamede, I have had no joy to write, nor indeed to do anything in the world. The greatest misfortune imaginable is fallen upon me. In one word, I am married, wretchedly married, and have been above these two years. Yes, faith, the devil has had power over me in spite of my vows and resolutions to the contrary. She's young; and, for her humor, she laughs, sings, and dances eternally; and, which is more, we never quarrel about it, for I do the same. A great beauty, too, as

people say. But ask those who have smelled to a strong perfume two years together what's the scent. All that I know of her perfections now is only by memory. I remember, indeed, that about two years ago I loved her passionately; but those golden days are gone, Palamede. Yet I loved her a whole half year, double the natural term of any mistress, and think in my conscience I could have held out another quarter. But then the world began to laugh at me, and a certain shame of being out of fashion seized me. At last we arrived at that point that there was nothing left in us to make us new to one another. Yet still I set a good face upon the matter and am infinite fond of her before company; but, when we are alone, we walk like lions in a room, she one way and I another, and we lie with our backs to each other so far distant as if the fashion of great beds was only invented to keep husband and wife sufficiently asunder. Considering the damned disadvantages of a married man, I have provided well enough for another poor humble sinner that is not ambitious of great matters. She's a woman, one of the stars of Syracuse, I assure you: young enough, fair enough, and but for one quality, just such a woman as I would wish. But my mistress has one fault that's almost unpardonable; for, being a town-lady without any relation to the court, yet she thinks of herself undone if she be not seen there three or four times a day with the princess Amalthea. And for the king, she haunts and watches him so narrowly in a morning that she prevents even the chemists who beset his chamber to turn their mercury into his gold. With all this, she's the greatest gossip in nature; for besides the court, she's the most eternal visiter of the town, and yet manages her time so well that she seems ubiquitary. For my part, I can compare her to nothing but the sun: for like him she takes no rest, nor ever sets in one place but to rise in another. No lady can be so curious of a new fashion as she is of a new French word; she's the very mint of the nation, and as fast as any bullion comes out of France, coins it immediately into our language.

No naming; that's not like a cavalier. Find her if you can by my description and I am not so ill a painter that I need write the name beneath the picture. 'Tis yet in the bud, and, what fruit it may bear I cannot tell, for this insufferable humor of haunting the court is so predominant that she has hitherto broken all her assignations with me for fear of missing her visits there. That's the hardest part of the adventure. I'll tell you at more leisure my adventures. The walks fill apace, I see.

good girls: wanton wenches **great beds**: double beds, a recent fashion **chemists**: alchemists **ubiquitary**: ubiquitous, omnipresent

90
RHODOPHIL RESOLVES THAT HE AND DORALICE MUST FOREVER SUFFER THE MISFORTUNE OF THEIR MARRIAGE
(1672) JOHN DRYDEN, Marriage-a-la-Mode, *Act 3, Sc. 1*

Faced with the prospect of confronting one another in the presence of a court lady, Rhodophil and Doralice, the husband and wife who cannot bear one another [see I, #89], play a well-practiced charade of love and devotion, in which they parody the verbal exertions of a blissful marital state. With the realization a moment later that the court lady Artemis has gone, they separate quickly, and return to the behavior of mutual aversion.

But Rhodophil is getting fed up with the labor of sustaining hostilities, and offers, tentatively, the terms of a truce. But before he's articulated them, he remembers the most galling of his disaffections: that he's run out of pictures of substitute ladies to sustain him during sessions in bed with his wife. Nothing of their truce having been accomplished here, they continue their mutual acrimony until the plot, at the last moment, effects their reconciliation.

> *(Enter Rhodophil, meeting Doralice and Artemis,*
> *Rhodophil and Doralice embrace.)*

RHODOPHIL

My own dear heart! My true love! I had forgot myself to be so kind;
indeed I am very angry with you, dear; you are come home an hour
after you appointed. If you had stayed a minute longer, I was just considering whether I should stab, hang, or drown myself.

> *(Kissing her hand.)*

Betwixt us, Artemis? It is always thus! this is nothing. I tell you there is
not such a pair of turtles in all Sicily; there is such an eternal cooing
and kissing betwixt us, that indeed it is scandalous before civil company. If I had imagined I should have been this fond fool, I would never
have married to be happy, and have made myself miserable by over-
loving. Nay, and now, my case is desperate; for I have been married
above these two years and find myself every day worse and worse in
love: nothing but madness can be the end on't.

> *(Embracing each other.)*
Sweet Doralice! *(looking up)* What, is she gone?

> *(parting from her)*
Then there's enough for this time. The scene's done.

> *(They walk contrary ways on the stage; he, with his*
> *hands in his pocket, whistling; she, singing a dull melan-*
> *choly tune.)*

Pox o' your damned tune; you can neither be company to me yourself,
nor leave me to the freedom of my own fancy. Thou art the most pro-
voking wife! For myself, I was never thought dull till I married thee;
and now thou hast made an old knife of me; thou hast whetted me so
long, till I have no edge left. Prithee leave me to my own cogitations; I
am thinking over all my sins, to find for which of them it was I married thee. My comfort is thou art not immortal; and when that
blessed, that divine day comes of thy departure, I'm resolved I'll make
one holy-day more in the almanac for thy sake. Then, setting my victorious foot upon thy head, in the first hour of thy silence (that is, the

first hour thou art dead, for I despair of it before), I will swear by thy ghost, an oath as terrible to me as Styx is to the gods, never more to be in danger of the banes of matrimony.

(He sighs, and wonders)

Yet, prithee, Doralice, why do we quarrel thus a-days? ha? This is but a kind of heathenish life and does not answer the ends of marriage. If I have erred, propound what reasonable atonement may be made, before we sleep, and I shall not be refractory; but withal consider, I have been married these three years, and since we must live together, and both of us stand upon our terms, as to the matter of dying first, let us make ourselves as merry as we can with our misfortunes.

Why there's the devil on't! If thou couldst make my enjoying thee but a little less easy, or a little more unlawful, thou shouldst see what a termagant lover I would prove. I have taken such pains to enjoy thee, Doralice, that I have fancied thee all the fine women in the town to help me out. But now there's none left for me to think on, my imagination is quite jaded. Thou art a wife, and thou wilt be a wife, and I can make thee another no longer.

(Exit Rhodophil.)

turtles: turtledoves, lovers **almanach**: calendar **banes**: an obsolete spelling of "banns," published announcement of a proposed wedding; but the pun is intended **termagant**: violent, turbulent; after the mythical deity Termagant

91

HORNER EXPLAINS TO HIS DOCTOR THE ADVANTAGES OF PRETENDING TO BE A EUNUCH

(1675) WILLIAM WYCHERLEY, The Country Wife, *Act 1*

When the exiled court of Charles II returned from France after the English Puritan demise, they took with them on permanent loan a large measure of French manners, dress and plays, but left behind the moral refinement if not decorous prudishness of French comedy in the time of Molière. Morality, if taught at all in Restoration comedy, is taught by bad example. If so, nowhere is its lesson pushed further than in the character of Horner, the ultimate Restoration libertine, nor in this comedy of Wycherley's, in which the moral norm of behavior for most of the characters and for society at large is the unvarnished, untempered pursuit of sexual conquest. Horner—and by implication Wycherley—defers to the hypocritical mode of this pursuit, which needs only the thinnest veneer of propriety to function well. And it's that thin veneer that Horner, with the practical sagacity of the born sexual strategist, pays homage to in the scheme he outlines here for his physician-accomplice: to suggest that, owing to the "English-French disaster," (i.e., syphilis) an inept surgeon, in his mistaken attempt to cure the malady, left him a eunuch. If with such reputation he can "abuse the husbands" to be thoroughly off their guard, it follows that he will soon "disabuse the wives." The scheme, needless to say, succeeds beyond libertinism's wildest dreams.

But it's a mistake to dismiss Horner's—and Wycherley's—conceit as little more than a scurrilous joke. Note how Horner advances his notion: not as whimsical, but as soundly observed fact. Note the style: soberly argued, with the assurance of, and the wisdom of, experimental certainty. There is lurking under the drollery of the conceit an attitude toward human hypocrisy as excoriating as that in Swift's soberly argued suggestion in *A Modest Proposal* to use the skin of economically burdensome children of the Irish peasantry to make gloves and other usable items of commerce.

Horner is as emotionally neutral in his pursuit as Swift is in his style of telling; both insist, given the nature of the human animal, on the certainty, the accuracy, and the efficacy of their separate proposals. Marginally, Swift hasn't yet had Horner's opportunity to prove his point; Horner in the play proves his triumphantly.

(Enter Horner and Quack following him at a distance.)

HORNER

A quack is as fit for a pimp, as a midwife for a bawd; they are still but in their way, both helpers of Nature. *(aside)* Well, my dear doctor, hast thou done what I desired? Have you told all the midwives you know, the orange wenches at the playhouses, the city husbands, and old fumbling keepers of this end of the town, for they'll be the readiest to report it, and whisper'd it as a secret to 'em, and to the whisperers of *Whitehall*; so that 'twill spread, and I will be as odious to the handsome young women, as the small pox. And to the married women of this end of the town, as the great ones; nay, as their own husbands. I am only afraid 'twill not be believ'd; you told 'em 'twas by an *English-French* disaster, and an *English-French* Chirurgeon, who has given me at once, not only a cure, but an antidote for the future, against that damn'd malady, and that worse distemper, love, and all other womens evils. Dear Mr. doctor, let vain rogues be contented only to be thought abler men than they are, generally 'tis all the pleasure they have, but mine lies another way. Doctor, there are quacks in love, as well as physick, who get but the fewer and worse patients, for their boasting; a good name is seldom got by giving it ones self, and women no more than honour are compass'd by bragging: Come, come doctor, the wisest lawyer never discovers the merits of his cause till the tryal; the wealthiest man conceals his riches, and the cunning gamster his play; sly husbands and keepers like old rooks are not to be cheated, but by a new unpractis'd trick; false friendship will pass now no more than false dice upon 'em, no, not in the city. Don't you see already upon the report and my carriage, this grave man of business leaves his wife in my lodgings, invites me to his house and wife, who before wou'd not be acquainted with me out of jealousy. If I can but abuse the husbands, I'll soon disabuse the wives: Stay—I'll reckon you up the advantages, I am like to have by my stratagem: First, I shall be rid of all my old acquaintances, the most insatiable sorts of duns, that invade our lodgings in a morning: And next, to the pleasure of making a new mistriss, is that of being rid of an old one, and of all old debts; love when it comes to be so, is paid the most unwillingly. As but all the young fellows of the town, if they do not lose more time like huntsmen, in starting the game, than in running it down; one knows not where to find 'em, who will, or will not; women of quality are so civil, you can hardly distinguish love from good breeding, and a man is often mistaken; but now I can be sure, she that shews an aversion to me loves the sport, as those women that are gone, whom I warrant to be right: And then the next thing, is your women of honour, as you call 'em, are only chary of their reputations, not their persons, and 'tis scandal they wou'd avoid, not men: Now may I have, by the reputation of an eunuch, the priviledges of one; and be seen in a ladies chamber, in a morning as early as her husband; kiss virgins before their parents, or lovers; and may be in short the *pas par tout* of the town.

Keepers: guardians **Whitehall**: the Royal Palace in London at the time **Chirurgeon**: surgeon **Rooks**: crooks **Dun**: a persistent creditor **chary**: careful, wary ***Pas par tout***, Fr, *passe par tout*: that which passes everywhere

92

RAMBLE DECLARES A "NEW ORDER OF NATURE" FOR TRUE WITS AND AGAINST FOOLS

(1675) JOHN CROWE, The Country Wit, *Act 2*

Ramble rambles, even from Christina who loves him and is being tormented by her father to marry a fool of a country squire with 2000 pounds a year. Ramble loves her too—more or less—but in the tradition of Wycherley's Horner [see I, #91], the quintessential Restoration rake (and in the footsteps of Don Juan, the quintessential libertine of Western literature), Ramble's pursuit is sex, his devotion the enjoyment of desirable women.

He has, like Don Juan, a valet—Merry—who serves as advance guard for his seductions, arranging his assignations and setting fiddlers to serenade for him beneath ladies' windows. But unlike Don Juan's servant, Merry rambles too, on his own.

Both are currently, in the dead of night, at the sport when Merry chances to speak of people's complaints of the two of them turning night into day. It's Ramble's cue. He seizes the moment to spell out his credo: "The world is Nature's house of entertainment," and the masters of that entertainment are the "men of wit and pleasure" who have the wisdom to follow appetite alone, to escape the burdens that Nature places, in varying humiliating degrees, on the world's fools who subordinate themselves to serve her various mundane functions.

Ramble's is the ultimate credo of the libertine, possibly the most fully articulated statement of it in Restoration comedy. Its logic, when a century later it was drawn to its most exuberant consequence, became the apologia of the Marquis de Sade.

> **RAMBLE**
> The order of nature? The order of nature is to follow my appetite: am
> I to eat at noon, because it is noon, or because I am hungry? To eat

because a clock strikes, were to feed a clock, or the sun, and not myself. Let dull grave rogues observe distinction of seasons, eat because the sun shines, and when he departs lie drown'd some nine hours in their own flegm; I will pay no such homage to the sun, and time, which are things below me; I am a superior being to them, and will make 'em attend my pleasure.

The world is Nature's house of entertainment, where men of wit and pleasure are her free guests, tied to no rules and orders. Fools indeed are her household-stuff, which she locks up, and brings forth at seasons; handsome fools are her pictures; studious, plotting, engineering fools are her mechanic implements; strong laborious fools are her common utensils; valiant bold fools are her armoury; and dull insignificant fools are her lumber, which, by wars, plagues, and other conveniences, she often throws and sweeps out of the world.

And, Merry—let me think—what fool are you? An amphibious creature, that livest in both elements of wit and fool; the major part of thee is fool; but that part of thee that is wit is true wit; and so thou are a nobler animal than many of those poor creatures that thou seest swim after men of wit and sense, for the scraps and orts of wit that fall from them; they leap and play out of the water, as high as they can, but they are but fish still; folly in their element, and there they must stay. I pity the poor poets; these creatures do but spoil our mirth, but they ruin the poets' labours. They are to them as the fox is to the badger; when the badger has with great pains scratch'd himself a hole, the fox comes and stinks him out of it. But enough of this.—Come, to the business in hand! however 'tis in other affairs I am for reducing love to the state of nature; I am for no propriety, but every man get what he can: however invasion in this case I am sure is lawful. When a pretty young woman lies in the possession of an old fellow, like a fair fertile province under the dominion of the Turk, uncultivated and unenjoy'd, no good Christian but ought to make war upon him:—that mine is a kind of holy war, and I deserve a benediction. And so my musical pilgrims to your arms.

orts: leavings **under the dominion of the Turk**: at the time the Turkish (Ottoman) Empire was expanding threateningly into Europe, eventually reaching Vienna

93

SIR FOPLING FLUTTER DISPLAYS ON HIS PERSON THE FRENCH MODE

(1676) GEORGE ETHEREGE, The Man of Mode, *Act 3, Sc. 1*

The male targets of Restoration comedy's satiric contempt above all others were the country bumpkins and the Frenchified fops, one native to the lowest, the other imitations of the highest, models of maleness: the boor with no manners, the fop with too many. The model of all Restoration fops is certainly Etherege's Sir Fopling Flutter, newly arrived from Paris with his new equipage—a half-dozen French valets; his new *caleche* (coach); his new manners, language, and clothes. Dorimont, the play's commanding rake, reveals his secret: "He went to Paris a plain, bashful English blockhead, and is returned a fine, undertaking French fop."

In this scene, Sir Fopling reintroduces himself to the London *beau monde* with a flourish. He first greets Dorimont, whom he ran into in Paris, and for a start, makes much of their meager connection. Then he pays address to the others, but finally he comes to the real business at hand: his French clothes, his shops, his tailors.

In the play's original text, the others are joined in a choral catechism on his adornments, but here, in this monologue version, the dialogue is collapsed into an eager, self-propelled monologue for Sir Fopling alone. What's lost is the universal duping of Sir Fopling; what's not lost, and possibly gained, is his rapt eagerness to display his novel acquisitions together with their attributions—owning the height of fashion, sourcing the exclusiveness of its makers.

But to represent Sir Fopling Flutter's "style" as characteristic of Restoration manner and behavior—hand on hip, nose tilted, flipping kerchief, making a leg, lisping French—is to be guilty of the deepest betrayal of the Restoration mode. Sir Fopling's "style" is close to its direct opposite. There is a gamut—not too wide—in its true modes of self-presentation. The genuine "wits" possess the single most defining characteristic of their town-and-court society: diffidence. It was the most distinctive characteristic of the "gentleman" since the Renaissance, set out in detail by Castiglione in his *The Courtier*, the single characteristic that determines the difference between the true gentleman and the mere artisan, the mere doer, the mere man of skill or attainment, the mere emulator. Diffidence translates into never noticing one's own manner, retreating from its exhibition, holding to the mean of social behavior—in other words, behaving as non-distinctively and non-excessively as possible. Ease, not effort, is its mark. The gentleman is witty without deigning to notice it; modest without show; graceful and adept without consciousness. If for an instant his attainments *do* show, instant self-denigration follows. He never lets a compliment pass without diverting its credit to some other source than his own.

What is the difference between these, the "true wits," and the posturing Sir Foplings, the excessive fools? Fundamentally, only one: the fools lack diffidence. In manner, in behavior, they range from those moderate fools who are too visibly proud of their dress, or wit, or attainments, or opinions, whatever, and those, like Sir Fopling, who are positively gleeful in their presentation of these things in themselves. They exhibit—they can't help it—visible, voluble glee in what they are. They may even be as witty as the truewits—Pope wondered whether "Congreve's fools were fools indeed"—but they smack their lips and grin over hitting their mark.

The cap of folly is not only the fool's visible pride or glee, but his fundamental certainty that he too has diffidence. He never notices the difference between his self-congratulation on what he supposes are his attainments, and the careful blanketing of them in the wit. He's helpless to conceal his delight at compliments thrown, even mockingly, his way. The self-revealed fool—like Sir Fopling here—lays out his wares, urges them, applauds them—the sum, in Restoration mode, of folly.

The reverse of the usual stage-crime committed in playing Restoration comedy is the ideal to be pursued: a suppression, as much as possible, of the puppetry of "manners."

(Enter Sir Fopling Flutter with his Page after him)

SIR FOPLING

Page, wait without. *(To Lady Townley)* Madam, I kiss your hands. I see yesterday was nothing of chance ; the *belles assemblees* form themselves here every day. *(To Emilia)* Lady, your servant.—Dorimant, let me embrace thee! Without lying, I have not met with any of my acquaintance who retain so much of Paris as thou dost—the very air thou hadst when the marquise mistook thee i'th Tuileries and cried, "Hey, Chevalier!" and then begged thy pardon. Thou art a man of wit and understands[t] the town. Prithee, let thee and I be intimate; there is no living without making some good man the confidant of our pleasures, let me perish! I knew a French count so like thee! *(To Emilia)* A thousand pardons, madam; some civilities due of course upon the meeting a long absent friend. The *éclat* of so much beauty, I confess, ought to have charmed me sooner. I never saw anything prettier than this high work on your *point d'Espagne.* Dorimant, is not that Medley? Forgive me, sir; in this *embarrass* of civilities I could not come to have you in my arms sooner. You understand an equipage the best of any man in town, I hear. Have you taken notice of the *caleche* I brought over? 'Tis as easily known from an English tumbril as an Inns-of-Court man is from one of us. The world is generally very *grossier* here, indeed. A slight suit I made to appear in at my first arrival—not worthy your consideration, ladies. The pantaloon is very well mounted. The tassels are new and pretty. I never saw a coat better cut. It makes me show long-waisted, and, I think, slender. The breech, though, is a handful too high, in my eyes. I have wished it lower a thousand times, but a pox on't! 'twill not be. The gloves are well fringed, large and graceful. I was always eminent for being *bien gante.* The suit? Barroy. The garniture? Le Gras. The shoes? Piccar. The periwig? Chedreux. The gloves?

Orangerie! You know the smell, ladies. Dorimant, I could find in my heart for an amusement to have a gallantry with some of our English ladies. Here was a woman yesterday—Mistress Loveit. Methoughts she seemed, though, very reserved and uneasy all the time I entertained her. Prithee, let thee and I take the air together. All the world will be in the park to-night. Ladies, 'twere pity to keep so much beauty longer within doors and rob the Ring of all those charms that should adorn it.—Hey, page!

(Enter Page)

See that all my people be ready.

(and goes out again)

— Dorimant, au revoir.

(Exit Sir Fopling)

belles assemblees, Fr: fashionable gatherings **Tuileries**: the Royal Palace in Paris **eclat**, Fr: splendor **point d'Espagne**, Fr: Spanish lace **embarras**, Fr: an embarrassment (of civilities) **equipage**: a retinue of personal attendants **caleche**, Fr: an elegant open carriage **tumbril**: a heavy cart for carrying dung (later for carrying the victims to the guillotine) **Inns-of-Court man**: of the legal profession **grossier**, Fr: coarse **bien gante**, Fr: well-gloved **Barroy, Le Gras, Piccar, Chedreux, Orangerie**: fashionable Paris tradesmen **garniture**: trimming **the Ring**: a circular course in Hyde Park, used for riding and driving

94

WHITTMORE, UNDER INSTRUCTIONS FROM LUCIA, MUST "FEIGN A COURTSHIP" TO ISABELLA

(1678) APHRA BEHN, Sir Patient Fancy, *Act 2, Sc. 1*

Whittmore must struggle with his conscience. He loves Lucia who wholly reciprocates, although she is the wife of ancient hypochondriac Sir Patient Fancy. Caught in the garden by the suspicious old man, the two had instantly to justify their interview. Ah, they explain, Whittmore was seeking assistance for his suit to Sir Patient's daughter Isabella, whereupon it becomes Whittmore's task, under anxious instructions from Lucia, to pretend it.

Meeting with Isabella, he is momentarily in a quandary. She's young, beautiful, thoroughly eligible, and sorely tempting. And she might, conceivably, believe his suit. He wavers. But almost alone among Restoration rakes, he tilts to the side of loyalty to his first love, Lucia, and conscientiously assumes the role he had planned for the wooing of Isabella: fashionably silly Frenchified fop—one of the standard butts of Restoration comedy. Under the watchful eye of Maundy, Lucia's servant, he performs almost too convincingly—mumbling to Maundy, then to himself, astonished at his own steadfastness—and finally, to avoid the danger of being smitten, scurries out as quickly as possible.

Betterton, one of the most brilliant actors of the time, played this role, performing the impressive feat of slipping convincingly from self to fool to self and back to fool again, with no aid from costume.

WITTMORE

Take heed, Wittmore, whilst you only design to feign a courtship, you do it not in good earnest. I'll make such awkward love as shall persuade her, however she chance to like my person, to think most lewdly of my parts. Now Foppery assist to make me very ridiculous.—Death, she's very pretty and inviting; what an insensible dog shall I be counted to refuse the enjoyment of so fair, so new a creature, and who is like to be thrown into my arms too, whether I will or not?—But Conscience and my vows to the fair mother. No, I will be honest.— Madam,—as Gad shall save me, I'm the son of a whore, if you are not the most belle person I ever saw, and I be not damnably in love with you; but a pox take all tedious courtship, I have a free-born and generous spirit; and as I hate being confined to dull cringing, whining, flattering, and the Devil and all of foppery, so when I give an heart, I'm an infidel, Madam, if I do not love to do't frankly and quickly, that thereby I may oblige the beautiful receiver of my vows, protestations, passions, and inclination. Upon my reputation, Madam, you're a civil, well-bred person, you have all the *agreemony* of your sex, *la belle taille, la bonne mine,* and *repartee bien,* and are *tout oure torre,* as I'm a gentleman, *fort agreeable.*—If this do not please your lady, and nauseate her, the Devil's in 'em both for unreasonable women. *(To Maundy.)* Well, if I do hold out, egad, I shall be the bravest young fellow in Christendom. But, Madam, I must kiss your hand at present; I have some visits to make, *devoirs* to pay, necessities of gallantry only, no love engagements, by Jove, Madam, it is sufficient I have given my *parole* to your father, to do him the honor of my alliance; and an unnecessary jealousy will but disoblige, Madam, your slave.

(Exit.)

the *agreemony...agréable*, Fr: the agreeableness of your sex, a beautiful shape, a lovely face, good repartee, and all the rest (*tout autour*) are extremely agreeable ***devoirs*,** Fr: respects, compliments ***parole*,** Fr: word

95

PETRO DEMONSTRATES HOW THE BODY CAN TELL A TALE AND PICK A POCKET, WITH SMALL AID FROM WORDS OR SENSE

(1679) APHRA BEHN, The Feign'd Courtesan, *Act 2, Sc. 1*

Petro is a chameleon; he's described as "your brokering Jew, your fencing, dancing, civility-master, your linguist, your antiquary, your bravo, your pathic, your whore, your pimp, and a thousand more excellencies he has to supply the necessities of the wanting stranger." "The wanting stranger[s]" are for the most part Englishmen traveling in Rome, somewhat desperately needing his salutary services. But he's in fact none of these; rather, he's the servant of two young virtuous maidens who pose as courtesans after running away to Rome to escape an uncle who's importuning one of them to marry a man she doesn't love. And Petro, we discover late in the play, is their protector, a sort of anti-pimp, playing tricks that shield them from the "wanting strangers" who pursue them.

But his shielding of them is extravagantly supplemented by pleasures of his own: multiple disguises that pretend to serve, but thoroughly gull, these foreign fools. His particular targets are Sir Signal Buffoon, a signal buffoon, and his guardian Mr. Tickletext, your standard Puritan hypocrite inhabiting two centuries of English comedy.

Before this scene, he had already played—in appropriate quick-change disguises—pimp, barber and French dancing master, but before his dancing lessons were launched he was challenged by Mr. Tickletext to display his fencing-master's prowess. And he failed. Tickletext knew swords, and Petro looked foolish. Harboring this affront, he bides his time until—as a civility-master—he has both

Tickletext and Buffoon where he wants them: being taught by him the civilities of the town—the *bonne grace* of a gentleman's behavior.

Lesson one: taking snuff with grace (which makes for their non-stop sneezing for the rest of the lessons). Lesson two: the art of "giving" with grace (which offers up to Petro two diamond rings). Final lesson: "How to act a story" with no words or sense (which offers up the opportunity for Petro to pick their pockets). Revenge accomplished.

This last lesson is a show-piece: zanni-like mime (accompanied by unintelligible Italian gibberish) distantly out of *commedia dell'arte*, exhibiting the kind of brilliance in both mime and patter for which the Arlecchinos of England were to become hugely popular in the next century—this last is the comic dazzle of the scene.

PETRO
The first lesson you shall learn, is, how to give and how to receive, with a bone grace. This unfrequented part of the garden, signior, will fit our purpose as well as your lodgings,—first then—signiors, your address—

(Puts himself in the middle. Petro bows on both sides, they do the like.)
Very well! That's at the approach of any person of quality; after which you must take out your snuff-box. You take no snuff? Then sir, by all means you must learn: for besides the mode and gravity of it, it inviveates the pericranium! That is, sapientates the brain,—that is, inspires wit, thought, invention, understanding, and the like—you conceive me signiors—

(bowing)
Then signiors, it keeps you in confidence, and countenance! And whilst you gravely seem to take a snush, you gain time to answer to the purpose and in a politic posture—as thus—to any intricate question. It helps the memory better than rosemary, therefore I have brought each of you a snuff-box. Ah, bagatelles signior, bagatelles, and now signiors, I'll teach you how to take it, with a handsome grace, signior your hand;—and yours signior.

(Lays snuff on their hands.)

—So now draw your hand to, and fro under your noses, and snuff it hard up:—excellent well.

(They daub all their noses, make grimaces, and sneeze.)

What scent do you call this? Cackamerda Orangate, a rare perfume I'll assure ye, sir. 'Tis your right dulce piquante, believe me:—but come signiors, wipe your noses and proceed to your giving lesson. Present me with something—that—diamond on your finger! To show the manner of giving handsomely. Oh fie, signior—between your finger and thumb—thus—with your other fingers at a distance—with a speech, and a bow. Now a fine turn on your hand—thus—oh that sets off the present, and makes it sparkle in the eyes of the receiver. Now kiss your fingers ends, and retire back with a bow. There is such a certain relation between a finger and a ring, that no present becomes either the giving or the receiving half so well.

But now signiors, I'll teach you how to act a story. Aye, sir, no matter for words or sense, so the body perform its part well. Oh sir, I have taught it men born deaf and blind:—look ye, stand close together, and observe—

(gets between them)

—closer yet. A certain Ecclesiastico,

(makes a sign of being fat)

plump and rich—

(galloping about the stage)

riding along the road,—meets a paver strapiao—un pavero strapiao, paure strapiao:

(puts himself into the posture of a lean beggar, his hands right down by his sides—and picks both their pockets)

—strapiao—strapiao—strapiao—elemosuna per un paure strapiao, par a moure de dievos—at last he begs a julio—

(makes the fat bishop)

neinte—

(lean)
the paure strapiao begs a mezzo julio—

(fat)
neinte—

(lean)
une bacio—

(fat)
neinte—at last he begs his blessing—and see how willingly the Ecclesiastico gave his benediction—

(opening his arms, hits them both in the face)
—scusa, scusa mea, patrons—Your pardon signior;—

(begs their pardons)
but come Sir Signal—let's see how you will make this silent relation—come stand between us two—

I think I have revenged my backsword-beating.

(goes off)

inviveates: enlivens, awakens (Petro's invention) **pericranium**: n, the skull or brain **sapientates**: makes wise or sage (Petro's invention) **snush**: a pinch of snuff **bagatelles**: trifles **Cackamarda Orangate**. orange-scented feces (another Petro invention) **dulce piquante**: sweet-sharp **Ecclesiastico...patronas**: the story that Petro tells in bad Italian mixed with some Spanish and French elements, and some obscure elements which may be meant as Petro's imitation of beggars' dialect. An English translation of the story would be: "A certain priest, plump and rich...meets a poor cripple. A poor cripple, poor criple; cripple, criple, cripple!...Charity for a poor cripple, for the love of God!" At last he begs a julio. "Nothing!" Then the poor cripple begs half a julio..."Nothing!"..."A kiss."..."Nothing!"..."Pardon, pardon, my masters." A coherent summary of the entire story would be: a fat bishop meets a lean beggar, and refuses to give him money, or a kiss, but when the beggar asks for a blessing, the bishop is enthusiastic to oblige. In his 'enthusiasm' Petro hits the two gentlemen, and finishes the aphorism with apologies.

96

BELFONT SENIOR, THE "SWINISH" RUSTIC SON OF A BRUTISH FATHER, EMBRACES LONDON'S LOW LIFE

(1688) THOMAS SHADWELL, The Squire of Alsatia, *Act 1, Sc. 1*

Belfont Senior, brought up in the country after his father's "rustic, swinish" manner, on his first visit to London falls in with the dregs of London's underworld, and, susceptible dupe that he is, celebrates his good luck. He is drawn after his original model, Ctesipho, who is the product of a harsh father's discipline in Terence's classic Roman comedy, *The Brothers*, which contrasts the effects of gentle vs. disciplinary upbringing of young sons. Shadwell follows Terence's guidance in plot and theme, but domesticates the play in the world of London riffraff, the effects of which, on the manners and behavior of "swinish" Belfont, gets detailed and realistic study.

In this, the very first scene, he's already met the companions of his undoing: Cheatly, the "debauched" fellow who lends goods and money to well-heeled young heirs, to their undoing; Shamwell, Cheatly's "decoy," a ruined heir himself who now cadges a living by helping Cheatly ruin others; "Captain" Hackum, a blustering ex-sergeant, now a pimp; and the like. "Alsatia" is the slang name for Whitehall, the London district where the law, wisely, rarely ventures.

During this very first night in London, Belfont is at once recognized by the leeches as the heir to an "entailed" estate—one that is legally bound to be inherited by a firstborn—and they swarm. He's thrilled by the generous good fellowship of their company, and in this speech, thanks them with a very full heart.

BELFONT SENIOR

Cousin Shamwell, well met. Good morrow to you. You know we were boozy last night. I am a little Hot-headed this morning, and come to take the fresh air here in the Temple Walks. Ne'er stir, I could never have thought there had been such a gallant place as London. Here I can be drunk over night, and well next morning; can ride in a coach for a shilling as good as a Deputy-Lieutenant's; and such merry wags and ingenious companions—! Well, I vow and swear, I am mightily beholding to you, dear cousin Shamwell. Then for the women! Mercy upon us! so civil and well bred. And I'll swear upon a Bible, finer all of them than knight-baronets' wives with us. Ay, I vow, pretty rogues! No pride in them in the world, but so courteous and familiar, as I am an honest man, they'll do whatever one would have them presently. Ah, sweet rogues! While in the country, a pize take them! There's such a stir with "pish, fy, nay, Mr. Timothy, what do you do? I vow I'll squeak, never stir, I'll call out," ah hah—

And I am in that fear of my father besides, adad. To say truth, he's so terrible to me, I can never enjoy myself for him. Lord! What will he say when he comes to know I am in London? Which he in all his life-time would never suffer me to see, for fear I should be debauched, forsooth; and allows me little or no money at home neither. Well, I'll endur't no longer! If I can but raise money, I'll teach him to use his son like a dog, I'll warrant him.

But sure that Mr. Cheatly is as fine a gentleman as any wears a head, and as ingenious, ne'er stir, I believe he would run down the best scholar in Oxford, and put 'em in a mousehole with his wit, a rare fellow. I'll speak a bold word: he shall cut a sham or banter with the best wit or poet of 'em all. He is so, and a worthy brave fellow, and the best friend where he takes, and the most sincere of any man breathing. Nay, I must needs say I have found him very frank, and very much a gentleman, and am most extremely obliged to him and you for your great kindness.

I am mightily beholding to you both, I vow and swear. My uncle, Sir Edward, took my brother when he was a child, and adopted him. Would it had been my lot! I was resolved not to let my brother see me till I was in circumstances, d'ye see? And for my father, he is in Holland. My mother's brother died, and left him sole executor. He'll not be here these six weeks. I'll cast off all the relations in the world before I'll part with such true, such loving friends, adad. Pox o' the country, I say! The best team of horses my father has shall not draw me thither again.

pize: mild imprecation, as in "the Devil take them"

97

SOSIA, PLAYING TWO PARTS, REHEARSES THE NEWS HE IS BRINGING TO ALCMENE
(1690) JOHN DRYDEN, Amphitryon, *Act 2, Sc. 1*

In Dryden's *Amphitryon*, there are, according to divine decree, two Sosias. One is the legitimate slave of Amphitryon, who has hurried back this night to his master's wife Alcmene to give her happy news. Her husband, having won a battle for Thebes and killed the enemy King, is happily on his way home to his wife, ready to resume marital bliss. But the other Sosia prevents this one from banging at the door. He's the God Mercury, the "porter," he calls himself, condemned to serve *his* master too, the Lord of all the Gods, Jupiter. Most particularly, he is on porter's duty tonight during the Divine One's amatory adventure: seducing Alcmene disguised as the living replica of her husband. And so Mercury, disguised as the replica of Sosia, stands at the door to the confounding of the real Sosia, to prevent his interrupting the God's pleasure with the unwelcome news that the real Amphitryon is not due to return until the morning.

Like most of the clever servants in classical comedy, Sosia is no abject drudge. He has a character of his own, and a mind of his own, and his mind has no problem acknowledging happily that he is, first and foremost, a coward. Even before the meeting with the confounding replica of himself, he's been through a night of substantial terrors: the journey home during which the trees in the night looked like thieves and the bulrushes shook like spears. And so, first and foremost, he accommodates his cowardice, trusting nothing and no one, not even himself, to accomplish without special care whatever task lies before him.

Having gotten through the terrors of the night and arrived home, he anticipates a new chore—one that might even give pleasure rather than fright: spelling out his news to Alcmene. And for this, characteristically, he prepares with excruciatingly detailed foresight lest he fail. So thoroughly does he rehearse his message that he prepares not only his own answers but Alcmene's breathless queries too. Like his forebears in comedy for the previous 2,200 years, his practical cowardice produces carefully calculated, sometimes even successful, cunning. But no success this time: he's forestalled, later in the scene, by One Above. His message does not get through, and the Divine One's pleasure is not interrupted.

> SOSIA
>
> Was not the devil in my master, to send me out in this dreadful dark night to bring the news of his victory to my lady? And was not I possessed with ten devils, for going on his errand without a convoy for the safeguard of my person? Lord, how am I melted into sweat with fear! I am diminished of my natural weight, above two stone. I shall not bring half my self home again to my poor wife and family. I have been in an ague-fit ever since shut of evening, what with the fright of trees by the highway, which looked maliciously like thieves by moonshine, and what with bulrushes by the riverside, that shaked liked spears and lances at me. Well, the greatest plague of a servingman is to be hired to some great lord! They care not what drudgery they put upon us, while they lie lolling at their ease abed, and stretch their lazy

limbs in expectation of the whore which we are fetching for them.

The better sort of 'em will say 'Upon my honour' at every word. Yet ask 'em for our wages, and they plead the privilege of their honour and will not pay us, nor let us take our privilege of the law upon them. These are a very hopeful sort of patriots, to stand up as they do for liberty and property of the subject. There's conscience for you!

(Looking about him)

Stay; this methinks should be our house, and I should thank the gods now for bringing me safe home. But I think I had as good let my devotions alone, till I have got the reward for my good news, and then thank 'em once for all; for if I praise 'em before I am safe within doors, some damned mastiff dog may come out and worry me, and then my thanks are thrown away upon 'em.

Now am I to give my lady an account of my lord's victory. 'Tis good to exercise my parts beforehand and file my tongue into eloquent expressions, to tickle her ladyship's imagination.

(Setting down his lanthorn)

This lanthorn, for once, shall be my lady-because she is the lamp of all beauty and perfection. Then thus I make my addresses to her.

(Bows)

'Madam, my lord has chosen me out, as the most faithful, though the most unworthy of his followers, to bring your ladyship this following account of our glorious expedition.' Then she.

(In a shrill tone)

'O my poor Sosia, how am I overjoyed to see thee!' She can say no less. 'Madam, you do me too much honour, and the world will envy me this glory.' Well answered on my side. 'And how does my lord Amphitryon?' 'Madam, he always does like a man of courage, when he is called by honour.' There I think I nicked it. 'But when will he return?' 'As soon as possibly he can; but not so soon as his impatient heart could wish him with your ladyship.'

'But what does he do, and what does he say? Prithee tell me something more of him.' 'He always says less than he does, madam, and his
enemies have found it to their cost.' Where the devil did I learn these
elegancies and gallantries?

(staring up to the sky)

What, is the devil in the night! She's as long as two nights. The seven
stars are just where they were seven hours ago! High day—high night,
I mean, by my favour. What, has Phoebus been playing the good-fellow and overslept himself, that he forgets his to us mortals? Well, this
is our house, and when I am got in, I will tell you more.

ague: a fever, chill, shivering **lanthorn**: lantern **nicked**: guessed exactly, "nailed"
high day: an exclamation (Sosia's invention) **playing the good-fellow**: reveling

98

MELLEFONT RECOUNTS HOW LADY TOUCHWOOD INVADED HIS BEDCHAMBER AND WOOED WITH FURY

(1694) WILLIAM CONGREVE, The Double Dealer, *Act 1, Sc. 3*

Before the encroachment of 18th century Sentimentality, Love was
understood as often as not to be an illness, an aberration. In the
last years of the Restoration, the game of sex as it was boldly pursued
in its first years was genteelly upgraded, and was more politely spoken
of as Love. But even in the guise of Love, it still could enter the game
as an irrational force with mad intent, to the game's confusion and
detriment. When Love was moderately subscribed to by equal lovers,
and was harnessed by them to their mutual and more serious pursuit
of Fortune (life-income by way of inheritance), it remained perfectly
amenable to reasonable alliances and happy endings—as the success of

so many well-matched lovers in Restoration comedy testifies. Unequal love was a different matter altogether. In its erratic course, it provoked a succession of responses: chagrin, cunning, mad daring, triumph, repletion, indifference, hatred—more or less in that order. And each of these stages evoked its appropriate rhetoric, its appropriate postures, its appropriate plan of action. But for love spurned outright, there was only one response: vengeful fury.

Mellefont, before the play's opening, became the victim of such a love, in which the distinction between passionate lover and mad murderer was entirely erased. His aunt, Lady Touchwood, is madly in love with him. He's rejected her for practical as well as virtuous reasons: his inheritance depends on his uncle's will, and therefore on his aunt's having no offspring. She has learned of his impending marriage to Cynthia and gambles everything on one last chance. The "chance"— invading his bedroom, and being again repulsed—leads first to her attempting to murder him with his own sword, and that failing, planning thenceforth his utter destruction.

Here the play's plot begins. Its interest is not at all in tracking the scorned woman's or the endangered lover's emotional "journeys," but given their relative societal and political strengths and weaknesses, its interest is exclusively in their game-maneuvers, one to destroy, the other to forestall. The means? Diplomatic alliances [see I, #100]. Mellefont at once plans his campaign: his friend Careless is assigned the job of keeping Lady Pliant, a potential ally of Lady Touchwood's, out of the way, and as a bonus to getting her "secured" to Careless's "interest," "you may incline her to mine." (Careless follows up his "interest" to the last degree.) Mellefont takes for himself the assignment of watching his uncle, to prevent Lady Touchwood from getting his ear (her persuading Lord Touchwood of Mellefont's iniquities would be the ruin of Mellefont's own incidental design, which is to marry Cynthia for both her love and her money). And—his almost fatal mistake—assigning Maskwell the task of spying in the enemy's camp, and "giving me notice of any suspicion." And what does Mellefont suppose Maskwell's "interest" would be? "Obligations of gratitude" for helping him to his uncle's favor. (Mellefont's strategic error: Gratitude, in this conniving world, is not an "interest.") Lady Touchwood, with equal zest, collects her alliances, and the two camps are ready to begin their maneuvers through the play's action. In whispers, in overhearings, in reports from the enemy camp, intelligence battles intelligence, and beneath the chatter and wit of Congreve's banter, hard-headedness works its blunt, self-advancing will.

> **MELLEFONT**
> I am jealous of a plot. I would have noise and impertinence keep my Lady Touchwood's head from working: for hell is not more busy than her brain, nor contains more devils than that imaginations.
> You shall judge whether I have not reason to be alarmed. None besides you and Maskwell are acquainted with the secret of my Aunt Touchwood's violent passion for me. Since my first refusal of her addresses, she has endeavoured to do me all ill offices with my uncle; yet has managed 'em with that subtlety that to him they have borne the face of kindness; while her malice, like a dark lantern, only shone upon me, where it was directed. Still it gave me less perplexity to prevent the success of her displeasure, than to avoid the importunities of her love; and of two evils, I thought myself favoured in her aversion: but whether urged by her despair, and the short prospect of time she saw to accomplish her designs; whether the hopes of revenge, or of her love, terminated in the view of this my marriage with Cynthia, I know not; but this morning she surprised me in my bed.—
>
> 'Tis well Nature has not put it into her sex's power to ravish. What at first amazed me; for I looked to have seen her in all the transports of a slighted and revengeful woman: but when I expected thunder from her voice, and lightning in her eyes, I saw her melted into tears, and hushed into a sigh. It was long before either of us spoke, passion had tied her tongue, and amazement mine.—In short, the consequence was thus, she omitted nothing that the most violent love could urge, or ten-

der words express; which when she saw had no effect, but still I pleaded
honour and nearness of blood to my uncle, then came the storm I
feared at first: for starting from my bedside like a fury, she flew to my
sword, and with much ado I prevented her doing me or herself a mischief: having disarmed her, in a gust of passion she left me, and in a
resolution, confirmed by a thousand curses, not to close her eyes, till
she had seen my ruin. But does she think I have no more sense than to
get an heir upon her body to disinherit myself? For as I take it this set-
tlement upon me is with a proviso, that my uncle have no children.

I must get you to engage my Lady Plyant all this evening, that my
pious aunt may not work her to her interest. And if you chance to
secure her to yourself, you may incline her to mine. She's handsome,
and knows it; I'll observe my uncle myself; and Jack Maskwell has
promised me, to watch my aunt narrowly, and give me notice upon
any suspicion. He has obligations of gratitude to bind him to me; his
dependence upon my uncle is through my means.

jealous: suspicious **imaginations**: plots

99

MASKWELL STRENGTHENS MELLEFONT'S CONFIDENCE IN HIS LOYALTY BY CONFIDENTLY CONFESSING HIS TREACHERY
(1694) WILLIAM CONGREVE, The Double Dealer, *Act 2, Sc. 7*

Jack Maskwell has promised me," confides Mellefont. to his friend
Careless, making his first and most costly strategic error, "to watch
my aunt narrowly, and give me notice upon any suspicion. He has
obligations of gratitude to bind me to him."

   In fact, he has none. Maskwell is the double dealer of the play's
title. He's the lover of Lady Touchwood, her ally in her campaign

against the hated Mellefont who spurned her passion [see I, #98]. He's also the friend of Mellefont, to whom he reports all of Lady Touchwood's treacheries, and to guarantee his trustworthiness, reports even his own ostensible role in them. But his genuine agenda is in fact winning from Mellefont his lover Cynthia, by the double betrayal of both his supposed allies.

Maskwell is later [in I, #100] to spell out for his own delectation the rules of the game, none of which countenance Gratitude. He's been party to one of the stratagems of Lady Touchwood's vengeance against Mellefont, persuading Lady Pliant that Mellefont is using the screen of pretended love for her daughter Cynthia "to procure the mother," Lady Pliant herself, and so provoke the rage of Lord Pliant, destroying Mellefont's "pretensions" to his daughter. Mellefont, astounded by their accusation, and by Lady Pliant's supposing he is really infatuated with her, confides in Maskwell, his supposed ally, hoping for explanation as well as consolation.

Maskwell provides both in abundance by his intelligent strategy — given those very rules of the game — of confessing the full extent of his treacherous alliance with Lady Touchwood against Mellefont himself. It's an advanced ploy, but is only the first example in the play of his art, which he visits with equal pretended frankness, and equal relish, on Lady Touchwood.

Here is his consoling confession of betrayal to Mellefont.

> MASKWELL
> The witch, Lady Touchwood, has raised the storm, and her ministers have done their work. I met Sir Paul towing away Cynthia. Come, trouble not your head. I'll join you together ere tomorrow morning, or drown between you in the attempt. No sinking, nor no danger — Come, cheer up; why you don't know, that while I plead for you, your aunt has given me a retaining fee; — Nay, I am your greatest enemy, and she does journey-work under me.
>
> What d'ye think of my being employ'd in the execution of all her

plots? Ha, ha, ha, by Heav'n it's true; I have undertaken to break the
match, I have undertaken to make your uncle disinherit you, to get
you turn'd out of doors; and to — Ha, ha, ha, I can't tell you for
laughing, — Oh. she has open'd her heart to me, — I am to turn you
a grazing, and to — Ha, ha, ha, marry Cynthia myself; there's a plot
for you.

Ha, ha, ha. — Well, you must know then, that all my contrivances
were but bubbles; 'till at last I pretended to have been long secretly in
love with Cynthia, that did my business; that convinc'd your aunt, I
might be trusted; since it was as much my interest as hers to break the
match: Then she thought my jealousy might qualify me to assist her
in her revenge. And, in short. in that belief, told me the secrets of her
heart. At length we made this agreement, if I accomplish her designs
(as I told you before) she has engag'd to put Cynthia with all her fortune into my power.

I would not have you stay to hear now how I have contrived it: for I
don't know, be she may come this way; I am to meet her anon; after
all, I'll tell you the whole matter; be here in this gallery an hour hence,
by that time I imagine our consultation may be over.

100

MASKWELL, SELF-CONGRATULATING, APOSTROPHIZES TREACHERY AND DOUBLE DEALING
(1694) WILLIAM CONGREVE, The Double Dealer, *Act 2, Sc. 8*

In the moral climate of the Restoration, Maskwell doesn't see himself
as evil at all, but simply as accurate. He is merely the extreme instance
of the policy followed by all of Congreve's sophisticated, worldly characters, heroes and villains alike. If we think of them for a moment not

as persons but as nations, their smoothly engineered maneuvers become altogether intelligible. Like nations, each is bound, under cover of diplomacy and its universal rhetoric, to pursue with single-minded devotion one national interest. Maskwell, like all the others, adheres to this cold policy. It is understood among all of them—the Maskwells most coldly of all—that like nation's diplomats, the business of getting what you want involves a tireless courting of alliances, and as occasion demands, dissolving and restructuring them according to the fixed principle of private interest. The Valentines, the Mirabels, the Angelicas, the Millimants as well as the Maskwells, all pursue their ends by way of the same exclusive allegiance: to self-interest alone.

And so Maskwell accurately delineates reality. Neither duty, nor devotion, nor gratitude, nor faithfulness, nor honesty is linked to practical wisdom. None of these or their counterparts are accurate guides for either national or personal advantage, which is best gotten at by fraud, treachery, baseness, hypocrisy and all the other moral iniquities. Note closely the strategies by which the Mirabels and the Angelicas and the Valentines and the other of Congreve's more admirable souls gain their objectives; Maskwell merely overdoes their practice. Only by overdoing is he caught out in the end, and so loses by the same gamesmanship by which the others win.

At the moment, his plotting is going perfectly; he stops for a spell to review, with glee, the precision of his policy, to savor the sheer pleasure of saying bluntly what all the others profess, but who rarely—with such unashamed frankness—confess.

> MASKWELL
> Cynthia, let thy beauty gild my crimes; and whatsoever I commit of treachery or deceit shall be imputed to me as a merit.—Treachery! What treachery? Love cancels all the bonds of friendship, and sets men right upon their first foundations.

Duty to Kings, piety to parents, gratitude to benefactors, and fidelity to friends, are different and particular ties: but the name of "rival" cuts 'em all asunder, and is a general acquittance—rival is equal, and love like death an universal leveler of mankind. Ha! But is there not such a thing as honesty? Yes, and whosoever has it about him bears an enemy in his breast: for your honest man, as I take it, is that nice, scrupulous, conscientious person who will cheat nobody but himself; such another coxcomb as your wise man, who is too hard for all the world, and will be made a fool of by nobody, but himself; but himself: ha, ha, ha. Well, for wisdom and honesty, give me cunning and hypocrisy; oh, 'tis such a pleasure to angle for fair-faced fools! Then that hungry gudgeon Credulity will bite at anything.—Why, let me see, I have the same face, the same words and accents, when I speak what I do think, and when I speak what I do not think—the very same—and dear dissimulation is the only art not to be known from nature.

Why will mankind be fools, and be deceived?
And why friends' and lovers' oaths believed?
When each, who searches strictly his own mind,
May so much fraud and power of baseness find.

hungry gudgeon Credulity: owing to the gudgeon being often used for bait, the word came to mean a gull, one that will bite at any bait

101
THE VALET JEREMY IS HORRIFIED AT HIS MASTER'S PLAN TO TURN PLAYWRIGHT
(1695) WILLIAM CONGREVE, Love for Love, *Act 1, Sc. 1*

When Voltaire visited Congreve to pay homage to England's most eminent living dramatist, Congreve, alert to condescension, begged that he not be addressed as a playwright but rather as a gentleman. In *Love for Love*, Valentine's valet Jeremy is horrified for the livelihood of both his master and himself, should Valentine succumb to the poverty of a writing career. But for Congreve, there was an additional horror: the playwright-artisan, like the merest tradesman, is of the workaday world. The gentleman, having no tangible talents and not stooping to labor for his livelihood, retains the pure status of the indefinable [see I, #109]. He is even loftier than the many "wits" whose vanity stooped to exploiting their gifts, and so descended into authorship.

But Valentine's urgency, as Jeremy so fully describes it, is enormous: lost estate, lost possessions, lost love, insurmountable debt, and all this owing to his own folly. There's a tradition in classical comedy of servants chastising their masters for such follies as these and others, and Jeremy takes full advantage of his tradition's license. He's irate on a number of scores: (1) the iniquity of learning's and wisdom's miserable, and likely, yoke to poverty; (2) the iniquity of Valentine's extravagance when he was rich; (3) the iniquity of being invited to share for good his master's poetic starvation; (4) the iniquity of Will's, the literary coffee house in London's bohemian slum, where "nothing thrives that belongs to it," neither the starving poets inhabiting it, nor the tobacco-and-liquor stink of the place, nor the proprietors supporting them on tick, nor the chairmen (= cabbies) carrying the poets to "visit some great fortune," paid with nothing but doomsday promises. Valentine's mad determination is proof against Jeremy's persuasions, and leaves Jeremy with the poor alternative of turning his task over to Scandal, Valentine's friend, just arrived.

> **JEREMY**
> Sir, you're a gentlemen, and probably understand this fine feeding; but does your Epictetus, or your Seneca here, or any of these poor rich rogues, teach you how to pay your debts without money? Will they shut up the mouths of your creditors? Will Plato be bail for you? or Diogenes, because he understands confinement, and lived in a tub, go

to prison for you? 'Slife, sir, what do you mean? to mew yourself up here with three or four musty books, in commendation of starving and poverty?

Ay, sir, I am a fool, I know it; and yet, Heaven help me, I'm poor enough to be a wit;—but I was always a fool when I told you what your expenses would bring you to; your coaches and your liveries, your treats and your balls; your being in love with a lady that did not care a farthing for you in your prosperity; and keeping company with wits that cared for nothing but your prosperity, and now, when you are poor, hate you as much as they do one another.

And now Heaven, of mercy, continue the tax upon paper! you mean to write a play?! You're undone, sir, you're ruined, you won't have a friend left in the world if you turn poet.—Ah, pox confound that Will's Coffee-house! it has ruined more young men than the Royal Oak lottery;—nothing thrives that belongs to't. The man of the house would have been an alderman by this time with half the trade, if he had set up in the city. For my part, I never sit at the door that I don't get double the stomach that I do at a horse-race:—the air upon Banstead downs is nothing to it for a whetter. Yet I never see it, but the spirit of famine appears to me, sometimes like a decayed porter, worn out with pimping, and carrying billets-doux and song; not like other porters for hire, but for the jest's sake:—now like a thin chair-man, melted down to half his proportion with carrying a poet upon tick, to visit some great fortune, and his fare to be paid him, like the wages of sin, either at the day of marriage, or the day of death.

(Enter Scandal.)

Mr. Scandal, for Heaven's sake, sir, try if you can dissuade him from turning poet.

fine feeding: Jeremy, angry at Valentine "a gentleman" for calling "reading for breakfast" the same as "feeding" **Epictetus** (AD 60?-120?): Greek stoic philosopher **Seneca** (see v. II, #24) **Diogenes**: a Greek philosopher, lived in a barrel and looked for 'the man' with a candle **mew**: to confine **Will's Coffee-house**: where Dryden reigned; gamblers, poets and other men of wit used to hang out in coffee houses **Royal Oak Lottery** for the benefit of the Royal Fishing Company; the only one not outlawed in 1698 **alderman**: a member of a borough or county council **double the stomach**: sick from the stench

102

LOVELESS, IMPOVERISHED BY RIOT, REMAINS THOROUGHLY WELL DISPOSED TOWARD PLEASURE

(1696) COLLEY CIBBER, *Love's Last Shift, Act 1, Sc. 1*

L oveless is a hardened case of cynical libertinism, and so, in the right hands, is ripe for reform. Being so absolute a debauchee, and proud of it, proud even of the impoverished condition to which it's brought him, he can go nowhere but up.

The case of Loveless initiates the story to which we've grown accustomed since the 18th century of the Journey from Cold Reason to the Wisdom of the Heart, from sad ignorance of the Self to the happy discovery of its inherent Virtue. To be sure, the adoption of that sentimental journey was part and parcel of the revulsion, moral and religious, that overtook the middle classes as they encroached more and more on the theatrical purlieus that had been ruled by the morals and manners of the idlers above the middle. But to bear any resemblance to reality, and to so thoroughly displace the reality of the previous age—the Restoration—required something more than a mere shift in polite taste. It required a revolution in the understanding of the prime channel through which the human psyche operates: "Head" and "Soul" gave way to a new chief engine: the "Heart."

Colley Cibber is the pied piper of that revolution in England, in which the Head, encouraged to lose its moorings, gave way, and the properties that had been traditionally attributed to the Soul were transferred wholesale to the Heart. The Heart, the newly secularized Soul, knew what the Restoration's Head denied, that humanity deep down is made of and therefore moved by Good. And so, it was Feeling that opened the door to True Reason, and what turned the key was a virtuous act, a gesture, an appeal, to which the Heart could not fail to respond. Deeply touched, the cold Heart warmed, and the ice that kept it cold melted in tears, the first and certain sign of virtue's triumph.

In 18th century serious comedy, toward which *Love's Last Shift* led the way, the reasons of the Heart took over, and a tearful comedy ended—characteristically—when the first step, sometimes only a small one, was taken by the converted reprobate. In Loveless's case, it was a large one, at least to hear him tell it in his rapturous recantation of former error.

But so significant is this step in the alteration of character psychology, and so dramatically does it happen within the action of this play, that the actor taking on Loveless must somehow come to terms with the fact that he's two distinct people—the rationalist before conversion who's governed entirely by the pragmatics of desire, and the alternate one whose action is governed by the psychological engine of the heart alone. That shift needs a bridge that, if its intensity is missed by a hair, provokes skeptical derision, not to say outright laughter, but if smoothly negotiated, with the commensurate inward shift of human nature's nature, can still provoke tears flowing from the spectator's equally activated Heart.

(Enter Loveless and Snap, his servant)

LOVELESS
Sirrah! leave your preaching. Your counsel, like an ill clock, either stands still or goes too slow. You ne'er thought my extravagancies amiss while you had your share of them; and now I want money to make myself drunk, you advise me to live sober, you dog. Ungrateful rogue, to murmur at a little fasting with me when thou hast been an equal partner of my good fortune. Canst not thou bear the frowns of a common strumpet, Fortune? No, sirrah! The world to me is a garden stocked with all sorts of fruit, where the greatest pleasure we can take is in the variety of taste; but a wife is an eternal apple tree—after a pull or two you are sure to set your teeth on edge.

(Enter Young Worthy)

Dear Worthy! Let me embrace thee; the sight of an old friend warms me beyond that of a new mistress. Faith, Will, I am a little out of repairs at present. But I am all that's left of honest Ned Loveless. Why, my last hopes, faith, which were to persuade Sir Will[iam] Wisewoud (if he be alive), to whom I mortgaged my estate, to let me have five hundred pounds more upon it, or else to get some honest friend to redeem the mortgage and share the overplus! Beside, I thought that London might now be a place of uninterrupted pleasure, for I hear that my wife is dead; and to tell you the truth, it was the staleness of her love was the main cause of my going over. Well, rest her soul.

What have I done with my estate? I pawned it to buy pleasure, that is, old wine, young whores, and the conversation of brave fellows as mad as myself. Pox! If a man has appetites, they are torments if not indulged. I shall never complain as long as I have health and vigor; and as for my poverty, why the devil should I be ashamed of that, since a rich man won't blush at his knavery?

Ah, Will, you'll find marrying to cure lewdness is like surfeiting to cure hunger—for all the consequence is, you loathe what you surfeit on and are only chaste to her you marry. But do you hear?—canst not thou lend me the fellow to that same guinea you gave my man; I'll give you my bond if you mistrust me.

flux: diarrhea

103

LOVELESS EMBRACES LOVE OF VIRTUE TOGETHER WITH BLISS, AND FULSOMELY REPENTS

(1696) COLLEY CIBBER, *Love's Last Shift, Act 5, Sc. 2*

[see I, #102]

LOVELESS

My wife! Impossible! Is she not dead? How shall I believe thee? These speaking characters, which in their cheerful bloom our early passions mutually recorded. Ha! It is here. It is no illusion, but my real name, which seems to upbraid me as a witness of my perjured love. Oh, I am confounded with my guilt and tremble to behold thee. Pray give me leave to think. I have wronged you. Basely wronged you! Oh, seal my pardon with thy trembling lips, while with this tender grasp of fond reviving love I seize my bliss and stifle all thy wrongs forever.

(He embraces her)

Oh, thou hast roused me from my deep lethargy of vice! For hitherto my soul has been enslaved to loose desires, to vain, deluding follies, and shadows of substantial bliss, but now I wake with joy to find my rapture real. Thus let me kneel and pay my thanks to her whose conquering virtue has at last subdued me. Here will I fix, thus prostrate sigh my shame, and wash my crimes in never-ceasing tears of penitence.

Have I not used thee like a villain? For almost ten long years deprived thee of my love and ruined all thy fortune? But I will labor, dig, beg, or starve to give new proofs of my unfeigned affection. While in my arms I thus can circle thee, I grasp more treasure than in a day posting sun can travel over. Oh, why have I so long been blind to the perfections of thy mind and person? Not knowing thee a wife, I found thee charming beyond the wishes of luxurious love. It is then a name, a word, shall rob thee of thy worth? Can fancy be a surer guide to happiness than reason? Oh, I have wandered like a benighted wretch and lost myself in life's unpleasing journey.

'Twas heedless fancy first that made me stray
But reason now breaks forth and lights me on my way.

posting: from post, to travel with speed, hasten

104

SIR NOVELTY FASHION DEMONSTRATES HOW HE MERITS HIS NAME
(1696) COLLEY CIBBER, *Love's Last Shift*, *Act 2, Sc. 1*

Oh, such an air!" Narcissa, pretending, praises Sir Novelty, "so becoming a negligence!" That negligence, diffidence [see I, #125] is precisely what he does not have, but cheerfully thinks he does. He is, as the play's subtitle has it, the Fool of Fashion, built along the lines of his predecessor, Sir Fopling Flutter. They are almost identical fops, and together they generated almost identical later imitations. Like his predecessor, Sir Novelty is a "coxcomb," that is, a show-off and a fool, and like him too, he believes he has the manner of a gentleman. Hopelessly, he doesn't; his vanities (even apart from his clothes) give him away. Like a gentleman, he deflects compliments, but can't sustain their deflection, letting his pleasure in them show; he's self-deprecating, but his modesty only pleads for contradiction; he imitates, as Narcissa cruelly noted, diffidence, but can't suppress his eagerness to flaunt what diffidence always slights. The true gentleman deflects detraction as well as compliment; Sir Novelty, incapable of letting detractions pass, hurries to their vindication.

He has already, before launching on this tirade of self-plumage and self-praise, brushed by all the tests of self-denigration, deflection of praise and blame, etc., etc., and failed them all. He is now in full unbridled flight, tumbling rapidly and decisively, display by display, brag by brag, from sham Gentleman to self-revealing Fool.

SIR NOVELTY FASHION

Madam, I was the first person in England that was complimented with the name of "Beau" which is a title I prefer before "Right Honorable" for that may be inherited, but this I extorted from the whole nation by my surprising mien and unexampled gallantry. Then another thing, madam: It has been observed that I have been eminently successful in those fashions I have recommended to the town, and I don't question but this very suit will raise as many ribbon-weaves as ever the clipping or melting trade did goldsmiths. In short, madam, the cravat string, the garter, the sword knot, the centurine, the b[u]rdash, the steenkirk, the large button, the long sleeve, the plume, and full peruke were all created, cried down, or revived by me. In a word, madam, there has never been anything particularly taking or agreeable for these ten years past, but your humble servant was the author of it.

Then you must know my coach and equipage are as well known as myself, and since the conveniency of two play houses, I have a better opportunity of showing them, for between every act, whisk! I am gone from one to the other. Oh, what pleasure it is at a good play to go out before half an act's done! It looks particular and gives the whole audience an opportunity of turning upon me at once. Then do they conclude I have some extraordinary business or a fine woman to go to at least, and then again it shows my contempt of what the dull town think their chiefest diversion. But if I do stay a play out, I always set with my back to the stage. Then everybody will imagine I have been tired with it before, or that I am jealous who talks to who in the King's box. And thus, madam, do I take more pains to preserve a public reputation than ever any lady took after the smallpox to recover her complexion.

the clipping...goldsmiths: shaving off the edges of coins **sword knot**: holds the sword **centurine**: a waist-belt **burdash**: either a fringed sash or a kind of cravat **steenkirk**: a loosely flowing cravat or neckcloth; named by the French in honor of the battle of Steinkirk **peruke**: a wig **two play houses**: the two licensed theatres Drury Lane and Lincoln's Inn Fields

105

LORD FOPPINGTON FAVORS A LADY WITH AN ACCOUNT OF HIS DAY

(1696) JOHN VANBRUGH, The Relapse, *Act 2, Sc. 2*

In *The Relapse*, the mocking sequel to the sentimental *Love's Last Shift*, Vanbrugh promotes Sir Novelty Fashion to the English peerage. At the play's opening, as Lord Foppington, he's purchased his title not 18 hours ago, mainly to win a wealthy heiress in marriage, but also for the advantage title offers for vanity's self-esteem. Looked at closely, behind the winning comedy of his self-revealing portrait in this monologue, satirical intent lurks, and is almost Chekhovian in its suggestion of wry melancholy inside the joke. Buying titles had become endemic corrupt practice since the days of James II in the early 1700's. Peers without function or point beyond the wearing of their titles were automatically subject to the necessary human anxiety that attends a life routine of simply filling time to no purpose; "filling time" in fact *becomes* its sole purpose (we're on the verge of the chimerical life of the *rococo*). Lord Foppington does it ideally, with as little volition or expenditure of imagination as possible: the waking at ten, the three-hour dawdle over dressing, the yawning gap of time between dinner after one and the play at six, which, when stretched, can occupy four hours until ten. "So there's twelve of the four and twenty pretty well over." For the rest, four hours of drunken stupor and eight hours to "sleep myself sober again."

Notable above all is his scrupulous avoidance of time expended on matters of conceivable value: the books that must never be looked into, the plays that must never be watched, the affairs (toward which his life is presumably aimed) that never, luckily, take their toll in time on his conscientious doing-nothing. Amusing, yes, but the bleakness of Lord Foppington's days hangs like a shadow over his cheerful narration. It is a wonderful self-revelation that avoids, entirely successfully, self-recognition. And it is this particular fact—the total lack of self-recognition—which defines Lord Foppinton as a quintessential Fool.

FOPPINGTON

I have a private gallery, where I walk sometimes, is furnished with nothing but books and looking-glasses. Madam, I have gilded 'em, and ranged 'em prettily, before Gad, it is the most entertaining thing in the world to walk and look upon 'em. For the inside of the book, that, I must confess, I am nat altogether so fand of. Far to mind the inside of a book is to entertain one's self with the forced product of another man's brain. Naw I think a man of quality and breeding may be much better diverted with the natural sprauts of his own. But to say the truth, madam, let a man love reading never so well, when once he comes to know this tawn he finds so many better ways of passing the four-and-twenty hours, that 'twere ten thousand pities he should consume his time in that. Far example, madam, my life; my life, madam, is a perpetual stream of pleasure, that glides through such a variety of entertainments, I believe the wisest of our ancestors never had the least conception of any of 'em. I rise, madam, about ten a'clock. I don't rise sooner, because 'tis the worst thing in the world for the complexion, nat that I pretend to be a beau, but a man must endeavour to look wholesome, lest he makes so nauseous a figure in the side-bax, the ladies should be compelled to turn their eyes upon the play. So at ten a'clack, I say I rise. Naw, if I find 'tis a good day, I resolve to take a turn in the park, and see the fine women; so huddle on my clothes, and get dressed by one. If it be nasty weather, I take a turn in the chocolate-hause, where, as you walk, madam, you have the prettiest prospect in the world; you have looking-glasses all round you. Why then, ladies, from thence I go to dinner at Lacket's, where you are so nicely and delicately served that, stap my vitals, they shall compose you a dish no bigger than a saucer, shall come to fifty shillings. Between eating my dinner, and washing my mauth, ladies, I spend my time till I go to the play, where, till nine a'clack, I entertain myself with looking upon the company; and usually dispose of one hour more in leading 'em aut. So there's twelve of the four-and-twenty pretty well over. The other twelve, madam, are disposed of in two articles: in the first four I toast myself drunk, and in t'other eight I sleep myself sober again. Thus, ladies, you see my life is an eternal raund O of delights. As to time for my intrigues, I usually make detachments of it from my other pleasures, according to the exigency. Far your ladyship may please to take notice, that those who intrigue with women of quality have rarely occasion far above half an hour at a time: people of that rank being under those decorums, they can seldom give you a longer view than will just serve to shoot 'em flying. So that the course of my other pleasures is not very much interrupted by my amours.

Gad: God (Lord Foppington's affected accent turns o's into a's)

106
LOVELESS IS DISQUIETED BY THE LOGIC OF HIS WAVERING MARITAL AFFECTIONS
(1696) JOHN VANBRUGH, The Relapse, *Act 3, Sc. 1*

In *Love's Last Shift,* Loveless, after abandoning his wife Amanda for a life of debauchery, returns years later to his native soil. Amanda, by a cunning stratagem, demonstrates so convincingly the strength and endurance of her love that his heart melts with reciprocal feeling, and with an invigorated determination to walk the path of marital virtue [see I, #102 and 103]. In *The Relapse,* Vanbrugh's skeptical incredulity moved him to append a sequel, the later story of the convert, the all too familiar story of lapsed virtue.

Loveless, not too surprisingly, is found wanting. In his soliloquy, he debates with himself: Is it Fate, he asks, that the very woman who, at a distance, so sexually aroused him at the theatre, should be the cousin whom his wife now invites to live with them? There are several stages to his argument with renewed temptation: (1) For all that Amanda has blessed him with, lifting him up from "the black tyrant Vice" to "envied fortune," is he not "bound" to her in gratitude? (Sudden halt in his reflections—the hinge on which his thoughts turn.) (2) Apart from his gratitude, does he in fact love her? (Here, an urgent reinforcement of his conviction.) He does, he does, and the proof is that he would sacrifice his life for her.

But now the old dominion of the libertinish Head returns, and undercuts the urgings of the melting Heart. (3) The real test is, whether he would not also save the life of cousin Berinthia; and assuredly he would. And so the not-loved-but-only-desired-in-the-old-way Berinthia subverts the proof: the willing sacrifice of life is no proof of love. But if so (4) it must be—ah!—that the sacrifice for the one is a strong proof of love, whereas the sacrifice for the other is merely a proof of friendship. But then (5) if so, it must be a friendship as mightily compelling as love itself. But how and when did such a friendship blossom? For mighty friendships demand long, long nurturing; and so his feeling for the recently-met Berinthia cannot pass for mighty friendship. It must therefore be—but (6) the terminal argument cuts short his speculation: Berinthia appears, and the other door is effectually reopened for renewed entrance, the one opposite his newfound door to Virtue.

The speech moves smoothly from Loveless's newly found sentimental discourse back to the discourse of old: logical scrutiny gradually turns its back on the language and principles of the Heart. The speech follows a similar progression of logical postulates as does a familiar, earlier one that ended: "Thus 'conscience' doth make cowards of us all." Loveless's, with parallel scrutiny, ends with "reason" making backsliders of us all.

LOVELESS
Sure fate has yet some business to be done,
Before Amanda's heart and mine must rest;
Else, why amongst those legions of her sex,
Which throng the world,
Should she pick out for her companion
The only one on earth
Whom nature has endow'd for her undoing?
Undoing, was't, I said!—who shall undo her?
Is not her empire fix'd? am I not hers?
Did she not rescue me, a grovelling slave,
When chained and bound by that black tyrant vice,
I labored in his vilest drudgery?
Did she not ransom me, and set me free?
Nay, more, when my follies sunk
To a poor, tattered, despicable beggar,
Did she not lift me up to envied fortune?
Give me herself, and all that she possessed,
Without a thought of more return,
Than what a poor repenting heart might make her?
Hasn't she done this? And if she has,
Am I not strongly bound to love her for it?
To love her!—Why, do I not love her then?
By earth and heaven I do!
Nay, I have demonstration that I do:
For I would sacrifice my life to serve her.
Yet hold—if laying down my life
Be demonstration of my love,
What is't I feel in favor of Berinthia?

For should she be in danger, methinks I could incline to risk it for her
service too; and yet I do not love her. How then subsists my proof?—
Oh, I have found it out! What I would do for one, is demonstration
of my love; and if I'd do as much for t'other ; if there is demonstration
of my friendship—Ay, it must be so. I find I'm very much her
friend.—Yet let me ask myself one puzzling question more: Whence
springs this mighty friendship all at once? For our acquaintance is of
later date. Now friendship's said to be a plant of tedious growth; its

root composed of tender fibres, nice in their taste, cautious in spreading, checked with the least corruption in the soil; long ere it take, and long still ere it appear to do so: whilst mine is in a moment shot so high, and fix'd so fast, it seems beyond the power of storms to shake it. I doubt it thrives too fast.

(Musing. Enter Berinthia)

Ha, she here!—Nay, then take heed, my heart, for there are dangers towards.

demonstration: evidence **towards**: ahead

107

LORD FOPPINGTON, IN THE EPILOGUE, CONDEMNS THE AUTHOR
(1696) JOHN VANBRUGH, The Relapse, *Epilogue*

In a brilliant about face, Vanbrugh gives Lord Foppington the chance to get even. He's portrayed him throughout the play as both "coxcomb" and "beau," as though they were automatically equivalent. But Lord Foppington at play's end is smarting from the insult: "beau," yes, by preference, but "coxcomb"? Not remotely the same.

Lord Foppington has his own principles concerning social and even national polity. A staunch "beau," he argues that each of the parties, the lowly and the beaux, can be recognized from their outward display alone as either the ornaments of that polity or its thieves, cutthroats, and rebels: clothes, manners, objects, define them and, more important, give them away. Somewhat buried in his anger is the telling, and most relevant, distinction between the two parties: the beaux never "squabble" with the court, i.e., are not part of the current political opposition to Charles II, whereas the lowly "coxcombs," in the anti-court, or "Country" party, are the Republicans, the Jacobites, the "men of mischief" fostering rebellion. What infuriates Lord Foppington is Vanbrugh's commingling the elegant with the fashion-less of the "vile, dirty nation," their lowly and dangerous opposite, and so be damned to him, this Vanbrugh.

> LORD FOPPINGTON
> Gentlemen and ladies,
> These people have regaled you here today
> (In my opinion) with a saucy play;
> In which the author does presume to show
> That coxcomb, *ab origine*—was beau.
> Truly I think the thing of so much weight,
> That if some sharp chastisement ben't his fate,
> Gad's curse, it may in time destroy the state.
> I hold no one its friend, I must confess,
> Who would discauntenance your men of dress.
> Far, give me leave t'abserve, good clothes are things
> Have ever been of great support to kings:
> All treasons come fram slovens; it is not
> Within the reach of gentle beaux to play;
> They have no gall, no spleen, no teeth, no stings,
> Of all Gad's creatures, the most harmless things.
> Through all recard, no prince was ever slain
> By one who had a feather in his brain.
> They're men of too refined an education,
> To squabble with a court—for a vile dirty nation.
> I'm very pasitive, you never saw
> A through republican a finished beau.
> Nor truly shall you very often see
> A Jacobite much better dressed than he:
> In shart, through all the courts that I have been in,
> Your men of mischief—still are in faul linen.
> Did ever one yet dance the Tyburn jig
> With a free air, or a well pawdered wig?
> Did ever highway-man yet bid you stand

With a sweet bawdy snuff-bax in his hand;
Ar do you ever find they ask your purse
As men of breeding do?—Ladies, Gad's curse,
This author is a dag, and 'tis not fit
You should allow him ev'n one grain of wit.
To which, that his pretence may ne'er be named,
My humble motion is—he may be damned.

ab origine, Lat: by definition **far**: for (see I, #105) **Tyburn jig**: suffer death by hanging; Tyburn was a place for public executions in London

108

FAINALL DISMISSES WIVES, MARRIAGE, CUCKOLDRY AND JEALOUSY
(1700) WILLIAM CONGREVE, The Way of the World, *Act 3, Sc. 3*

Fainall, deliberating warily, escapes the emotional trap of moral feeling. Ostensibly the villain of *The Way of the World*, he is only marginally different in his motives and schemes from the more reputable characters [see I, #100]. Mirabel pays pretended court to Millimant's aunt, Lady Wishfort, to further his suit to Millimant and her dowry. Lady Wishfort, having discovered his treachery, joins with Mrs. Marwood to oppose his suit. Just as Mrs. Marwood in turn is her accomplice in destroying Mirabel's suit because she is herself secretly in love with him, so Fainall, who is married to Lady Wishfort's daughter, and is the wearied lover of Mrs. Marwood, is maneuvering to control his wife's fortune as well as Millimant's.

In the complex weave of motives and strategies of all the principle characters, Fainall is perhaps the greediest, and certainly the only one with no love in his soul for any of the women, and no honesty in his friendship with any of the men. But the principle on which he operates is the same as all the others: calculated private advantage alone.

His wife, Mrs. Fainall, one of Mirabel's former mistresses before her marriage, is still attached to him in friendship and feeling; the discovery instinctively provokes the conventional response in Fainall, but in this private deliberation, he considers: what, given the world's real principles, is his suffering and loss? Carefully, he deconstructs: wife, marriage, honor, love, cuckoldry, jealousy. Rationally considered, the claim of each disintegrates. The emotional baggage clinging to them thoroughly neutralized, he is left composed, reassured, and renewed in his quest to fulfill his objectives with unobstructed rationality.

FAINALL

Why then, I, it seems, am a husband, a rank husband; and my wife a very arrant, rank wife—all in the way of the world. 'Sdeath, to be a cuckold by anticipation, a cuckold in embryo! sure I was born with budding antlers, like a young satyr, or a citizen's child. 'Sdeath! to be out-witted—to be out-jilted—out-matrimony'd!—If I had kept my speed like a stag, 'twere somewhat,—but to crawl after, with my horns, like a snail, and be outstripped by my wife—'tis scurvy wedlock.

How do I stand affected towards my lady? Let me see—I am married already, so that's over:—my wife has played the jade with me—well, that's over too:—I never loved her, or if I had, why that would have been over too by this time:—jealous of her I cannot be, for I am certain; so there's an end of jealousy:—weary of her I am, and shall be—no, there's no end of that—no, no, that were too much to hope. Thus far concerning my repose; now for my reputation. As to my own, I married not for it, so that's out of the question;—and as to my part in my wife's—why, she had parted with her's before; so bringing none to me, she can take none from me; 'tis against all rule of play, that I should lose to one who has not wherewithal to stake.

Besides, marriage is honourable. Hum, faith, and that's well thought on; marriage is honourable, and if so, wherefore should cuckoldom be a discredit, being derived from so honourable a root?

Jealous! No—let husbands be jealous; let husbands' doubts convert to endless jealousy; or if they have belief, let it corrupt to superstition and blind credulity. I am single, and will herd no more with 'em. True, I wear the badge, but I'll disown the order. And since I take my leave of 'em, I care not if I leave 'em a common motto to their common crest:—

All husbands must or pain or shame endure;
The wise too jealous are, fools too secure.

citizen's child: as in the seduction of citizens' wives by courtiers

109

MIRABEL OFFERS HIS CONDITIONS FOR MARRIAGE TO MILLIMANT
(1700) WILLIAM CONGREVE, The Way of the World, *Act 4, Sc. 1*

When the paragons of Restoration lovers, Mirabel and Millimant, contracted on the one hand to become "a tractable and compliant husband," and on the other to "dwindle into a wife," Restoration comedy, as one critic mourned, was over. Their surrender goes far beyond the range of other marital succumbings in other Restoration comedy's endings. Those acknowledge giving up their sexual independence. These surrender a great deal more.

What had been developing in Congreve's comedies and in their society's moment was an extraordinary sense of private worth, the value of the self as such. Not the "self" in its native state, as a given; but in its subsequent refinement: self-cultivation aimed at achieving the exquisite—a state of personal perfection which has no value or use beyond itself. Rooted in diffidence toward outward show [see I, #125], it also forbids invasion of its inward privacy. Its most cruel betrayal is by "the world's" defining it, diminishing it to a function, a role, a name. "Painter," for example, or "Poet", is bad; "Tradesman," or "Fool," is even worse; they're functions, roles. The "liberty" whose passing Millimant laments, a lamentation in which Mirabel concurs, is also her freedom from circumscription, from the imprisonment of definition: wife.

But there were contingencies; the private condition had to be attained at a price. It depended on both the easy assurance of love, and the equally comfortable assurance of money. The delicacy of the balance between the maintenance of their self-reflective self-image and the necessity of their stooping to its supportive needs (Mirabel's plotting all through the comedy for the guarantee that money will accompany marriage, and Millimant's walking backwards all through the comedy into the coils of marriage), is for both of them the desperate reason for their contract. It will guarantee their "world's" gross needs (marriage; money; possibly—"Name it not!" says Millimant—offspring) without compromising, not to speak of violating, their very being.

The overriding irony of their endeavor is that for each the provisos of the other are trivial, irrelevant, of small note; their own, on the other hand, are the binding assurances of their self-preservation.

> MIRABEL
> Well, have I liberty to offer conditions—that when you are dwindled into a wife, I may not be beyond measure enlarged into a husband? *Imprimis* then, I covenant that your acquaintance be general; that you admit no sworn confident, or intimate of your own sex; no she-friend to screen her affairs under your countenance, and tempt you to make trial of a mutual secrecy. No decoy-duck to wheedle you a 'fop-scrambling' to the play in a mask—then bring you home in a pretended fright, when you think you shall be found out—and rail at me for missing the play, and disappointing the frolic which you had, to pick me up and prove my constancy.

Item, I article, that you continue to like your own face as long as I shall; and while it passes current with me, that you endeavor not to new-coin it. To which end, together with all vizards for the day, I prohibit all masks for the night, made of oiled-skins and I know not what—hog's bones, hare's gall, pig-water, and the marrow of a roasted cat. In short, I forbid all commerce with the gentlewoman in What-d'ye-call-it Court. *Item,* I shut my doors against all bawds with baskets, and pennyworths of muslin, china, fans, atlases, etc.—*Item,* when you shall be breeding—Which may be presumed, with a blessing on our endeavors—I denounce against all strait lacing, squeezing for a shape, till you mould my boy's head like a sugar-loaf; and instead of a man-child, make me the father to a crooked billet. Lastly, to the dominion of the tea-table I submit,—but with proviso, that you exceed not in your province; but restrain yourself to native and simple tea-table drinks, as tea, chocolate, and coffee, as likewise to genuine and authorized tea-table talk—such as mending of fashions, spoiling reputations, railing at absent friends, and so forth—but that on no account you encroach upon the men's prerogative, and presume to drink healths, or toast fellows; for prevention of which I banish all foreign forces, all auxiliaries to the tea-table, as orange-brandy, all aniseed, cinnamon, citron, and Barbadoes waters, together with ratafia and the most noble spirit of clary—but for cowslip-wine, poppy water, and all dormitives, those I allow. These provisos admitted, in other things I may prove a tractable and complying husband.

imprimis, Lat: in the first place **no decoy duck…mask**: to wheedle you to the theatre to scramble after a fop **article**: to stipulate **atlas**: a variety of satin **billet:** thick stick; tree limb **orange-brandy…clary**: liqueurs **cowslip-wine…dormitives**: sleep-inducing drinks

110

BEAUMINE COMMISERATES WITH AND WARNS PHILLABELL, WHO IS IN DANGER OF MARRIAGE

(1700) CATHERINE TROTTER, Love at a Loss, *Act 1, Sc. 2*

Beaumine is serious; marriage is a danger. It is of course the ploy the professed libertine must stoop to, promising it in the interest perhaps of retaining a mistress, but though he dances on its brink, he finally, and decisively, avoids it. Phillabell argues the propriety and sincerity of a genuine love embracing marriage. Beaumine defends against this heresy with cogent, if by 1700 familiar, argument: the fade of wifely beauty after marriage, her disguise of virtue and good humor and flattering tendernesses before out of fear of losing her lover, and her cold civilities and dullness after. In contrast to the fate of the husband, there are the infinite pleasures of the libertine's swift, unhindered retreat from a fickle one to another "one in hand," his serenely easy shuttle back and forth between a cloyingly jealous mistress and an overly fond one.

Beaumine, strong in his libertine's principles and inflexible in their practice, is nevertheless trapped by the writer Trotter. Lesbia, the lover of whose loving behavior he brags to Phillabell as the great example of a mistress's tearful devotion, is in fact shrewder than Beaumine and fools him, according to Trotter's more virtuous standards, by the very tears he so admires, and reduces him by play's end to asserting, in a vein foreign to his tongue earlier in the play: "treating [wives] with rudeness or neglect / Does most dishonor on ourselves reflect." His projected marriage and the capitulating language the playwright here puts into his mouth is revenge enough for his career-long, conscientious debasement of women.

BEAUMINE

I came to condole with you; faith, Phillabell, I am heartily sorry for thee. You are certainly to be married tomorrow? Faith, I would willingly reclaim thee, if thou art not too far gone to hear reason. Are you sure you will always be of this mind? Do you imagine she will be always young, always handsome, and that you shall always love her? What if all that you call good humour should prove affectation, nothing else; and virtue, but the art of well dissembling?

The disguise is always laid aside when there's no further need of it. When you are entered into bonds, 'twon't be worth her pains. If you but saw the fond, endearing Lesbia, what arts she uses to engage me, how well she thinks 'em all return'd by one kind word or look. And then the tender niceness of her passion. She lost a ring the other day which I had given her; never was anything so moving as her complaints! I told her she shou'd have one twice the value, but she said 'twas the first present I had made her, and she fear'd the loss, a sad presage that she should lose my heart. Nothing could comfort her but my repeated vows of never changing. Are there such tender sentiments in marriage? You'll find a cold civility the best part of a wife's entertainment, after a month's enjoyment. What that's old can charm to ecstasy? Or not be dull with being repeated?

Fickle as women are, they must be plaguy quick to make me complain of losing them; for if any of 'em should run out of my arms to another's (for then she is sure to have the start of me), I have always one in hand that supplies the vacancy. When the coyness or jealousy of one has vex'd me, I fly to another that with kindness restores my good humour; and when her over-fondness has cloy'd me, I return to the first for fresh appetite; for by one of these extremes, the women always lose us: they are either so capricious, they grow troublesome, or so tender, they grow dull; but temper'd thus, they give the relish to each other. And I have the greater pleasure in the chase, to observe their different crossings, windings, and little arts; sometimes their very fear, you know, makes 'em run full into the hound's mouth. But if you do not give over too soon, there's none of 'em but may be wearied out; then seize but panting quarry, and she's yours.

But I need not endeavour to convince thee; thy wife will do it effectually, since thou art resolv'd to purchase wisdom at the dearest rate, experience. What a lamentable figure thou'lt make, preaching it to others, as a fellow at the gallows does honesty, when 'tis too late to make use of it himself.—But I'll leave you to prepare for your solid blessing. Will you meet me in the walk this evening?

Egad, I beg your pardon. I forget thou'rt a man of business. Honest matrimony. Adieu.

111

BEAUMINE, WHILE CHASTISING LESBIA, PRETENDS TO TALK HIMSELF INTO AN IMMEDIATE PROPOSAL OF MARRIAGE

(1700) CATHERINE TROTTER, *Love at a Loss, Act 3, Sc. 1*

Beaumine [see I, #110] is trapped; he's caught by the two women he was betraying, both of whom informed one another of his betrayal. To wit: Lesbia is engaged to Beaumine, but he has long ago stipulated that no one must know it. This leaves him free for other skirmishes. (The logic by which he had convinced her to agree to this arrangement is a particular tribute to the flexibility of the libertine's logic which is wreathed in paradox, and the equal flexibility of his mistress's compliance.) Nevertheless, Lesbia and Miranda, out of mutual jealousy as well as mutual self-interest, form an alliance against Beaumine, and so cancel all his secrets. Confronted by Lesbia's direct accusation of his duplicity, he's on his mettle, as he sees it, not so much to squirm out of it as to rise above it. He does, by "the old way of complaining first, when we know ourselves at fault," and then by the remarkable footwork that puts him in the right and Lesbia in the wrong. How? A suspicion crossed his mind, and so he approached

Miranda, he explains, and learned from her that Lesbia had given away their secret ("I did not imagine you had so much indiscretion"). He, shocked by the position she put him in, "was never so out of countenance in [his] life." The result was Miranda's, and by implication, "the world's" laughter at Lesbia (though their mutual laughter was in fact at him), against which he warns her for the future, but for his love, forgives her.

The aplomb, the skill which which he turns the scales on Lesbia is sufficiently successful for him to go a step further—the ultimate, completely cynical, thoroughly Don Juan-ish ploy: a promise that brings her teeterng to the edge of marriage, and in an instant, its eclipse. They will be married that very moment, he's off to fetch the priest— but the legitimate hour for marriage, the "canonical" hour, has—shucks!—already passed.

BEAUMINE
(Aside) [Well, I must take the old way of complaining first, when we know ourselves in fault.]

Indeed, Lesbia, I did not imagine you had so much indiscretion, but women can no more forbear talking of their *amours*, than an ill poet of his verses; tho' they equally expose their folly, by what they design to gratify their vanity with, and usually prove as tiresome to their hearers, unless such as have ill nature enough to divert themselves with every thing that's ridiculous in another. You'll guess what I mean, when I tell you I have seen Miranda, and know all you said to her. Really, madam, you gave me cause enough to suspect you had let her know of our engagement, and I resolv'd to see her, to find out how far you had discover'd. I was never so out of countenance in my life. To be so laugh'd at, to hear you so ridiculed for being overreach'd by a creature that professes abusing everybody; you wou'd have been asham'd to have seen yourself so describ'd, so mimic'd so—I did not know what to say for myself or you. O Lesbia, Lesbia, that you cou'd be caught by such a shallow artifice.

Well, you know I love you, and can forgive you anything; but I hope you'll be more cautious hereafter. I think 'tis time our engagement were made known to everybody. Ay, ay.

We'll write each other's names on every bark,
The winds shall bear our vows to distant climes,
And Echo every tender word rebound.

To show you I don't think your favours a trifle, and have no mind you shou'd lose me, I wou'd have 'em still favours, the more to engage me, and not turn all to duty. And had I talk'd thus to you at first, you had lost a great deal of pleasure, Leobia, and laugh'd at me for a fool. Which is something better than knave. Knaves are precise, protesting, plotting, thinking creatures; but you'll find this mad, maggoty fellow, a very honest fellow at last. Well, if you'll have me marry you just now, I'll run and fetch a priest immediately.

(Going)
Oh Gad, I forgot, the canonical hour is over.

Comedy

XVII CENTURY FRENCH

112

TARTUFFE ATTEMPTS TO SEDUCE ELMIRE, THE WIFE OF HIS PATRON

(1664) JEAN-BAPTISTE MOLIÈRE, Tartuffe, or The Imposter, *tr. Christopher Hampton,*
Act 3, Sc. 3

Molière's *Tartuffe* is the quintessential portrait in Western literature of the man of the cloth as hypocrite. So broad, so blatant is his sham piety that, together with his sham poverty, he moves Orgon, well-to-do bourgeois, to take him into his home as protegé and confessor. No one in Orgon's household but himself and his pious old mother is taken in by Tartuffe; he's held in contempt, not to say dread, by all with any measure of worldly common sense. It's Molière's conceit that such a menace is made possible not at all by his skill (which is plainly ridiculous in its exaggerated ineptitude), but by two factors: the passion of the dupe to be duped, and the proscriptive weight of religiosity to cow and shut the mouth of the undeceived. Orgon's dupe is a match for Tartuffe's charlatan, but his blindness is proof against detraction because of the weapon he shares with Tartuffe: the obligation of his household, and of all the King's subjects, to stop short of open defiance of sanctioned mummery, no matter how suspect its honesty. "Cleante," Orgon warns his brother-in-law who tries to talk sense to him, "this sounds to me like irreligion!/ You've had some tendency to that already;/ And as I've warned you a good dozen times,/ You'll get yourself in trouble some fine day." It takes both mindless piety and a suggestion of spiritually hovering police to stifle outrage against the predations of counterfeit sanctity.

Orgon is planning to give his daughter, in love with Valere, in marriage to Tartuffe. The family is horrified, and in a quandary as to how to rescue the child from Orgon-Tartuffe. Orgon's wife, Elmire, a model of common sense, takes on the job of persuading the imposter to relent. To her possible surprise, Tartuffe is not interested in the child Marianne but in attractive Elmire herself, and he diverts the interview between them from her urging him to his entreating her.

But his entreaty stays entirely in character: his actions, his lewdness, his desire, are unmistakable, but his language is unrelentingly heavenward. His address to her is not only an example—there are many in literature—of the ingenuity of the religious hypocrite to use the language of piety to mean invitation to fornication, but the very argument that language advances is a justification, as though on religious principles, of its propriety, arguing the heart's surrender to the divine when it is visibly to the human.

But like the monks and priests in Boccaccio's *Decameron* who are up to the same game, Tartuffe is no fool, and doesn't suppose his prey is a fool either. He assumes a similar distance from sanctity in her, and a similar acquaintance with the language-code he's exploiting. And so while his text is redolent of saintly ardor, his silent subtext—which never for a moment surfaces—is a nudge and a wink of common understanding. Unfortunately for Tartuffe, she not only gets it, she's ahead of him, as is Damis, Orgon's son, who is hiding in the cupboard and leaps out to entrap Tartuffe in his domestic chicanery.

> TARTUFFE
> My heart is not entirely made of stone.
> The love we feel for the eternal beauties
> doesn't preclude a love for what is temporal,
> and our senses can easily succumb
> under the spell of God's perfect creations.
> His glories are reflected in your sex,
> but in your case it's more than that, He's revealed
> His rarest wonders and lavished such beauties
> on you, we're dazzled, we're carried away;

and I can't look at you, you perfect creature,
without admiring the Almighty in you,
struck to the heart with blazing love in front of
God's loveliest self-portrait. Oh, at first,
I was afraid this secret passion was
a cunning subterfuge of the Prince of Darkness;
and I even determined to avoid you,
thinking you might jeopardize my salvation.
But finally I realized, my sweet beauty:
in such a feeling there could be no guilt,
it could be reconciled with purity,
and that's when I surrendered myself to it.
The indescribable tenderness of your
divine expression broke down my resistance,
overcame all my fasting, prayers, and weeping
and concentrated all my hopes on you.
If you could bring yourself to show some favour
to your unworthy servant's tribulations,
if you would deign to stoop down to my level
and out of kindness offer me relief,
delicious prodigy, I guarantee
my eternal, unparalleled devotion.
And your reputation would be safe with me,
you'd run no risk of notoriety.
People like us know how to love discreetly,
and how to keep it permanently secret.
Our own concern for our good character
acts as a guarantee for those we love,
and once you've given way, you'll find we offer
love without scandal, pleasure without fear.

113

SGANARELLE REVEALS THE TRUE NATURE OF HIS MASTER DON JUAN

(1665) JEAN-BAPTISTE MOLIÈRE, Don Juan, *tr. G. Graveley and I. Maclean, Act 1, Sc. 1*

"A great gentleman who is really wicked is a terrible thing," Sganarelle mourns, "but…fear makes me his accomplice." Sganarelle is a comic 17th century French version of Jacobean tragedy's tool villain [see I, #/4] who does, if not the criminal acts, at least the legwork for the "great and powerful" villain whom he serves. And like his counterpart, other than to starve, he has little option but to serve him. Riddled with fear, certain he will ultimately gain nothing from his service, sickened by what he must witness and join, he nevertheless, even while cringing, keeps his underdog's comic perspective, which is not all that different from the bitterly satiric and tragic perspective of his English version in Webster's *The White Devil.*

At the play's opening, he is gently hinting to Gusman, the servant of Donna Elvira, that his lady's pursuit of Don Juan is a waste of time. It's hard for Gusman to take this in; after all, Don Juan wooed her, a recluse in a nunnery, urged her out, offered marriage, bedded her— but, unaccountably, left her soon after. Gusman, like his pious mistress, supposes they are pursuing a man of the nobility, and so certainly a man of honor. But at last Sganarelle can bear deception no longer, and out of sheer compassion, blurts out the truth, airing his pent-up rage and disgust with greater and greater abandon until he's revealed a telling list of Don Juan's depravities. And all of them, he insists, are only a glimpse, the merest sketch. But having unveiled that glimpse, he remembers his precarious position, and warns: if he learns of this, I'll swear you're lying.

SGANARELLE

Oh, my poor Gusman, my dear friend, I'm afraid you don't know what kind of man Don Juan is. I ought to warn you, strictly between the pair of us, that in Don Juan my master you see the greatest scoundrel that ever walked the earth. He is a madman, a dog, a devil, a Turk. He is a heretic who believes in neither Heaven, nor saint, nor God, nor the bogeyman. He lives the life of an absolute brute beast. He is an Epicurean hog, a regular Sardanapalus who is deaf to every Christian remonstrance, and looks on all that we others believe as nothing but old wives' tales. You say he has married your mistress. He would have done far more than that to gratify his desires. He would have married you, and her dog and cat as well. It costs him nothing to marry. That is the best baited trap he has. He marries right and left. Fine lady, ward, town dweller or country girl, none are too hot or too cold for him. And if I were to give you the names of all the women he has married, in this place and that, it would be sundown before I had done. You seem surprised and upset at what I say. But this is only the merest sketch. To finish the picture I should have to paint with a broader brush still. One day the wrath of Heaven will strike him; that's for certain. I might as well wait on the devil as wait on him; and he makes me live with such horrors that I wish he was already I don't know where. A great gentleman who is really wicked is a terrible thing. But I must be faithful to him, however I feel. Fear makes me his accomplice. It stifles my feelings; and I often find myself applauding what I loathe with my very soul. Here he comes now to take a walk in the palace. We mustn't be seen together. I have taken you into my confidence quite frankly, rather too frankly perhaps; but I warn you that, if any of this ever comes to his ears, I shall swear black and blue that you're lying.

Epicurean: hedonistic; Epicurus (342?-270 BC) was a Greek philosopher who believed that the highest good in life is pleasure, which means freedom from disturbance or pain **Sardanapalus**: an Assyrian king, d. 876 BC, infamous for his luxury, licentiousness and womanizing

114

DON JUAN EXPLAINS HIS CONTEMPT FOR THE IDEA OF FIDELITY

(1665) JEAN-BAPTISTE MOLIÈRE, Don Juan, *tr. G. Graveley and I. Maclean, Act 1, Sc. 2*

In Molière's version of the legendary anti-hero, Don Juan, he is nei-ther romantically tittilating nor Byronically intriguing; he's morally disgusting. But the edge of revulsion toward which Molière pushes his portrait becomes the very strength, the enormity, of the character. Molière's Don Juan is the absolute of moral subversion. It is demon-strated less in his behavior during the play's action (his stage life exhibits fairly mild instances of iniquity), but in his exposition of his subversive principles. The play, far from following classical structure, is more a series of loosely connected disquisitions and demonstrations, each devoted to negating a major tenet of civilization's pieties: moder-ation, constancy, gallantry, veracity, courage, piety, chivalry, trustworthiness, familial reverence, divine reverence, repentance. At one moment (in Act 3, scene 3), Don Juan appears to respond to a victim's plight with honor and courage; Molière carefully vitiates his claim to either by the duplicity with which the Don later squirms out of the dangers his gesture initiated.

There is only one way in which Don Juan exhibits genuine integri-ty: in his devotion to his principle of moral subversion. More than a sensualist, more than an immoralist, more than a hedonist, he is an uncompromising apologist for sensuality, immorality, hedonism. What makes possible his unrestrained abandonment to these inverted ideals is, of course, what is named by Sganarelle and implied through-out the play: his privilege, which makes him, like de Sade's licentious aristocrats, scarcely subject to any worldly restraint. (His punishment is left, *faut de mieux*, to Heaven.)

In this speech—a reply to one of Sganarelle's querulous reproofs—
Don Juan pits insatiable Epicurean appetite against the constraint of
constancy. Note the emotional progression of the speech: it starts with
cool reason, gets caught up in the vision of what it is describing, and
ends with the enthusiasm of sexual repletion paralleled (not mimicked) in the words.

DON JUAN
So you think we should be tied for ever to the first object that takes
our fancy, forswear the rest of the world, and have no eyes for anyone
else? A nice thing indeed to take seriously to heart such a false point of
honour as fidelity; to bury myself for ever in one passionate affair, and
to be dead from henceforth to everything that my eyes tell me is worthy of devotion! No, no. Constancy is only fit for idiots. Every pretty
woman has the right to attract us, and the mere accident of being seen
first should not rob the others of their privilege of subjugating our
hearts. Beauty delights me wherever I find it, and I fall a willing slave
to the sweet force with which it seeks to bind me. However my heart
may be engaged, the love I have for one woman has no power to
make me unfair to the rest. My eyes see the merits of each, and pay
homage and tribute wherever it is due. If I see an attractive woman,
my heart is hers; and, had I ten thousand hearts, I would give them all
to a face that was worthy of them. After all, the growth of a passion
has infinite charm, and the true pleasure of love is its variety. How
deliciously sweet to lay siege to a young heart; to watch one's progress
day by day; to overcome by means of vows, tears, and groans, the delicate modesty of a soul which sighs in surrender; to break down little
by little the weakening resistance, the maidenly scruples that her honour dictates, and bring her at last where we would have her be. But
once we have had our way with her, there is no more to wish for. The
best is behind us. And so we slumber on, lulled by our love, until a
new object appears to reawaken our desire, and lure us on with the
charms of a new conquest. There in nothing so sweet as to overcome

the resistance of a beautiful woman; and, where they are concerned, I
have the ambition of a conqueror, who goes from triumph to triumph, and can never be satisfied. Nothing shall stand in the way of
my desire. My heart is big enough to love the whole world; and I
could wish, with Alexander, that there were more worlds still, so that I
might carry yet further my prowess in love.

Well, what answer can you make to that?

According to legend, **Alexander** the Great (356-323 BC), after conquest wept for
there were no more worlds left to conquer

115

DON JUAN EXPLAINS HIS DEVOTION TO "THE FASHIONABLE VICE," HYPOCRISY

(1665) JEAN-BAPTISTE MOLIÈRE, Don Juan, *tr. G. Graveley and I. Maclean, Act 5, Sc. 2*

Molière leaves the most reprehensible but the most serviceable of
Don Juan's iniquities [see I, #114] to the last: the strategem of
Tartuffe—religious hypocrisy [see I, #112]. It's the supreme imposture, the one that works best, that's always respected, and even if
found out, "no one dare open his mouth." Sganarelle is more shocked
by Don Juan's taking up with pious hypocrisy than by any of his other
transgressions because, it seems to him, it contradicts the principled
integrity with which the Don pursued all his other derelictions. But
it's no contradiction at all, Don Juan explains, and enumerates his reasons, reasons that Tartuffe might, in a lapse of honesty, have echoed as
well. But the reason that caps them all is that piety is the ideal cover:
behind its austerities, its glances to heaven, its groans of remorse, the
libertine is free to practice in secret "my favorite sins." It's the ultimate
victory of moral subversion—to betray the integrity of that subversion
in order to gain for it perfect license, and for one's behavior, perfect

freedom.

There are three parts to Don Juan's argument: hypocrisy is respectable and therefore privileged; hypocrisy easily wins defenders among its dupes; and, hypocrisy's pious fulminations are the ideal weapon against one's enemies.

DON JUAN

There's no longer any disgrace in it. Hypocrisy has become a fashionable vice, and all such vices pass for virtues. The mask of a good man is the best mask to wear. At no time could the profession of a hypocrite be carried on more advantageously than today. That sort of imposture is always respected; and, even if it is found out, no one dare say anything against it. All other vices come under censure, and everyone is free to rail against them; but hypocrisy is privileged and enjoys special immunity. No one dare open his mouth. By this kind of deceit, one forms a solid pact with all others of the same persuasion. If one is attacked, the rest rush to his defence at once; and even those who act in good faith, and are known to be genuinely religious, are always the dupes of the others. They fall head foremost into the hypocrites' trap, and blindly back them up in everything they do. Do you think I don't know hundreds of others who have glossed over in this way the debauchery of their youth; made themselves a shield out of the cloak of religion; and, under its cover, have continued to be the greatest scoundrels living? Even if you see through them, and know them for what they are, they still enjoy credit in the eyes of the world; and whatever ill they do is easily put right by hanging their head, groaning deeply and casting a pious glance up to heaven. It is in this safe harbour that I mean to take refuge, and set my affairs in order. I shall not give up my favourite sins, but I shall engage in them in secret; and take my pleasures without making such a noise about it. Then, if I am found out, the whole cabal will take up the cudgels without my stirring a limb, and defend me against all and sundry. That is the only way I can do whatever I like with no risk of being called to account for it. I shall set up as a censor of other people's actions, think the worst of everybody, and have no good opinion of anyone but myself. If anyone offends me, be it ever so slightly, I shall never forgive him, and have a secret grudge against him for ever after. I shall appoint myself the avenger of Heaven; and, under this convenient pretext, I shall harass my enemies, accuse them of impiety and let loose upon them a whole horde of crazy zealots, who, without the least knowledge of the matter, will preach against them in public, cover them with abuse, and consign them to perdition by their own private authority. It's only commonsense to take advantage of the weaknesses of mankind, and adjust one's behaviour to fit in with the vices of one's age.

cabal: a group of intriguers, plotters

116
ALCESTE, CONDEMNING CELIMENE'S FALSENESS, ALSO CONFESSES HIS LOVE
(1666) JEAN-BAPTISTE MOLIÈRE, The Misanthrope, *tr. Richard Wilbur, Act 4, Sc. 3*

Alceste, misanthropic because he sees nothing in the world but hypocrisy and deceit, is deeply in love with Celimene, who has no quarrel at all with hypocrisy and deceit; they are for her the understood rules of the game of social pleasure. Playing suitors against one another by open flattery and covert denigration, she is caught redhanded before "the world" with incriminating letters, but of all "the world," none is so horrified by the revelation of her culpability as Alceste, who confronts her with the shaming weapons of moral integrity and truth.

"I want to be angry! I don't want to listen!" cries Alceste at the play's opening, when his friend Philinte is trying to argue common sense into him. One of the keys to Alceste: he is not only in a state of fury because of human foibles, pained by society's hypocrisy, but takes a certain vain pleasure in his misery. It is his pride that he can prevision the world's treacheries, its deceptions, its cheats, anticipate them accurately in imagination, and take miserable pleasure in their confirmation when they come to light. Another key: He is a knight, in dream, lying in wait to save the world from its iniquities, waiting for that moment when its miseries are miserably manifest, at which moment he will reveal the magnanimity that lies behind his misanthrope.

This is the partially concealed Alceste who emerges fully at the climactic moment when he discovers—when the world discovers—the deceptions practiced by the young woman he loves. What lies buried in his soul never emerges so clearly as in his response to his discovery of Celimene's treachery. "I went insane," he confesses, "the day I fell/ A victim to your black and fatal spell," and at the heart of his lunge into those treacherously attractive waters, was an incipient longing, "to meet with some sincerity/ Among the treacherous charms that beckoned me." The attraction was the prize of "sincerity" that lay dark and distant in the heart of a most unlikely residence.

His fulmination against her has two parts, reflecting, halfway through, a change of intent. At first, out of his bitter disappointment he rails at her unmercifully, condemns her "double-dealing," justifies his "righteous wrath," his "savage feelings," that have "deprive[d him] of [his] senses." This is the blast of righteousness that refreshes.

But in Part Two, he slips into a new vein, contradicts his entire moral policy, and without noticing it, joins the cabal of the world's hypocrites in order not to lose the essential dream of that virtuous policy: to rescue Celimene from the slough of the world's misery. It begins as a challenge: justify, if you can, the evidence that plainly condemns you—your letter to Oronte. Inadvertently, this changes from a challenge into a plea: please, I beg, mouth any justification, and I'll pretend to believe it. Then the sluice-gates are opened: his love, irrespective of standards of moral worthiness, comes pouring out. But note the active image of that love in his imagination: the "purity and vastness" of his love would best be demonstrated if only he could find a Celimene enduring such abject misery that he, a knight, could "repair the great injustice of her plight." The precondition, it is to be noted, is a situation in which Celimene cannot conceivably be imagined; she, a self-assured, gregarious creature loving the world's compromising ways, is not at all the world's victim. She eludes Alceste's need; so much so that when he offers his final plan of reconciliation—to flee society with him and join in strict, unworldly solitude, she replies with instinctive worldliness, "But I'm twenty years old!"

ALCESTE

Sweet heaven, help me to control my passion.
Blush and hang your head; you've ample reason,
Since I've the fullest evidence of your treason.
Ah, this is what my sad heart prophesied;
Now all my anxious fears are verified;
My dark suspicion and my gloomy doubt
Divined the truth, and now the truth is out.
For all your trickery, I was not deceived;
But don't imagine that you'll go scot-free;
You shan't misuse me with impunity.
I know that love's irrational and blind;
I know the heart's not subject to the mind,
And can't be reasoned into beating faster;
I know each soul is free to choose its masters;
Therefore had you but spoken from the heart,
Rejecting my attentions from the start,
I'd have no grievance, or at any rate
I could complain of nothing but my fate.
Ah, but so falsely to encourage me—
That was a treason and a treachery
For which you cannot suffer too severely,
And you shall pay for that behaviour dearly.

Yes, now I have no pity, not a shred;
My temper's out of hand; I've lost my head;
Shocked by the knowledge of your double-dealings,
My reason can't restrain my savage feelings;
A righteous wrath deprives me of my senses,
And I won't answer for the consequences.

I went insane the day I fell
A victim to your black and fatal spell,
Thinking to meet with some sincerity
Among the treacherous charms that beckoned me.
But you'll not victimize me any more.
Look: here's a document you've seen before.
This evidence, which I acquired today,
Leaves you, I think, without a thing to say.
You take this matter lightly, it would seem.
Was it no wrong to me, no shame to you,
That you should send Oronte this billet-doux?
Kindly construe this ardent closing section
As nothing more than sisterly affection!
Here, let me read it. Tell me, if you dare to,
That this is for a woman...
Just show me how this letter could be meant
For a woman's eyes, and I shall be content.
Defend this letter and your innocence,
And I, poor fool, will aid in your defence.
Pretend, pretend, that you are just and true,
And I shall make myself believe in you.
Destiny requires me to entrust
My happiness to you, and so I must.
I'll love you to the bitter end, and see
How false and treacherous you dare to be.
You take advantage of my helpless passion,
And use my weakness for your faithless charms
To make me once again throw down my arms!
I love you more than can be said or thought;
Indeed, I wish you were in such distress

That I might show my deep devotedness.
Yes, I could wish that you were wretchedly poor,
Unloved, uncherished, utterly obscure;
That fate had set you down upon the earth
Without possessions, rank, or gentle birth;
Then, by the offer of my heart, I might
Repair the great injustice of your plight;
I'd raise you from the dust, and proudly prove
The purity and vastness of my love.

117

ARLECCHINO'S ACCOUNT OF HIS TRIP TO THE MOON

(c1660s) GIUSEPPE DOMENICO BIANCOLELLI (ARLECCHINO) *tr. Pierre Louis Duchartre*

B iancolelli, the greatest Arlecchino of his time, was one of the actors in the Italian *commedia dell'arte* company who for some years shared a theatre in Paris with Molière, the two companies splitting the week. His great contribution to the legacy of the Arlecchino mask was its elevation from the *zanni* who jumped, danced and turned somersaults and played the ignorant and gluttonous coward, to a character still remarkable for his acrobatics, but also for his wit, quick cunning, and wild invention. When his career was over, Biancolelli published a book of his "sides"—his monologues, his legendary *lazzi,* his dialogues—from which we get the clearest notion of the verbal and theatrical inventiveness with which he endowed his upgraded Arlecchino.

Like his other *lazzi*—both verbal and physical—the "trip to the moon" could be serviceable in any number of scenarii. Used over years, these set pieces can hardly be thought of as "improvisations."

Tried and polished, they were part of the actor's thoroughly rehearsed repertory, their improvisation consisting of little more than their injection into the performance of the moment—but even these insertions were rehearsed in advance with the other actors performing.

Delivery of "Accounts" like this one depend on the momentum of their incredibility being reinforced—as silliness mounts—by an escalating sort of inner glee. What spurs them on is the sheer pleasure of invention, the sheer madness of the conceit's being not only tolerated by the teller but insisted on as though it were gospel truth, and most of all the sheer pride of the teller in his glib prowess.

HARLEQUIN

Well, it was like this. I had arranged with three friends to go to Vaugirard to eat a goose. I was deputed to buy the goose. I went to the valley of misery, made my purchase, and set out for the place of our rendezvous. When I had arrived in the plain of Vaugirard six famished vultures appeared, seized my goose, and tried to make off with it. But I held on to its neck for dear life, and the vultures carried us both away. When we had gone rather high a new regiment of vultures came to help the others. They threw themselves upon us, and in a moment neither the goose nor I could see the peaks of the highest mountains…I fell into a lake. Fortunately some fishermen had stretched their nets there, and I fell into them. The fishermen pulled me out of the water, and, taking me for a fish of some consequence, loaded me on their shoulders and carried me as a present to the Emperor. They put me on the ground, and the Emperor and all his Court gathered round to look at me.

'What kind of a fish is that?' they said. The Emperor replied, 'I believe it is an anchovy, and let him be fried for me right away just as he is.' When I heard that they were going to fry me I commenced to bawl and shout. I told the Emperor of the Moon that I was not a fish, and related how I happened to arrive in his empire. He asked me immediately, 'Do you know Doctor Grazian Balouard?' 'Yes, my lord.' 'Do you know his daughter Isabelle?' 'Yes, my lord.' 'Well, I want you to be my ambassador and ask him for her hand in marriage. I shall send you to Paris in an exhalation of rheumatism, catarrh, inflammation of the lungs, and other similar trifles.' 'But, my lord.' I said, 'what will you do about Doctor Grazian Balouard? He is a man of no mean merit, and a scholar who knows rhetoric, philosophy, and spelling.' 'The Doctor! Ha, ha!' he answered; 'I'm reserving one of the best places in my empire for him.'

Do they eat in the same way as we do here? Yes and no. When the Emperor is at table he has a line of twenty men on his right, each armed with a solid gold crossbow loaded with humming-birds, pork-sausages, little pasties, and other like delicacies. On his left are twenty other men with silver syringes, solid also, one filled with Canary wine, another Muscatel Champagne, *et sic de coeteris*. When the Emperor is ready to eat he turns to the right, opens his mouth and *bing!*...the crossbowman shoots a little pasty directly at him. Then when he wishes to drink he turns to the left, and *whisht!* he receives a syringeful of St. Laurent wine or good Canary or Normandy, according to his taste. A marvelous method of eating, provided the crossbowman take good aim. There was an accident once, and since then no one is hired unless his arm has been tested first.

The Emperor once wished to eat some eggs fried in black butter. A clumsy crossbowman shot one at him, but, instead of aiming at his mouth, the fellow aimed at his eye, which was in a sorry mess for a long time afterward. The doctors feared that he might lose his eye, but luckily it did not prove dangerous, and his sight was restored after wearing a plaster for several days. And that is why the dish has been called poached eggs ever since.

The people of that country have extremely long noses, which they put to good use by fastening a catgut string from one end of the nose to the other; then placing the left hand on the lip and holding a bow in the right hand, they play the nose for you just as we play the violin. It gives an enchanting nasal twang.

Vaugirard: a town in the Southeast of France **Dr. Grazian Balouard**: Arlecchino is telling the story to that doctor *et sic de coeteris*, Lat: and so forth **poached eggs**: a pun in French derived from two meanings of the word *pocher*, "to poach" (eggs) and "to black" (eyes)

118

ARLECCHINO'S HEROIC ATTEMPT TO COMMIT SUICIDE

(c1660s) GIUSEPPE DOMENICO BIANCOLELLI (ARLECCHINO), *ad. L. Katz*

Commedia dell'arte [see I, #117] shares with low comedy everywhere the staple comic motives: food, sex and money. And all the masked characters in *Commedia,* especially the servants, the *zanni,* are usually plotting and yearning to get one or another of these good things. But beyond these motives, there's a wisdom which defines great comedy as Chaplin defined it: "Comedy," he remarked, "is tragedy." The more devastating, the more humiliating the situation is for the comic fool, the more hilarious he seems. The two funniest situations in *Commedia lazzi,* funnier even than hunger, sexual frustration and beggary, are madness and suicide.

In Biancolelli's *lazzo* of suicide, *Commedia* touches on one of comedy's deepest veins: an understanding of the greatest loss of all. Is Arlecchino's loss Columbina? Only partly. Self-esteem? Entirely. The more the loss of his self-esteem, the more he's faced with his own nonentity, the more he's tempted to settle for death.

Biancolelli's procedure to accomplish death involves a parody of the classical Speech of Justification—on the one hand, on the other, no this, yes that—together with the problem of its physical execution. What turns tragedy into comedy is juxtaposing noble misery and silly ineptitude. Arlecchino's thoughts are tragically lofty: he wants the symbolism of his way of dying to match the enormity of the great Arlecchino's death; but his technology is a flop. How do you manage to die? He settles for a questionable technique, one that, with grim irony, turns the intention of comedy on its head: usually, comedy tries to make the audience, not the actor, die laughing.

> *(Arlecchino plays the scene with many changes of voice, gesturing wildly and raging from one side of the stage to the other.)*

ARLECCHINO
Misery, Arlecchino! Dottore is marrying Columbina to a farmer. How can I live without Columbina! I would rather be dead. Idiot Dottore! Treacherous Columbina! Villainous farmer! Doomed Arlecchino! Let me die, and it will be written in ancient and modern history : Arlecchino died for Columbina. I'll go to my room, tie a rope to a crossbeam, climb up on a chair, put a rope around my neck, kick away the chair, and ough! I'm hanged. (*He imitates a hanged man.*) And so it's done. Good. To the gallows! (*He stops.*) The gallows? What are you thinking? You would be a very great fool, Arlecchino, to kill yourself for a woman. Agreed. Then, we go. *(He stops.)* But when you're hanged, will you be any the fatter for it? No, you'll be thinner, and there's nothing you want more in this world, Arlecchino, than to have a fine, plump figure. What do you say to that?—What do I say?—That if you want to see the hanging, you'd better come along right now.—Oh, no! Oh no! You're not going to any hanging!—Oh yes, I'm going!—You're not going to any—!—I'm going, I tell you!

> *(He takes out his knife, and stabs himself with it.)*

Good. I'm rid of that meddler. Now there's no one to stop me. We go to the hanging! (*He starts with a will, then stops.*) No. Hanging is too ordinary. It's a death you see every day, and would I gain any honor by it? No. It must be an unusual death. A heroic death. An Arlecchinoesque death. (*He thinks.*) Ah! I'll stop up my nose and mouth so that no air can escape, and then I can die.

> *(He does, and remains in that position for some time, and then says:)*

No. The air comes out below. Besides, it isn't worth the trouble. Oh, how hard it is to die! *(To the audience:)* Ladies, gentlemen, if one of you would be kind enough to die to show me how, I'd be very much obliged. *(He waits.)* No one.—Ah, but look, Arlecchino! They're laughing. What do people say? "I laughed," they say "till I nearly died." Well—try! *(He tries to squeeze out a laugh. Nothing.)* But what have you got to laugh about; you're miserable. Think. *(He thinks hard, not too hopeful.)* Well, I'm very ticklish. If I tickle myself for a long long time, I could probably die laughing. I'll tickle myself, yes. And then—ah, then!—I can die.

> *(He starts to tickle himself. At first, a bit of a laugh. He warms up to it, and at last, is rolling across the stage floor in convulsions, trying to tickle himself to death until Pasquariello interrupts him.)*

Comedy
XVIII CENTURY ENGLISH

119

YOUNG BOOKWIT, NEWLY ARRIVED IN LONDON, PREPARES TO PUT INTO PRACTICE HIS SCRUPULOUS STUDY OF WOMEN

(1703) RICHARD STEELE, The Lying Lover, *Act 1, Sc. 1*

"Oh London, London! Oh woman, woman!" cries Bookwit, thrilled to have made it out of the cloister of Magdalen College, Oxford, and into the city and its seductions. He is terrified only that he will be mistaken for a bookish lout and not for a military man of passion, "brisk and very ignorant...bold, negligent and erect." His fellow journeyer Jack and he have cast lots for who would play footman to the other for "the necessity, in intrigues, for a faithful...prating servant." Bookwit has won, Jack is to play his servant, and now Bookwit is ready to conquer womankind. He stakes out St. James's Park, costumes himself as a red-coated soldier, and sends friend—now footman—Jack to scout for useful intelligence on one of the Park's ladies from a fellow footman. So unknowing, so bumbling, yet Bookwit finds somewhere in his soul the gift of lying glibly and immeasurably. Lying becomes the springboard for his lovemaking, its triumph and finally its disaster.

The easy humor of this opening scene is hardly preparation for the steep decline of Bookwit's fortunes that follows. First, he is laughed at and exposed as an unconscionable liar by the very ladies he and Jack are pursuing. Then he is caught in a duel by a rival whom Bookwit presumably kills, and subsequently sentenced to hanging for murder before his merciful, last-minute rescue. Steele, a pioneer in the sentimental "lesson" plays that resulted from Jeremy Collier's and other prelates' denunciation of the morals of Restoration theatre, chastises two moral ills: one societal (dueling), one personal (lying). But chastisement with a heavy hand, as in the last act of *The Lying Lover,* was a bit in 1703 premature for audiences, and the play, as Steele confessed, was "damned for its piety," and failed.

But in this early scene, long before he tumbles, Bookwit is rubbing his hands in glee at the freedom he's been granted to find love in the welcoming city, and at the opportunities he dreams are lying in wait.

> **BOOKWIT**
>
> You prate as if I came to town to get an employment;—No, hang business,—hang care, let it live and prosper among the men;—I'll ne'er go near the solemn ugly things again—I'll keep company with none but ladies,—bright Ladies—Oh *London! London!* Oh woman! Woman! I am come where thou livest, where thou shinest. I had study'd 'em, and know how to make my approaches to 'em by contemplating their frame, their inmost temper:—I don't ground my hopes on the scandalous tales and opinions your wild fellows have of 'em,—Fellows that are but mere bodies,—machines,—which at best can but move gracefully,—No, I draw my pretences from philosophy, from nature—and have so accurately observ'd on woman, that I can know her mind by her eye, as well as her doctor shall her health by her pulse.—I can read approbation through a glance of disdain:—Can see when the soul is divided by a sparkling tear that twinkles and betrays the heart; a sparkling tear's the dress and livery of love—Of love made up of hope and fear, of joy and grief. Were't not a taking complement with my college face and phrase t'accost a lady— Madam, I bring your ladyship a learned heart, one newly come from the university.—I, I've read *Aristotle* twice over, compar'd his jarring commentators too, examin'd all the famous peripateticks.
>
> This certainly must needs enchant a lady. No, no! The name of soldier bids you better welcome: 'Tis valour and feats done in the field, a man shou'd be cry'd up for;—nor is't so hard to achieve. 'Tis but looking big, bragging with an easie grace, and confidently mustering up an hundred hard names they understand not: thunder of *Villeroy, Catinat,* and *Bouffleurs,* speak of strange towns and castles, whose barbarous names, the harsher they're to the ear, the rarer and more

taking.—Still running over lines, trenches, outworks, counterscarps, and forts, citadels, mines, countermines, pickeering, pioneers, centinels, patroles, and others, without sense or order, that matters not, the women are amaz'd, they admire to hear you rap 'em out so readily; and many a one that went no rather for't, retailing handsomely some warlike terms, passes for a brave fellow.—Don't stand gaping, but live and learn, my lad—I can tell thee ten thousand arts, to make thee known and valued in these regions of wit, and gallantry, the parks— the playhouse—

Oh! Sir, I have put so much of the soldier with my red-coat, that I came here t'observe the ground I am to engage upon.—Here, ay here,—I stood and gaz'd at high Mall, 'til I forgot 'twas winter, so many pretty she's marched by me.—Oh! to see the dear things trip, trip along, and breath so short, nipt with the season.—I saw the very air not without force leave their dear lips.—Oh! they were intolerably handsome.

Peripatetics: the followers of Aristotle from the Lyceum in ancient Athens **Villeroy, Catinat, Bouffleurs**: Marshals of France who fought against the English (under Marlborough) and their allies in the Eurpoean wars of the 1690s and 1700s **outworks**: fortifications outside the main "work" (fort, etc.) **counterscarp**: the exterior slope or wall of the ditch of a fort, supporting the covered way **coutermines**: mines to intercept/destroy enemy mines **pickeering**: skirmishing **pioneers**: scouts **Mall**: a fashionable promenade adjoining St. James's Park in London

120

CAPTAIN CLERIMONT, DISGUISED AS A PAINTER, OFFERS A YOUNG LADY HER CHOICE OF COMPELLING ATTITUDES FOR HER PORTRAIT

(1707) RICHARD STEELE, The Tender Husband, *Act 4, Sc. 2*

S teele lays out the predicament of "younger sons" under the laws of primogeniture (under which the eldest gets it all) more explicitly than most: the undesirable options for the unfortunate second son are the law, the college, the "shops" (trade). There are two other alternatives, and second son Captain Clerimont is losing the good of one of them—he's been safe from starving in the army, but now "the General makes such haste to finish the war that we redcoats may be soon out of fashion." That leaves him with one only remaining option—marrying a rich heiress, and with the help of an understanding elder brother, they hire an experienced hand, Pounce, to fix it up.

There are three obstacles to overcome. The lady, worth a fortune, is chaperoned by a sharp-eyed aunt whose intent is to see her married that day to an already chosen one. The chosen one is a country bumpkin with another fortune. The lady is addled with French romances, and talks the pseudo-language and dreams the dreams of medieval fantasy.

The entirely resilient Captain Clerimont, who at the recitation of her income, she still unseen, has instantly fallen in love with her, through Pounce finds a moment alone with her and woos her in the language of romance (he suddenly as adept as the young lady herself). She responds, they are in love, but according to the medieval chivalric code, it takes years for the wooer to be granted the lady's hand. Yet the Captain must accomplish abduction and marriage that very day.

Disguised as a painter by Pounce, he is introduced into the assembled presence of the lady, the sharp-eyed aunt, and the bumpkin. The country lout and the lady have already agreed to hate one another eternally, and he is therefore only too eager to help the abduction once he knows of it. The aunt, and the years of required chivalric penance for lovers, are still problematic. It is the Captain's feat to accomplish his wholly successful wooing while in disguise, and speaking only the words of the fashionable portraitist, makes himself, his mission and his urgency known to the lady, and wins her assent to forego the lover's obligatory penance and elope that day. The feat for the actor is to accomplish Clerimont's task in subtext alone, nobody present following its sense but the lovers.

CAPTAIN CLERIMONT

Madam, I'm generally forced to new-mould every feature, and mend nature's handy-work; but here she has made so finish'd an original, that I despair to my copy's coming up to it. To see the difference of the fair sex!—I protest to you, madam, my fancy is utterly exhausted with inventing faces for those that sit to me. The first entertainment I generally meet with, are complaints for want of sleep, they never look'd so pale in their lives, as when they sit for their pictures—Then so many touches and retouches, when the face is finish'd—That wrinkle ought not to have been, those eyes are too languid, that colour's too weak, that side-look hides the mole on the left cheek: In short, the whole likeness is struck out. But in you, madam, the highest I can come up to will be but rigid justice.

Madam, be pleas'd to place your self near me, nearer still, madam, here falls the best light—You must know, madam, there are three kinds of airs which the ladies most delight in—There is your haughty—your mild—and, your pensive air—The haughty may be express'd with the head a little more erect than ordinary, and the countenance with a certain disdain in it, so as she may appear almost, but not quite inexorable: This kind of air is generally heightened with a little knitting of the brows—I gave my lady *Scornwell* her choice of a dozen frowns, before she cou'd find one to her liking. The mild air is compos'd of a languish, and a smile—But if I might advise, I'd rather be a pensive beauty; the pensive usually feels her pulse, leans on one arm, or sits ruminating with a book in her hand—which conversation she is suppos'd to chuse, rather than the endless importunities of lovers.

You seem indeed, madam, most inclin'd to the pensive—The pensive delights also in the fall of waters, pastoral figures, or any rural view suitable to a fair lady, who with a delicate spleen has retir'd from the world, as sick of its flattery and admiration.

And if you please, there shall be a *Cupid* stealing away to shew that love shou'd have a part in all gallant actions. I'll place that beauteous boy near you, 'twill look very natural—He'll certainly take you for his mother *Venus*. Now—please, madam, to uncover your neck a little; a little lower still—a little, little lower.—Ah!

(He begins painting.)

Ladies, have you heard the news of a late marriage between a young lady of a great fortune and a younger brother of good family? This young gentleman, ladies, is a particular acquaintance of mine, and much about my age and stature (look me full in the face, madam). He accidentally met the young lady, who had in her all the perfection of her sex; (hold up your head, madam, that's right.) She let him know that his person and discourse were not altogether disagreeable to her. The difficulty was how to gain a second interview (your eyes full upon mine, madam,) for never was there such a sigher in the Valley of the Arcadia, as that unfortunate youth, during the absence of her he loved.

At length, ladies, he thought himself of an expedient. He dressed himself just as I am now, and came to draw her picture (your eyes full upon mine, pray, madam.) And by that means, found an opportunity of carrying her off and marrying her.

The gentleman has often told me he was strangely struck at first sight, but when she sat to him for her picture, and assumed all those graces that are proper for the occasion, his torment was so exquisite, his passion so violent, that he could not have lived a day, had he not found means to make the charmer of his heart his own. The young painter turned poet on the subject. I believe I have his words by heart.

spleen: ill humor, peevish temper

121

BEVIL JR., CONSTRAINED BUT COURTEOUS, COUNTERS HIS FATHER'S CHOICE OF WIFE FOR HIM

(1722) RICHARD STEELE, The Conscious Lovers, *Act 1, Sc. 2*

By 1722, when *The Conscious Lovers* was written, English sentimentality, like middle-class manners, had added to its four-square virtues a continental refinement it very much emulated and very much needed: French sensibility. Sensibility was a drawing-room version of *generosité,* a code that had thrived in French novels and drama; a codicil, a sort of footnote, to the code of "Honor," which itself had thrived at least in fictional report on the battlefield, at court, and in imitation by the lower orders. For the practitioners of *generosité,* those who added refinement of feeling to heroic acts, it meant a dignified forbearance, an indulgent understanding, a generous granting of a rival's or an enemy's claim to considerations of personal honor, or even, in its most generous form, to considerations of the heart. For the heroes of French tragedy back in the 1650s, it had added a delicacy of touch to honorable behavior, and separated altogether the boor on the battlefield from the refined warrior of *generosité*.

Off the battlefield and out of court, in the 18th century the man of *generosité* became the Man of Feeling. He was not only responsive to the feelings of the other, and also and equally deeply responsive to his own, but became feeling's votary, feeling itself becoming the supreme moral guide to his conduct. Knowing the flutterings, the whims and desires, the shames and mortifications, within his own heart, he was honor bound to detect them with equal accuracy, intensity and forbearance in the other, and to respond first and foremost to the claims of that forbearance. To violate, or even in very small ways to impinge on the feeling of the other, was the equivalent of physical assault.

Social intercourse—in drama, at least—was as much hobbled as improved by such delicacy. In Chekhov (sensibility, of course, continued to thrive into and through the 20th century), "I understand you, Masha" is the sign of this heart-to-heart compassionate mutuality, but when it fails by a hair in Chekhov's dramas, that failure is the very sign of each character's tragic isolation. In 18th century plays of sensibility, no allowance was made for such failure. For dramatic characters to qualify for Feeling's status, they had to be ideally attuned to the operative codes of conduct and feeling in the other, to act on the other's silent instructions and exhortations silently, and to give no sign that they were even aware that they were playing that game, lest it cause the numbing shame in the other to be read like an open book. Consider, then, the plight of characters who have reason to have feeling for one another—lovers, fathers and sons, devoted siblings, equally devoted masters and servants, close friends. To profess sentimental feelings in their raw state might, for all one knew, impinge painfully on the other who may or may not have feelings of precisely the same fervor, or, even if so, might, for all one knew, have reason not to air them. And so politesse required a mutual paralysis of open expression.

Consider the condition of Bevil Jr.'s father, who at the opening of the play is explaining to his devoted servant Humphrey his difficulties in dealing openly with his son. The father hesitates to confront his son about the woman he has seen him with in masquerade, having never so confronted him out of principle. The son, for his part, has never made mention of what both know well: he has an independent income from his deceased mother and, therefore, no dependency on his father; "afraid of appearing to enjoy it before you," recalls Humphrey in admiration. The servant sums up the admirable impasse between them: "their fear of giving each other pain is attended with constant mutual uneasiness."

The uneasiness threatens to come to a head in this scene. Sir John is wishing his son would rise to the occasion of an advantageous marriage he, as a generous father, has planned for him. Gingerly, he is pushing as far as sensibility will allow, for the explanation of his son's apparent indifference to the match. Bevil Jr. has sufficient reason for disobeying his father: a secret love, which, out of generous sensibility of his own, has not even been confessed to his loved one.

Not to be guilty of the smallest rupture with his father, Bevil Jr. intends in this scene to resolve his dilemma by pretending to submit with filial devotion to his father's wish (having already written to the lady urging her, with honest reasons, to refuse him). But in doing so—professing earnestly to submit to his father's will, protesting his anxiety never to give his benefactor a moment's uneasiness—he becomes testy under the very constraint he's imposed on himself, and gradually allows intimations of insubordination to escape from his lips. By the end of the speech, he has moved to the point, unheard of in their relation, of almost open rebellion.

> **BEVIL JR.**
> I am still your son, sir. Sir, you have been married, and I have not. And you have, sir, found the inconvenience there is when a man weds with too much love in his head. I have been told, sir, that at the time you married, you made a mighty bustle on the occasion. There was challenging and fighting, scaling walls, locking up the lady, and the gallant under an arrest for fear of killing all his rivals. Now, sir, I suppose you, having found the ill consequences of these strong passions and prejudices, in preference of one woman to another, in case of a man's becoming a widower—
>
> I say, sir, experience has made you wiser in your care of me; for, sir, since you lost my dear mother, your time has been so heavy, so lonely, and so tasteless, that you are so good as to guard me against the like unhappiness, by marrying me prudentially by way of bargain and sale.

For as you well judge, a woman that is espoused for a fortune, is yet a better bargain if she dies; for then a man still enjoys what he did marry, the money, and is disencumbered of what he did not marry, the woman.

Pardon me, sir, I don't carry it so far neither. I am rather afraid I shall like her too well; she has, for one of her fortune, a great many needless and superfluous good qualities.

My father commands me as to the object of my affections, but I hope he will not as to the warmth and height of them. You may assure yourself I never will marry without my father's consent. But give me leave to say, too, this declaration does not come up to a promise that I will take whomsoever he pleases.

in the way: near at hand

122

SHARP IMPLORES HIS DESTITUTE MASTER TO MARRY
(1740) DAVID GARRICK, The Lying Valet, *Act 1, Sc. 1*

Leaning heavily on the first scene of Congreve's *Love for Love*, Garrick's Sharp, like Valentine's valet Jeremy [see I, #101], lectures his young master Gayless on the necessity of getting married before starvation overtakes them both. Here again, the master is without fortune, has been disinherited by his father, pursued by creditors, bereft of friends, and still holding on to some odd quirk of conscience that the servant finds, given their condition, lunatic. His lunacy: before marrying the wealthy heiress who would be their salvation, Gayless, as a matter of honor, insists on confessing to her his true condition, and his motive—at least in part—for marrying her. Sharp counters this with two arguments: one, that starving with honor is still starving, and two, if his master persists in this suicidal determination, relying on "so great uncertainties as a fine lady's mercy and good-nature," then Sharp runs.

Sharp's speech is a study in gradually growing exasperation. His argument, unlike Jeremy's, hammers away at one main point: the stupidity of honor in the face of hunger. Since he and his master have reached destitution, they're on a par. And so—again, in the classical tradition of the scolding servant—he automatically inherits the privilege, through the force and tone of his argument, of reversing their roles. But try as he might, he doesn't get Gayless's agreement. He wins only when he supposes he's lost; at the end of his harangue, as he sets off for good, Gayless, hit by the force of that terminal argument, calls him back.

(Enter Gayless and Sharp.)

SHARP

How, sir! shall you be married tomorrow? Eh, I'm afraid you joke with your poor humble servant. Fixed tomorrow for the happy day. 'Twas well she did, sir, or it might have been a dreadful one for us in our present condition: all your money spent; your movables sold; your honor almost ruined, and your humble servant almost starved; we could not possibly have stood it two days longer. But if this young lady will marry you and relieve us, o' my conscience, I'll turn friend to the sex, rail no more at matrimony, but curse the whores, and think of a wife myself. But you propose, good sir, to throw yourself at her feet, tell her the real situation of your affairs, ask her pardon, and implore her pity. Yes, after marriage, will all my heart, sir; but don't let your conscience and honor so far get the better of your poverty and good sense, as to rely on so great uncertainties as a fine lady's mercy and good-nature.

What, because you are poor, shall you abandon your honor? Yes, you must, sir, or abandon me: so pray, discharge one of us; for eat I must, and speedily too: and you know very well that that honor of yours will neither introduce you to a great man's table, nor get me credit for a single beefsteak.

Why, you must certainly be a very great philosopher, sir, to moralize and declaim so charmingly, as you do, about honor and conscience, when your doors are beset with bailiffs, and not one single guinea in your pocket to bribe the villains.

Do you be wise! You certainly have spent your fortune, and outlived your credit, as your pockets and my belly can testify: your father has disowned you; all your friends forsook you, except myself, who am starving with you. Now, sir, if you marry this young lady, who as yet, thank heaven, knows nothing of your misfortunes, and by that means procure a better fortune than that you squandered away, make a good husband, and turn economist, you still may be happy, may still be Sir William's heir, and the lady too no loser by the bargain: there's reason and argument, sir, and make no more objections to the marriage. You see I am reduced to my waistcoat already; and when necessity has undressed me from top to toe, she must begin with you; and then we shall be forced to keep house and die by inches. Look you, sir, if you won't resolve to take my advice, while you have one coat to your back, I must e'en take to my heels while I have strength to run, and something to cover me: so, sir, wishing you much comfort and consolation with your bare conscience, I am your most obedient and half-starved friend and servant.

guinea: a golden coin worth 21 shillings (almost 2 pounds) **turn economist:** become frugal **keep house:** stay indoors

123

PUFF REVEALS THE SECRETS OF HIS CRAFT
(1779) RICHARD BRINSLEY SHERIDAN, The Critic, *Act 1, Sc. 2*

Puff the playwright is on holiday from his real profession. According to his self-advertisement, he's a "practitioner in pane-gyric," "a professor of the art of puffing," in other words, an advertising man, a PR man and a con-man rolled into one.

Puff is the 18th century poet of virtual reality. He outdoes our time's TV commercials, fundraisers, schlock journalism, and infomer-cials with a range of conning that puts contemporary conning to shame. He doesn't bother with market research or ferreting out actual cases of misery to shake down the gullible; he invents them. And he doesn't locate them in the wide world; he keeps them very close to home. Puff advertises himself, anonymously, as a walking calamity with a menu of misfortunes that bilk tears and money out of the ten-derhearted, and on which he lives with comfort. Some memorable scams: he was a bankrupt five times over, an unfortunate with no limbs (and "went about collecting the subscriptions myself"), and pushing the envelope, a sick widow with six helpless children, and none of her past eleven husbands around to pay for hospital. Only slightly less outrageous, his PR: he's a master at planting news items, starting rumors, exploiting the whole repertoire of journalistic sleaze. And only incidentally, a playwright.

In *The Critic,* Sheridan surrounds Puff with a burlesque of the Drury Lane Theatre (of which he himself was the manager), of his company of actors (who actually performed the play), of his own man-agement, and even of the theatre's technical machinery. Most especially, he's ridiculing the kind of bombastic/poetic/scenery-cluttered play the theatre occasionally would have to do for its commercial good. (He himself was to be guilty in later years, in *Pizzaro,* of a play no less ridiculous than the one for which he's pillorying Puff here.)

But Puff, incapable of feeling shame, revels in all his talents, even playwriting. He brags with gusto about his play, and he explains away with equal gusto any detractions concerning his life and works. He's a well-adjusted man.

> PUFF
>
> I dare say, now, you conceive half the very civil paragraphs and adver-tisements you see to be written by the parties concerned, or their friends?—No such thing—nine out of ten manufactured by me in the way of business. Even the auctioneers now—the auctioneers, I say—though the rogues have lately got some credit for their language—not an article of the merit theirs!—take them out of their pulpits, and they are as dull as catalogues!—No, sir; 'twas I first enriched their style—'twas I first taught them to crowd their advertisements with panegyrical superlatives, each epithet rising above the other, like the bidders in their own auction-rooms!—From *me* they learned to inlay their phraseology with variegated chips of exotic metaphor: by *me,* too, their inventive faculties were called forth.—Yes, sir, by *me* they were instructed to clothe ideal walls with gratuitous fruits—to insinu-ate obsequious rivulets into visionary groves—to teach courteous shrubs to nod their approbation of the grateful soil! or on emergencies to raise upstart oaks where there never had been an acorn; to create a delightful vicinage without the assistance of a neighbor; or fix the tem-ple of Hygeia in the fens of Lincolnshire! If they had any gratitude they would erect a statue to me; they would figure me as a presiding Mercury, the god of traffic and fiction, with a hammer in my hand instead of a caduceus. But what first put me on exercising my talents in this way? Egad, sir, sheer necessity—the proper parent of an art so nearly allied to invention: you must know, Mr. Sneer, that from the first time I tried my hand at an advertisement, my success was such that, for some time after, I led a most extraordinary life indeed!

Sir, I supported myself two years entirely by my misfortunes. Yes, sir, assisted by long sickness and other occasional disorders; and a very comfortable living I had of it. Harkee!—By advertisements—'To the charitable and humane!' and 'to those whom Providence hath blessed with affluence!' And, in truth, I deserved what I got; for I suppose never man went through such a series of calamities in the same space of time!—Sir, I was five time made a bankrupt, and reduced from a state of affluence by a train of unavoidable misfortunes. Then, sir, though a very industrious tradesman, I was twice burnt out, and lost my little all both times!—I lived upon those fires a month.—I soon after was confined by a most excruciating disorder, and lost the use of my limbs!—That told very well; for I had the case strongly attested, and went about to collect the subscriptions myself. I was afterwards twice tapped for a dropsy, which declined into a very profitable consumption!—I was then reduced to—O no—then, I became a widow with six helpless children;—after having had eleven husbands pressed, and being left every time eight months gone with child, and without money to get me into an hospital! And bore all with patience.

Well, sir,—at last, what with bankruptcies, fires, gouts, dropsies, imprisonments, and other valuable calamities, having got together a pretty handsome sum, I determined to quit a business which had always gone rather against my conscience, and in a more liberal way still to indulge my talents for fiction and embellishment, through my favorite channels of diurnal communication—and so, sir, you have my history.

panegyrical: from panegyric, a praise, eulogy **variegated:** varied, diverse, multi-colored **viginage:** neighborhood **Hygeia:** Greek mythology, goddess of health **fens:** a marsh **caduceus:** the staff of Mercury (Hermes) as herald or messenger of the gods **dropsy:** illness caused by excessive accumulation of serous fluid in a serous cavity **pressed** into naval service **gout:** painful inflamation of the joints **diurnal:** daily

Comedy
XIX/XX CENTURY GERMAN/SCANDINAVIAN/ENGLISH

124

LEONCE CONTEMPLATES WITH CHEER LOVE, EMPTINESS, AND BOREDOM

(1836) GEORG BUCHNER, Leonce and Lena, *tr. Carl Richard Mueller, Act 1, Sc. 3*

Why must I be the one to know" complains Leonce, that bore-dom alone is what moves mankind—whether saint, sinner, genius or fool—to do anything at all? Because none of them know it, don't understand why, they seriously go about the business of study-ing, praying, loving, marrying, multiplying, and finally dying, with never a clue that the motive for all of it is emptiness and boredom. Leonce has separated himself from this charade, mocks but at the same time envies anyone who does it, anyone who dresses the "pup-pet" of himself in "a frock coat and put[s] an umbrella in his hand" so that he can act in the world as a proper, useful and moral being.

This is the Leonce we meet at the beginning of the play, playing a fairy-tale character in a fairy-tale play taking place in a mythical card-board kingdom. He is, as a "character" in the play, a Prince in the kingdom of Popo who is soon to be put under obligation, for the sake of dynasty, to marry Lena, the Princess of Pipi.

But later, ignorant of this impending plot event, he is with his "love" Rosetta, and is on the verge of so-to-speak "staging" his renun-ciation of their love. "Staging" it because Leonce has distanced himself from the character Leonce as much as he has from what, in the minds of the world's "puppets," passes for the real world. To understand Leonce and the perspective from which he imagines and invents and manipulates the "puppet" of himself, one must understand the nature and the reason for that distance.

Leonce, like Buchner himself in the 1830s when he was writing this comedy, is at a stage of disenchantment several steps beyond his

French contemporary Lorenzaccio's [see I, #75 and 76]. His disenchantment is not merely political but metaphysical. "Nothing to be done" is Lorenzaccio's conclusion about political action; for Leonce, nothing's to be done, period. His alienation from the world, from existence itself, doesn't end, like Lorenzaccio's, in an ironic, meaningless political gesture for its own sake, or like Byron's, in a suicidal cauldron of rage and guilt; but in a posture—supine, mordant, absurd, but free. In that reclusiveness, the mind has infinite leisure, and infinite possibilities within its own orbit, for inventing its role and its reality, according to its taste. The desperate alienation from the ordinary runs so deep, is so imbedded, in Leonce's being that it permits him to redefine himself, his own psychology, his own landscape, at will. His essential motive is to keep that immeasurable distance between the world and his reinventions at permanent arm's length.

But—another wrinkle—what seems like the infinite comfort of creative self-indulgence is not a pleasure. Buchner's motto for the play is taken from *As You Like It*: "Oh! that I were a fool,/ I am ambitious for a motley coat." If either Leonce or his author Buchner were capable of wrapping themselves in a role and believing themselves in reality to be inside that "coat"—a "fool's" would be best—how much more comforting that fool's sleep would be than is his awakened awareness.

But he's condemned to be free from his self's "puppet." And in his freedom, games are his serious occupation, and serious occupations, should they intrude, would be so pointless as to deserve punishment. An example (in a sequence not represented here): how he plays the game of bidding farewell to his love, Rosetta.

He has already set the stage for the scene of farewell: before she entered, he had banished daylight, and the room was stage set for a candle-lit night. When she entered, there was a formal, symmetrical lovers' exchange of kisses and patter, until he informs Rosetta that his love and his boredom, both of which he loved, were the same. She dances for him, and while she does, he imagines he is a Roman emperor, and imagines he is watching Rosetta's decline into death. Her weeping is not sorrow but the "sampling" of sorrow. Her tears, he instructs her, are transformable into "diamonds." But the cap of his metaphorizing the death of his love comes when Rosetta attempts to embrace him. "Careful," he warns her, and explains that his head must not be jarred because within it, as though lying in its coffin, is their dead love. He must not be touched lest one of the corpse's "tiny arms be broken off" by her sudden motion. Taking her cue, Rosetta leaves, and Leonce, alone, is free to indulge both his playfulness of mind and his boredom.

First, a couple of improvisatory reflections on love, and then wondering if he can get drunk enough to reach oblivion tonight. And then Leonce, like Hamm in Beckett's *Endgame* and for the same reasons (although Leonce is suffering a lot more comfortable a desperation), splits into two, actor and observer, and instructs himself: "Come, Leonce, let's have a monologue," and does another improvisation on emptiness, boredom and sameness, treating them to metaphorical fancy dress, and cheered by his rhetorical flourish, applauds. And he's saved from the need for further invention by an intruder [see I, #125].

> **LEONCE**
> The bees sit so languidly upon the flowers, and the sun's beams lie so lazily upon the ground. What dreadful indolence it brings with it. Indolence is the beginning of all evil. What people won't do out of mere boredom! They study out of boredom, pray out of boredom, they love, they marry and multiply out of boredom, and then at last they die out of boredom, and—what makes it so amusing—they do it with the most serious of countenances, without ever understanding why, and God knows what all else. These heroes, these geniuses, these simpletons, these saints, these sinners, these fathers of families, are, after all, nothing more than refined indolent idlers. Why must *I* be the

one to know this? Why can't I be important to myself and dress this poor puppet in a frock coat and put an umbrella in his hand so that it will become very proper and very useful and very moral? The man who left me just now is a man whom I envy. I should have liked to thrash him out of envy. My God, to be able to be someone else! For only a moment.

(Valerio, somewhat inebriated, enters.)

Look at the fool run! I wish I knew of only one thing under the sun that still could make me run like that.

125

LEONCE CONTEMPLATES WITH CHEER LOVE, EMPTINESS, AND BOREDOM

(1836) GEORG BUCHNER, Leonce and Lena, *tr. Carl Richard Mueller, Act 1, Sc. 3*

[see I, #124]

LEONCE

What a curious thing love is. One lies in bed for a whole year in a somnambulistic trance, and then wakens suddenly one beautiful morning, and runs his hand across his forehead and reflects…and reflects. My God, how many women we need to be able to sing the scale of love up and down again! One is scarcely enough to provide a single tone. Why must this haze over our earth be a prism to break down love's white ray of passion into a rainbow?

(He drinks.)

In what bottle is the wine hiding that's to make me drunk today? Or won't I ever get that far! I feel as if I were sitting under an air pump. The air's so rare and thin it makes me freeze, as if it wants to skate around in nankeen trousers.—My lords, my lords, tell me, do you

know what Caligula and Nero were? Tyrants out of boredom. Yes.—
Come, Leonce, let's have a monologue, I want to listen.—My life
gapes at me like a vast expanse of white paper which I'm to fill, but I
can't produce so much as a single letter. My head is an empty ball-
room: some wilted flowers and crumpled ribbons on the floor, cracked
violins in the corner, the last dancers have taken off their masks and
look at one another with eyes tired as death. Twenty four times a day I
turn myself inside out like a glove. Oh, I know myself, I know what
I'll be thinking and dreaming in a quarter of an hour from now, in
eight days, in a year from now. God, how have I sinned that like a
schoolboy Thou shouldst so often scold me?—Bravo, Leonce! Bravo!

(He applauds.)
It does me good to cheer myself that way. Ho, Leonce! Leonce!

126
VALERIO RETURNS TO COURT WITH TWO "MECHANISMS:" LEONCE AND LENA
(1836) GEORG BUCHNER, Leonce and Lena, *tr. Carl Richard Mueller, Act 3, Sc. 3*

Valerio appears miraculously from under Leonce's table, interrupting Leonce's applause over his own rhetorical prowess [see I,
#125]. And just as miraculously, Valerio has turned out to have
already arrived at the same rationale and the same habits of mind as
Leonce, who, having found so perfect a philosophic kin, had taken
Valerio into his service.

At the play's end, when Leonce returns to his kingdom with Lena,
it's Valerio who introduces them to King and Court because, like himself, they are masked. But not as thoroughly as he is himself; Valerio
wears layers of masks.

What's happened to the three of them? Why are they masked? They've become confused identities—their story identities and real identities are commingled. The silly tale of the plot—how both Prince and Princess, each having no desire to be victims of prearranged marriages for the sake of dynasty, had both fled their courts, then met by chance and fallen in love—becomes fairy-tale representation of the accidental design that willy-nilly, in Buchner's belief, fixes destiny. The very three who in their own minds are separated from their "puppet" selves have fallen into the "puppet" trap, inadvertently accomplishing the plot and confirming its predestined logic.

And so in answer to the King's question, "Who may you be?" Valerio treats the King to a display of put-on identities, taking off one mask after the other and challenging the King to choose among them. He then, as the plot's new major-domo, introduces his unmasked exhibits—the "puppets" or "mechanisms" that were predestined to arrive at this symmetrical ending. Valerio's description, in his presentation, is of those "puppets," not of the detachable, only *self*-identifying, Leonce and Lena.

But at the *very* end of the play, when the three are left to themselves, they recover their detachable, alienated personae. Having satisfied their functions in the plot, they plan their future outside its frame, when all clocks and calendars will be destroyed, when "every man who prides himself on eating bread earned by the sweat of his brow will be declared insane," and when the three will "all year long live amidst roses and violets…" once having risen, through a process of distillation, "as high as Ischia and Capri." At which point they will have escaped the coopting machinery of both reality and plot.

The inverse of Buchner's *Danton's Death* [see II, #60 and 61], *Leonce and Lena* is the comic version of the same tragedy.

(Valerio, Leonce, and Lena enter, masked.)

VALERIO

However, what I really wanted to announce to this high and honorable assembly was that the two world-famous automatons had arrived, and that I am perhaps the third and most curious of them both, if only I knew who I am, a topic about which we are not permitted to think, since I haven't the faintest idea what I'm talking about, in fact I don't even know that I *don't* know, so that it's highly probable that I'm merely being *let* talk, because after all it's only some tubes and hot air that's saying this. *(In a raspy voice.)* Here, ladies and gentlemen, you see two individuals of either sex, a man and a woman, a gentleman and a lady! They are nothing more than artifice and mechanical ingenuity, pasteboard and watch springs! Each is equipped with a delicate, delicate ruby spring under the nail of the small toe of the right foot. Press this lever ever so gently and the mechanism will be set in motion for fully fifty years. These individuals are so consummately constructed that they cannot be distinguished from other human beings, unless one knows that they are merely pasteboard; they might even be accepted as members of human society. They are very well born, because they speak High German; they are very moral, because they rise punctually at the stroke of a bell, because they eat punctually at the stroke of another bell of midday, and because they retire punctually at the stroke of another bell; and then, too, they have a good digestion, which attests to a clear conscience. They possess a delicately ethical sense of feelings, because the lady never has leave to speak of the concept of women's drawers, and it is utterly impossible for the gentleman to precede the lady, in either climbing or descending a flight of stairs, by so much as a single step. They are very well educated, because the lady sings all the new operas and the gentleman wears cuffs. Pay attention now, ladies and gentlemen, for they are now in an interesting stage of their development: the mechanism of love is beginning to set itself in motion. The gentleman has already given the lady her scarf a number of times, and several times now the lady has rolled her eyes and turned them toward heaven. Both of them have whispered together a number of times: about faith, and love, and hope! They already seem very much in accord, all that's lacking now is that paltry word: Amen.

nankeen: a firm, durable, yellow or buff fabric, made originally from natural-colored Chinese cotton

127

PEER GYNT DRIVES HIS DYING MOTHER TO HEAVEN

(1867) HENRIK IBSEN, Peer Gynt, *tr. Wm. Archer, ad. L. Katz, Act 3, Sc. 4*

"Peer, you're lying!" cries Asa, Peer Gynt's mother, in the first line of the play. Peer Gynt is the quintessential liar, the Loki, the Baron Munchausen, of Norwegian folklore, but transmuted by Ibsen into the symbol of moral backsliding and cowardice on the one hand and of redemptive human value on the other. At the time of his mother's death, he's already made up his mind to leave his native Norway and ship to America. For good reason. He's absconded with the bride at a wedding, carried her into the mountains, and then abandoned her; the townsfolk are after him for that. Climbing to the Trolls in the mountains so that he might marry the Troll Princess, he barely escapes with his body intact—to commit to Trolldom, he would have had to have a tail tied to his bottom and his eyes slit. The Trolls are after him for that. He forsakes Solveig—who for love of him left her home and joined him in the mountains—when the Troll Woman turns up with the brat he'd fathered, and swears she'll turn up every day.

Sneaking down to the valley to see his mother once more, he discovers that she is dying. But then his innate good feeling and liar's playfulness offer his mother, who adores him notwithstanding all his sins, a gentle farewell. In the play's most lyrical passage, together they play the game of Peer's driving his dying mother to the gates of heaven.

(Peer enters.)

PEER GYNT
Good evening!
Departing?
Where are you planning to go?

> *(Writhing and walking towards the back of the room.)*

I? I'm fleeing from trouble;
I thought at least here I'd be free — !

Your hands and your feet — are they cold?
(Sits on the edge of the bed.)

Now, mother, we'll chat together;
But only of this and that, —
Forget what's awry and crooked,
And all that is sharp and sore. —
Why see now, the same old pussy,
So she is alive then, still?
What news is there here in the parish?
Mads Moen, is he content?
The smith, what's become of him now?

No, now we will chat together,
But only of this and that, —
Forget what's awry and crooked,
And all that is sharp and sore.
Are you thirsty? I'll fetch you water.
Can you stretch? The bed is short.
Let me see; — if I don't believe, now,
It's the bed that I had when a boy!
Remember how oft in the evenings
You sat at my bedside here,
And spread the fur-coverlet o'er me,
And sang many a ballad and song?

Ah, but the best of all, though, —

Mother, you mind that too?
The best was the fleet-foot horses —

To the castle west of the moon, and
The castle east of the sun,
To Soria-Moria Castle
The road ran both high and low.
A stick that we found in the closet,
For a whip shaft you made it serve.

Ay, ay; you threw loose the reins,
And kept turning round as we travelled,
And asked me if I was cold.
God bless you, ugly old mother, —
You were ever a kindly soul —

Stretch yourself; I'll support you.
There now, you're lying soft.
Spread o'er you the bed-fur.
Let me sit at your bedside here.
There; now we'll shorten the evening
With ballads and songs and such.

In Soria-Moria Castle
The King and the Prince give a feast.
On the sledge cushions lie and rest you;
I'll drive you there over the heath —
What? Are we invited?
Ay, that we are, both of us.

> (*He throws a string round the back of the chair on
> which the cat is lying, takes up a stick, and seats
> himself at the foot of the bed.*)

Gee-up! Will you stir yourself, Blackee?
Mother, you're not a-cold?
Ay, ay; by the pace one knows it,
When Grane begins to go!

Why, what is it that's ringing — ?

The glittering sledge-bells, dear!
Hear how hollow it's rumbling.
We're just driving over a fjord.
Hear the sign of the pine-trees, mother,
On the heath. Do you but sit still.

There's a sparkling and gleaming far off now;
See all that blaze of light?
From the castle's windows and doorways.
Don't you hear, they are dancing? And there,
Outside the door stands St. Peter,
And prays you to enter in.
He greets us, he does, with honour,
And Pours out the sweetest wine.
And he has cakes as well.
Cakes in a heaped-up dish.
And the dean's wife is getting ready
Your coffee and your dessert.

(*Cracking his whip.*)
Gee-up; will you stir yourself, Blackee!
There's the castle rising before us;
The drive will be over soon.
Lie back and close your eyes, mother,
And trust me to get you there.

Come up with you, Grane, my trotter!
In the castle the throng is great;
They bustle and swarm to the gateway:
Peer Gynt and his mother are here!
What say you, Master Saint Peter?
Shall mother not enter in?
You may search a long time, I t i ell you,
Ere you find such an honest old soul.
Myself I don't want to speak of;
I can turn at the castle gate.
If you'll treat me, I'll take it kindly;
If not, I'll go off just as pleased.
I have made up as many flim-flams

As the devil at the pulpit desk,
And called my old mother a hen, too,
Because she would cackle and crow.
But her you shall honour and reverence,
And make her at home indeed;
There comes not a soul to beat her
From the parishes nowadays. —
Ho-ho; here comes God the Father!
Saint Peter! you're in for it now!

> (*In a deep voice.*)

"Have done with these fancy airs, sir;
Mother Ase shall enter free!"

> (*Laughs loudly, and turns towards his mother.*)

Ay, didn't I know what would happen?
Now they dance to another tune!
(*Uneasily*) Why, what makes your eyes so glassy?
Have you gone out of your wits — ?

> (*Goes to the head of the bed*).

You mustn't lie there and stare so — !
Speak, mother; it's I, your boy!

> (*Feels her forehead and hands cautiously; then throws
> the string on the chair, and says softly.*)

Ay, ay! —
You can rest yourself Grane;
For now the journey's done.

(*Closes her eyes, and bends over her.*)
For all of your days I thank you,
For beatings and lullabys!
But see, you must thank me back, now —

(*Presses his cheek against her mouth.*)
There; that, was the driver's fare.

Soria-Moria castle: the name derives from a group of small islands in the Red Sea which the Arabs believed to be the Isles of the Blessed **Grane**, Scandinavian mythology: was Sigurd Fafnirsbane's horse; Grane was gray

128

TANNER, EXHORTING ANN TO ASSERT HER INDEPENDENCE, PUTS HIS OWN IN JEOPARDY

(1903) BERNARD SHAW, Man and Superman, *Act 1*

John Tanner bitterly denounces old Whitefield's will, which names him guardian to Whitefield's daughter Ann, a young woman he finds detestable, hypocritical, cunning in her exploitation of conventional pieties for her own ends, and otherwise shameless and unscrupulous. His own relation to convention is spelled out in a pamphlet he wrote (which is to be distributed, as Shaw requires, at performances of the play) called *The Revolutionist's Handbook.* In it, he denounces fictions concerning love and marriage, parenthood, and an extended catalogue of other moral rigidities and cultural anomalies.

He's frank to the point of self-delusion in explaining his doctrine to Ann, and rails at her as a supreme offender against a genuine as opposed to a factitious understanding of the true relations between men and women, mother and daughter, self and society. She's ahead of him: Ann has already learned the lessons of Tanner's book, and plays on the field he's outlined very accurately, but does so with impunity behind the standard facades of propriety. Tanner believes that Step One in his revolution is to rail at and get rid of the facade— his own practice, which makes him unbearable in civilized society. Unscrupulous Ann, on the other hand, uses every cover afforded by propriety to get what she wants.

But what does she want? Exactly what Tanner in principle understands to be the business of life: to foster the progress of the Life Force. In principle, he's for it; in practice, it scares the hell out of him, since it involves exactly what Ann thoroughly understands: the selection and capture of the man by the woman for the purpose of—as Dona Ana puts it in Act 3—"the Life to Come."

In their early encounter in Act I, Tanner is beginning his guardianship by teaching Ann one of his Handbook lessons: daughters, like sons, should openly break their chains. His lesson backfires.

> **TANNER**
>
> *(his eye flashing)* Ha! I might have known it. The mother! Always the mother! Oh, I protest against this vile abjection of youth to age! Look at that fashionable society as you know it. What does it pretend to be? An exquisite dance of nymphs. What is it? A horrible procession of wretched girls, each in the claws of a cynical, cunning, avaricious, disillusioned, ignorantly experienced, foul-minded old woman whom she calls mother, and whose duty it is to corrupt her mind and sell her to the highest bidder. Why do these unhappy slaves marry anybody, however old and vile, sooner than not marry at all? Because, marriage is their only means of escape from these decrepit fiends who hide their selfish ambitions, their jealous hatreds of the young rivals who have supplanted them, under the mask of maternal duty and family affection. Such things are abominable: the voice of nature proclaims for the daughter a father's care and for the son a mother's. The law for father and son and mother and daughter is not the law of love: it is the law of revolution, of emancipation, of final supersession of the old and worn-out by the young and capable. I tell you, the first duty of manhood and womanhood is a Declaration of Independence: the man who pleads his father's authority is no man: the woman who pleads her mother's authority is unfit to bear citizens to a free people.
>
> Break down your chains. Go your way according to your own conscience and not according to your mother's. Get your mind clean and vigorous; and learn to enjoy a fast ride in a motor car instead of seeing nothing in it but an excuse for a detestable intrigue. Come with me to Marseilles and across to Algiers and to Biskra, at sixty miles an hour. Come right down to the Cape if you like. That will be a Declaration of Independence with a vengeance. You can write a book about it afterwards. That will finish your mother and make a woman of you.

(aghast)
You'll come!!! But—

(he stops, utterly appalled; then resumes feebly)
No: look here, Ann: if there's no harm in it there's no point in doing it.

the Cape of Good Hope, the southern extremity of Africa

129
DON JUAN SPEAKS HIS CONTEMPT FOR THE USES OF LIFE ON EARTH
(1903) BERNARD SHAW, Man and Superman, *Act 3*

"Life's incessant aspiration," Don Juan explains, "is the law of my life." It was Shaw's as well, and the contempt Don Juan feels for his incarceration in a Hell that so remarkably resembles English leisure class life is thoroughly shared by his author.

"Don Juan in Hell" is the third act of *Man and Superman,* originally a dialogue written as an independent piece, later wholly interpolated into the play where it pretends to be a "dream sequence" interrupting the play's action. It is, in fact, a discursive fantasia using the characters in Mozart's *Don Giovanni* as its discutants, in which "my hero," as Shaw explains in his Preface to the play, "has a dream in which his Mozartian ancestor appears and philosophizes at great length in a Shavio-Socratic dialogue with the lady, the statue and the devil."

Shaw substitutes the musical cadences of prose for the notations of the original, and carries the debate of his principles concerning "the higher life" vs. the comfortable life into territory that is trod only once in a great while in modern English prose, exhibiting some of the most dazzling rhetorical display that the language affords. Among the most dazzling is the passage here, which verges on the acrobatic in the technical skill needed for its delivery.

The burden of Shaw's whole thesis carries as its major codicil the profound, almost religiously felt optimism of the social reformer of the early 20th century, who "looked at the world and, unlike God who saw that it was good, saw rather that it could be improved." Ameliorative socialism was known then as Fabian Socialism, and Shaw was its most notable exponent.

In this particular passage, the power of the Don's argument is not in its Fabianish optimism, but in its violent condemnation of the class—the leisure class—who betrayed the greatest responsibility that life afforded it: "striving to bring into existence"—What? For Shaw, it was quite literally the meaning of life, the "striving" that yearned to bring into existence a great deal more than social, political, economic amelioration, but—the crux of the matter—to give birth to a level of rationality and wisdom in humanity capable of overcoming its moral charades, its moral lies, its moral sloth. Probably nowhere in literature is there so succinct and yet so comprehensive a diatribe against a class's failure, one that articulates so fully and so precisely its compendium of sham.

The burden of Don Juan's attack on the Devil who governs this kingdom of sloth is his argument to escape from it. His recourse is naturally to Heaven, and the Devil happily accedes to his desire to change venue, but it's a sad alternative. The Commendatore (whom Don Juan on earth dispatched to heaven) makes it his business to escape from there to lounge in the Tempter's domain whenever feasible, because, as he's already reported, of the stultifying conformity in which Heaven is mired. And so between the backsliders in Hell and the conventional pietists in Heaven, there's little for the Don to choose. The intent of the dialogue as a whole is to intimate a novel and transcendant way, a third way, one that Shaw borrowed from Nietzsche, who called it the transvaluation of values, its accomplishment anticipated by both Nietzsche and Shaw in the regeneration of man as superman.

DON JUAN

Here I have everything that disappointed me without anything that I have not already tried and found wanting. I tell you that as long as I can conceive something better than myself I cannot be easy unless I am striving to bring it into existence or clearing the way for it. That is the law of my life. That is the working within me of Life's incessant aspiration to higher organization, wider, deeper, intenser self-consciousness, and clearer self-understanding. It was the supremacy of this purpose that reduced love for me to the mere pleasure of a moment, art for me to the mere schooling of my faculties, religion for me to a mere excuse for laziness, since it had set up a God who looked at the world and saw that it was good, against the instinct in me that looked through my eyes at the world and saw that it could be improved. I tell you that in the pursuit of my own pleasure, my own health, my own fortune, I have never known happiness. It was not love for Woman that delivered me into her hands: it was fatigue, exhaustion. When I was a child, and bruised my head against a stone, I ran to the nearest woman, and cried away my pain against her apron. When I grew up, and bruised my soul against the brutalities and stupidities with which I had to strive, I did again just what I had done as a child. I have enjoyed, too, my rests, my recuperations, my breathing times, my very prostrations after strife; but rather would I be dragged through all the circles of the foolish Italian's Inferno than through the pleasures of Europe. That is what has made this place of eternal pleasures so deadly to me. It is the absence of this instinct in you that makes you that strange monster called a Devil. It is the success with which you have diverted the attention of men from their real purpose, which in one degree or another is the same as mine, to yours, that has earned you the name of The Tempter. It is the fact that they are doing your will, or rather drifting with your want of will, instead of doing their own, that makes them the uncomfortable, false, restless, artificial, petulant, wretched creatures they are. Your friends are all the dullest dogs I know. They are not beautiful: they are only decorated. They are not clean: they are only shaven and starched. They are not dignified: they are only fashionably dressed. They are not educated: they are only college passmen. They are not religious: they are only pewrenters. They are not moral: they are only conventional. They are not virtuous: they are only cowardly. They are not even vicious: they are only "frail." They are not artistic: they are only lascivious. They are not prosperous: they are only rich. They are not loyal, they are only servile; not dutiful, only sheepish; not public spirited, only patriotic; not courageous, only quarrelsome; not determined, only obstinate; not masterful, only domineering, not self-controlled, only obtuse, not self-respecting, only vain; not kind, only sentimental; not social, only gregarious; not considerate, only polite; not intelligent, only opinionated; not progressive, only factious; not imaginative, only superstitious; not just, only vindictive; not generous, only propitiatory; not disciplined, only cowed; and not truthful at all—liars every one of them, to the very backbone of their souls.

the foolish Italian: Dante

GLOSSARY

Aphrodite: Greek mythology — goddess of love, daughter of Zeus

Apollo: Greek mythology — god of the sun, healing, music, prophecy, patron of the Oracle at Delphi, son of Zeus

Ares: Greek mythology — god of war, husband of Aphrodite

Argive: poetic epithet for Greek or Grecian

Artemis: Greek mythology — virgin goddess of the hunt, also identified with the Moon, twin sister of Apollo

Ate: Greek mythology — Avenger, goddess of rage and mischief, daughter of Eris (Strife) and Zeus; she personifies infatuation, with guilt its cause and evil its consequence

Athena Pallas: Greek mythology — a warrior goddess of Wisdom, the Arts and Sciences, daughter of Zeus, patroness of Athens

Bacchus: Roman equivalent of Dionysus

Charon: Greek mythology — with his boat, he takes the souls of the dead across the river Lethe/Styx to Hades

Cypris: see *Aphrodite*

Delphi: a town in northern Greece, site of the famous oracular shrine of Apollo (see *Pytho*)

Demeter: Greek mythology — goddess of agriculture, sister of Zeus, mother of Persephone

Dionysus: Greek mythology — god of wine, patron of drama in Athens, son of Zeus

Elysium: the equivalent of Heaven in Greek mythology

Erynyes: see *Furies*

Furies: Greek mythology — spirits of Divine Vengeance, especially transgressions that touch on the basis of human society. They punish violations of filial duty, the claims of kinship, rites of hospitality, murder, perjury, and the like; eventually reconciled by Athena to Athenian law

Hades: Greek mythology — god of the Underworld where the souls of the dead are kept, brother of Zeus; also used as a name for the Underworld

Hecate: Greek mythology — a confusing divinity, identified with the Moon, Artemis and Persephone, and invoked by sorcerers; she is the great sender of visions, of madness, and of sudden terror; Medea was her witch-priestess before falling in love with Jason

Helios: Apollo

Hera: Greek mythology — sister and wife of Zeus

Hermes: Greek mythology — messenger of the gods, guide of souls departing to Hades

Hymen: Greek mythology — god of marriage

Ilion: Troy

Ilium: Troy

Jove: see *Jupiter*

Jupiter: Roman mythology — chief deity (equivalent of Zeus)

Lethe: Greek mythology — the river in Hades from which the souls of the dead drank and became oblivious of their past lives; then they were carried across by Charon in his boat

Neptune: Roman mythology — god of the sea

Orpheus: Greek mythology — a Thracian philosopher, poet and musician, won permission by his music to bring his wife back to earth from Hades

Pallas: Athena

Persephone: Greek mythology — wife of Hades, queen of the underworld, daughter of Demeter

Phoebus: Apollo

Phrygian: of Phrygia, an ancient country in Asia Minor, one of whose cities was Troy

Pluto: Roman equivalent of Hades

Poseidon: Greek mythology — god of the sea, brother of Zeus and Hades

Pytho: ancient name for Delphi, Apollo's seat of prophecy, which was conducted by the prophetess Pythia (a girl or woman) seated on a tripod over the Oracle proper, which was a cleft in the ground in the innermost sanctuary from which rose cold vapors that had the power of inducing the ecstasy that gave rise to the priestess's prophetic vision. Her responses were ambiguous, but though always true, gave rise to misinterpretation.

Styx: see *Lethe*

Tartarus: Greek mythology — the infernal depths of Hades

Zeus: Greek mythology — chief of the gods, master of the lightning bolt